To Jack

With Best Wishes

for.

HORNCHURCH SCRAMBLE

HORNCHURCH SCRAMBLE

THE DEFINITIVE ACCOUNT OF THE RAF FIGHTER AIRFIELD, ITS PILOTS, GROUNDCREW AND STAFF

VOLUME ONE
1915 TO THE END OF THE BATTLE OF BRITAIN

RICHARD C SMITH

GRUB STREET · LONDON

First published in hardback in 2000 by
Grub Street
The Basement
10 Chivalry Road
London SW11 1HT

Copyright this edition © 2002 Grub Street, London
Text copyright © Richard C Smith

British Library Cataloguing in Publication Data
Smith, Richard C
Hornchurch scramble: the definitive account of the RAF
fighter airfield, its pilots, groundcrew and staff
Vol. 1: 1915 to the end of the Battle of Britain
1. Great Britain. Royal Flying Corps – History
2. RAF Hornchurch – History 3. RAF Hornchurch
I.Title
358.4′009422′09041

ISBN 1-904010-01-6

Typeset by Pearl Graphics, Hemel Hempstead

Printed and bound in Great Britain by Biddles Ltd
www.biddles.co.uk

This book is dedicated to all the men and women
who served at Sutton's Farm and RAF Hornchurch

CONTENTS

ACKNOWLEDGEMENTS

During the seven years of research and the writing of this first volume on Sutton's Farm and RAF Hornchurch, it has been a great honour and privilege for me to meet, talk and correspond with the men and women listed below. Without their help, enthusiasm and hospitality during this project, this book would be far less complete or interesting to those who like to peer back into history for first-hand accounts. I thank them also for the use of their personal papers and photographs, log books and historical documents. Sadly, some of these great personalities have since passed on.

Wing Commander Eric Barwell, DFC, RAF Retd
Flying Officer Fred Barker, DFM, RAF Retd
Squadron Leader George Bennions, DFC, RAF Retd
Squadron Leader Robert Beardsley, DFC, RAF Retd
The late Air Chief Marshal Sir Harry Broadhurst, GCB, KBE, DSO, DFC, AFC
Squadron Leader Peter Brown, AFC, RAF Retd
Squadron Leader John Carpenter, DFC, RAF Retd
The late Air Commodore Alan Deere, OBE, DSO, DFC
Wing Commander Frank Dowling, OBE, RAF Retd
Squadron Leader 'Dave' Glaser, DFC, RAF Retd
Wing Commander John Freeborn, DFC, RAF Retd
The late Group Captain Colin Gray, DSO, DFC
Flight Lieutenant Trevor Gray, RAF Retd
Warrant Officer Reginald Gretton, RAF Retd
Group Captain D.S 'Sammy' Hoare, RAF Retd
Flight Lieutenant Les Harvey, RAF Retd
Wing Commander Thomas Hayes, DFC, RAF Retd
Squadron Leader Iain Hutchinson, TD, RAF Retd
The late Group Captain Brian Kingcome, DSO, DFC
The late Air Commodore James Leathart, CB, DSO
Squadron Leader Arthur Leigh, DFC, DFM, RAF Retd
Squadron Leader Ludwick Martel, VM, KW, RAF Retd
The late Air Commodore Donald MacDonell, CB
Squadron Leader Percy Morfill, DFM, RAF Retd
Wing Commander Tom Rowland, RAF Retd
The late Wing Commander Gerald Saunders, DFC
The late Air Vice-Marshal David Scott-Malden, DSO, DFC
Air Marshal Sir Frederick Sowrey, KCB, CBE, AFC, RAF Retd
The late Squadron Leader Arthur Spears, AFC

Squadron Leader Gerald Stapleton, DFC, RAF Retd
Wing Commander William Stapleton, CBE, RAF Retd
The late Squadron Leader Jack Stokoe, DFC, AE
Wing Commander Harborne Stephen, CBE, DSO, DFC, AE, RAF Retd
Wing Commander George Swanwick, RAF Retd
The late Squadron Leader Henryk Szczesny, VM, KW, DFC
Wing Commander Tim Vigors, DFC, RAF Retd
Group Captain Edward Wells, DSO, DFC, RAF Retd
Mr Robert Ballard
Lady Dorothy and Mr Derek Bouchier
Mrs Joan Bowell
Lady Jane Broadhurst
Mr Neil Burgess
Mrs Joy Caldwell
Mrs Margaret Crabtree
Mr Joe Crawshaw (Chairman of No.222 Natal Squadron Association)
Mr Dave Davis
Mr John Gill
Mr Frank Mileham
Mr 'Ricky' Richardson
Mr William Sainsbury
Mr Jack Shenfield
The late Ronald Shelley

Special thanks go to my wife Kim, for her understanding, patience and help with driving the many miles we have travelled together to meet many of the interviewees, and for her assistance in typing the manuscript. Thanks also to David and Robert for putting up with Dad's time-consuming hobby, and my mother, Muriel Smith, brother Paul and my late father Robert for their unending support in all my ventures over the years.

An extra big thank-you goes to Squadron Leader Peter Brown for the outstanding support, contribution and advice he has given on the pre-publication editing of this book, also for suppling the superb Introduction. Also to Air Marshal Sir 'Freddie' Sowrey, with his vast knowledge of First War aviation; it is an honour to have him write the Foreword to this first volume.

Thank you to Honorary Secretary Wing Commander 'Pat' Hancock, OBE, DFC, RAF Retd, and Wing Commander John Young, AFC, RAF Retd, of the Battle of Britain Fighter Association, for their help with my first contact with the Few and subsequent information which is greatly appreciated, also the Imperial War Museum, especially Mr Brad King, the RAF Museum Hendon, the Air Historical Branch and the Public Record Office, Kew. Thanks also to Mr Stuart Leslie and Mr John Barfoot of the Cross & Cockade Society for photographs and information.

My thanks go out to my friends and fellow researchers who have helped and encouraged me over the years: Jack and Pamela Broad, Steve Butler, David and Alison Campbell, Joy Caldwell, John Coleman, Joe Crawshaw,

Dave Davis, Squadron Leader E.D. Dave Glaser, Alan and Sue Gosling, John Jones, Geoff and Lesley Nutkins, Peter Reynolds, David Ross, Michael Shelley, Squadron Leader Gerald 'Stapme' Stapleton and the late Squadron Leader Jack Stokoe.

And finally to Mr John Davies and all at Grub Street, for taking on the project and turning a dream into reality.

FOREWORD

by

Air Marshal Sir Frederick Sowrey, KCB, CBE, AFC, RAF Retd

This is the history of an airfield in war and peace, triumph and tragedy.

From rural farmland, emerged one of the most successful airfields in two world wars and the peace between them.

The outbreak of the First World War saw the aeroplane in its infancy, and it was the pressure of the conflict that accelerated its development. The crucible of war meant that technical advances which would have taken years in peacetime were achieved in a matter of months; generations of new aircraft and weapons were being produced by designers for specific roles – and for Sutton's Farm that was the interception of enemy raiders at night, ideally before they reached London.

At a time when aircraft (and particularly their engines) lacked reliability, each trip was a step further up the learning curve.

Night flying was regarded as being particularly hazardous: if the engine stopped there was little chance of seeing a suitable field for a forced landing – and there were no parachutes. However, the pilots of Sutton's Farm, as the first of the night fighters, learnt from the hard school of experience, and had the unique distinction that three pilots from the same flight of the same squadron in the space of one month shot down Zeppelins in flames within sight of the previously dispirited citizens of London.

With this blunting of the Zeppelin raids the main threat switched to Gotha bombers operating by day and night.

But the story told here is a more personal one involving people. Expert use has been made of combat reports and interviews. The personalities involved speak from these pages of their difficulties and dangers and ultimate success. This includes civilians living locally who, for the first time, became part of the front line in the twentieth century. Step by step the reader appreciates the long struggle for air superiority in the first war in the air.

Peacetime between the wars brought change with greater concentration on the development of people. In the First War, training was the minimum to teach a pilot to fly and be launched into combat. Now there was time to practise and practise again with the emphasis laid on fighting skills. Life was more relaxed – and fun – in a service which thrived on youth and vigour.

In both war and peace there are setbacks and successes along the way. Military aviation is an exacting profession, and we should salute all those in the air and on the ground who feature in this epic book on Sutton's Farm/RAF Hornchurch airfield.

INTRODUCTION

by

Squadron Leader M.P. Brown, AFC, RAF Retd
Flying Officer No. 41 Squadron, Hornchurch 1940

Hornchurch Scramble is the story of Sutton's Farm airfield and Royal Air Force station Hornchurch, from 1915 to 1940. Sutton's Farm airfield was built for the RFC for the fighter protection of London in World War I, and was later rebuilt and extended from 1924 to become RAF Hornchurch, a key fighter defence station. An operational fighter station is more than a base – it is a complex equation of its pilots, aircrew, its aircraft and the men that care for them, the operations team, and the support groups. The personnel and buildings changed over the 25 years, but the great fighting spirit and traditions of Hornchurch and its squadrons lived on. They were built up and enhanced by each generation of a special breed of young men, who flew the aircraft in peace and war. In the two wars Sutton's Farm/Hornchurch had the special responsibility and privilege of defending London from the German terror raids.

The book tells of young pilots in 1915, who flying alone, attacked the formidable Zeppelins at night; Davids fighting Goliaths. It tells of young Spitfire pilots in 1940 attacking German bomber and fighter formations that outnumbered them five or ten times. It is clear that whatever else changed over the years, our young pilots at Hornchurch always maintained the highest levels of courage, sacrifice and dedication for the safety of our country.

It is not normally realised that, quite differently from all other fighting services, the fighter pilot fights alone. Once the decision to attack has been made, then all further decisions are his. After his attack he can dive for home, or he can look for another enemy aircraft to attack. If his aircraft is hit and damaged, or he is injured, there is no help at hand; he decides whether to take to his parachute, or to stay with his aircraft, and try for base, or to crash-land in a field. If he is killed, he dies alone.

It is about these men, that the author has written his book. It is not a social diary; it is a diary of their lives in action. In his pages covering the Battle of Britain, he does not discuss strategy or tactics. He does not tell us, with hindsight wisdom, how the battle should have been fought more effectively.

When the pilots were at readiness or in action, their sole concern was in shooting down the German aircraft attacking England and its people; as many as possible, and as quickly as possible. The urgency and uncertainty of the battle gave little time for the introduction of tactics. Unless, and until Fighter Command was destroyed, there could be no Nazi invasion. This book tells of how, day by day and even hour by hour, they fought the Luftwaffe, and, with the sacrifice of more than 500 pilots and aircrew of Fighter Command, they achieved victory.

There are few media heroes in these pages. Our pilots who shot down the Zeppelins in 1916 were pioneers and few in number. Their great courage deserved the praise and recognition they received. Unusually, the British people saw the young pilots actually attacking the enemy in their defence, and watched the Zeppelins crash in flames. In the battle in 1940, at least a thousand of our pilots actually engaged the enemy. Some of them shot down several enemy aircraft and the top British scorer was a young Volunteer Reserve pilot serving at Hornchurch. Many of these pilots were awarded decorations. But the words 'hero' and 'ace' were not in common use in the squadrons, except in jest. For wherein lies the greatest courage? The most dangerous position in the squadron or flight was that of 'top cover', above and behind, to watch out for Me109s; this was normally undertaken by junior members of the flight. There was little chance for them to claim victories. The casualty rate was high; too often the 'top covers' just didn't return to base.

The history breaks down naturally into five periods. Firstly the establishment, in 1915, of the airfield at Sutton's Farm, to defend London from the German Zeppelin raids against the civilian population during the First World War. After the war had ended, it was finally closed at the end of December 1919.

The rebuilt airfield, RAF Hornchurch, was eventually brought into service again on 1st April 1928, commencing the second period. It became a permanent and vital fighter station for the protection of London and south-east England. The author presents a fascinating picture of life in a fighter squadron at a time of peace. Squadrons change, and personnel change. There is a presentation of the development of fighter aircraft, from the early two-gun Siskin biplanes, through to the eight-gun high speed monoplanes ready for World War II.

The third period starts with the declaration of war on 3rd September 1939, by which time the squadrons were equipped with Spitfires, and were controlled into action by a sophisticated system based on radar detection. Air Chief Marshal Sir Hugh Dowding, Air Officer Commanding in Chief of Fighter Command, was always deeply concerned about the welfare of his pilots, when Air Council Member for supply and research, had planned its structure and equipment. He led the Command to victory, but was then removed from office by the Air Ministry, without due honour. However the respect and affection held for him by his pilots have endured to this day.

This period also includes the miracle of Dunkirk, with more than 300,000 men brought safely home, helped by Hornchurch-based aircraft, fighting high above the beaches. It gave the Spitfire pilots their first major contact with the German Me109s; after ten days of fighting the squadrons engaged were well and truly bloodied. The squadrons were fighting a distant defensive battle and were faced with a sea crossing in each direction, which limited the time over the combat area. Often the Me109s were at height waiting for them. Air Vice-Marshal Keith Park, in command of 11 Group, of which Hornchurch was part, sent his squadrons over in pairs, and wings of three, four and even five squadrons. This was possible as they had time to form up and choose their time for action. The use of such wings would have been ineffective in the Battle of Britain, as time and immediacy were of the essence in a defensive action over England.

The fourth period, taking up almost half of the book, is dedicated to the Battle of Britain, and understandably so. For 16 weeks the pilots were locked in combat, day after day. The author's style and presentation creates an ambience that makes it possible for readers to feel that they were with the squadrons at the time.

After the victory had been won at the end of October, the final period of this book runs up to December 1940, dealing with the gradual run-down of the action, at the onset of winter. Britain's defensive battle by day had been won. The night defences would improve and grow, and in the coming year Hornchurch and 11 Group would go on to the offensive over France.

At the outbreak of war, the prime function of Hornchurch and all groups of Fighter Command was to defend Britain against enemy bombers coming across the North Sea. All fighter attack training was based on this, using formal formations of twelve, six, or three aircraft; the German bombers generally flew in formation in basic units of three or five aircraft. Fighting against Me 109 fighters at 30,000 feet had not been envisaged by Fighter Command. After the German armies reached Dunkirk, the Luftwaffe was only 23 miles, or ten minutes flying time from England's shores. Hitler made an opportunist decision to invade Britain. The Luftwaffe was given the task of destroying Fighter Command and bombing Britain into submission. The Germans soon realised that they could only operate their bombers by day, with a heavy fighter escort; three fighters for every bomber. The short range of the Me109s restricted the German bombers' day operations to the south-east of England, with London just within reach. Inevitably Hornchurch and other 11 Group stations would take the brunt of the battle, with back-up support from 10 Group.

The Luftwaffe had a strength of some 2,500 aircraft including 1,200 bombers and 1,000 Me109 and Me110 fighters. Against this formidable force, the largest in the world, Fighter Command had only 750 fighters, excluding the two-seater Defiants firing from a turret in the rear. Air Chief Marshal Dowding had to defend a coastline of some 1,000 miles, in addition to his defence of London and the south-east.

The Me109 pilots were battle trained from three previous campaigns, in Spain and against Poland and France, and were superior in tactics to our pilots. The Germans could mount raids when they chose, in any formation and at any target. This was the new, and taxing problem that Air Vice-Marshal Park, as commander of 11 Group, had to deal with.

At any time our pilots could be vectored on to massive German formations, typically of 50 bombers and 150 Me109s.

Our pilots always attacked, generally in single squadrons. It is not surprising that our squadrons continually found they were heavily outnumbered, with the German fighters above them. What our pilots lacked in battle experience, however, they made up for in courage and tenacity; at Hornchurch, they were fortunate to be flying Spitfires, the finest fighter aircraft of the period. The victory/kill ratio for the Hornchurch fighters averaged 3:2. For every three German aircraft that they shot down, two of our own aircraft were destroyed. Fortunately they were playing at home, so that all the German aircrews were either killed or captured. Many of our pilots baled out, or were not seriously hurt, and lived to fight another day. This was crucial in view of the dangerous shortage of trained pilots.

No.600 Squadron, with its night fighter Blenheims, battled on through the nights but without the success they deserved. Their time would come in 1941 when better aircraft and detection equipment were to hand.

The story of No.264 Squadron with their two-seater Defiants, is one of initial triumph, followed by unacceptable loss; but always with great courage and sacrifice. The experiences and the steadfast behaviour of the pilots in the book can be paralleled by the other squadrons that served in No.11 Group.

We now know that many of the claims of enemy aircraft destroyed, generally made within an hour of the heat of battle, were excessive. Fighter pilots and air gunners have always over claimed: the British by 2:1, and German Me109 pilots by 3:1. It is almost inevitable, since sometimes two Spitfires or Hurricanes would attack and claim for the same aircraft. Almost certainly, the most common reason was the assumption that an enemy bomber or fighter diving into cloud streaming black smoke was doomed; in fact, the pilot had probably pushed the throttle 'through the gate' to escape, the rich mixture resulting in black smoke streaming out of the exhaust. The German bombers could take a great deal of punishment, and many limped home on one engine. Over-claiming does not matter if the war is won. But if tactics are planned on the basis of inaccurate claims of three times the real enemy losses, then disaster is certain, as the Luftwaffe found out.

By early September, based on the over-claims of their pilots of 3:1, their commanders believed that Fighter Command was finished. On 15th September it learned the truth. The pilots came from all ranks and all walks of life. There were regular officers and NCO pilots, weekend Auxiliaries and Volunteer Reservists. By the beginning of the Battle of Britain they had been incorporated into squadrons, and fought together as a team, well able to challenge the professional pilots and aircrew of the Luftwaffe. Young VR pilots were among the top scorers in 11 Group. The squadrons were strengthened by pilots from the Dominions, and from countries that had been enslaved by Nazi Germany. They were truly the pilots of democracy.

Counselling for post traumatic shock was neither known nor wanted. Whatever the experience, pilots were ready to take off on their next sortie, or as soon as they had returned to the squadron, after baling out. Their next scramble could be even more traumatic.

The Royal Navy referred to some of their ships as 'happy ships'; RAF Station Hornchurch was a 'happy station'. Fighter pilots, with their tunic top-button undone, and flying boots in the Mess, jealously guarded breaches of regulations, were a special breed, and needed selective discipline and a loose rein. Their station commanders understood this. The pilots were bonded by their own deep and special sense of humour.

From May to December 1940, the name Hornchurch was synonymous with rugged fighting and high casualties. But pilots were aware of the value of the station support; the calm reassuring voice of the controller, at a time of crisis, was sometimes their only lifeline. Pilots remembered Hornchurch with affection, and with pride in being part of its great history.

Although most of the action took place many miles away from base, Hornchurch Station itself was bombed several times by the Luftwaffe, with casualties to its personnel. No history of Hornchurch would be complete, without reference to the courage under fire shown by ground personnel. During the enemy attacks, aircraft groundcrews worked in the open to help the pilots, and to service and re-arm their Spitfires. The Operations Room team of men and WAAFs, although underground, and knowing full well that Hornchurch was the target, stood fast even when the bombs could be heard and felt.

The authenticity of the book has been assured by the author. He has researched Hornchurch history for many years. The facts presented are mainly based on his studies of personal diaries and archive documents in the Public Record Office. The views expressed are based on numerous interviews with pilots, aircrew, and other RAF personnel and civilians. These interviews were taped or made by video and they form a valuable record of what really happened in the battle and of the personal experiences of some of those that played a part.

In *Hornchurch Scramble*, Richard Smith has written of sacrifice, bravery, and doggedness in the face of the enemy. It is a tale of daily fighting, with combat victories, combined with baling-out, forced landings, and death, as the normal pattern of life. He has also told some of the exciting history of the growing fighter defence squadrons when, even in peace, humour and tragedy lived side by side. I believe that this book will have a special place in Battle of Britain literature. Firstly because of the interesting history it recounts, but also as a fine record of defensive fighter action, that will be available for historians for years to come. It should be read by the young; it will serve to remind them of our great heritage in fighting for the cause of freedom and democracy.

When you read this book, you will walk with very special young men.

CHAPTER 1

ON A WING AND A PRAYER
1915-1919

On Sunday, 3rd October 1915, with the First World War just a year into the fighting, and the use of aircraft in war in its infancy, the airfield of Sutton's Farm, sited near the village of Hornchurch in Essex, began its life with the arrival of a small detachment of men from the newly formed Royal Flying Corps. The site of the new airfield had been chosen after much consideration by the War Office, who at the time were under a great deal of pressure with regard to the increasing activity over the British mainland by German airships. They had been making reconnaissance raids around the south-east of England and London to test out the British defences before embarking on bombing raids.

To prepare to act against such a threat, the War Office carried out a hurried search for suitable defensive airfield sites, which could be used to best effect to repel further attacks from raiding airships. After much consideration they decided on the site of Sutton's Farm, Hornchurch, along with a second airfield at Hainault Farm, near Barkingside, Ilford; these were designated landing grounds No.II and III. Other airfields already used in the defence of London included Northolt, Joyce Green and Rochford. The land on which the airfield was to be sited was purchased from the landowners, who at that time were New College, Oxford, who had owned the land for nearly six centuries. It was being used for farming during this period by a Mr Tom Crawford, and it consisted of 90 acres of fields that were flat and well drained. These had been used for corn crops, until it was officially requisitioned and given over to the RFC. The scene at Sutton's Farm was set for the arrival of a very basic operational unit.

On 3rd October, local residents witnessed the arrival from Gosport of Captain A.G. Moore with twelve men from No 23 Squadron, with a lorry, one light tender and provisions for their accommodation.

The aircraft arrived later in the day and consisted of two Royal Aircraft Factory BE2c biplanes, supplied by the 5th Wing RFC at Gosport with their pilots Lieutenant E. Powell and 2nd Lieutenant H. O'Malley, both of No.13 Squadron. The ground crew had the job of erecting the two RE5 canvas hangars for the aircraft, supplying the aviation fuel and armament, two bomb racks and eight 20lb bombs and anything else that was required to keep this small unit operational.

The ground staff were billeted in one of the local farmhouses, while the pilots were more comfortably housed in the local Hornchurch village public house, the White Hart, where their only means of communication to their commanders was by a newly installed telephone system, which was also relayed to the airfield.

By 8th October, two more pilots had arrived, Lieutenant R. Yates of No.23 Squadron and from No.14 Squadron, Lieutenant Jenkins. They relieved Lieutenants Powell and O'Malley.

On the 13th, another pilot arrived, a young 18-year-old by the name of John Cotesworth Slessor. He was about to embark on what was to be an outstanding career, which would lead eventually to his becoming in WWII, Commander in Chief of the Mediterranean and Middle East Air Force 1944-1945 and, post-war, Chief of Air Staff 1950-52.

It was somewhat of a twist of fate that the same evening the Zeppelin airship L.15, left its moorings at Nordholz, situated on the northern coast of Germany, along with five other airships, in what was to be the biggest raid yet of the war. The other airships were L.11, L.13, L.14, L.15 and L.16, and the majority of these made landfall over the Norfolk and Suffolk coasts.

Meanwhile L.15 had proceeded inland, and at 8 pm was sighted over Halstead, Essex. Then turning south-west, she headed for London, where with her engines now silent, to avoid detection, she dropped her bomb load at 9.25 pm causing the deaths of 72 civilians and injuring another 128. The local Air Defence had already been alerted to the raids, and the War Office had passed the information on to Sutton's Farm and three other airfields.

Earlier that evening Lieutenant Slessor had been talking with the farmer Tom Crawford about his agricultural machinery. He had then returned to one of the canvas hangars, where his folding cot had been erected, taken off his boots and covered himself with a warm blanket. The telephone rang: it was Lieutenant Colonel W.W. Warner from the War Office. John Slessor was ordered aloft, taking off in his BE2c biplane at 9.05 pm, to start the slow climb to an altitude of 10,000 feet, where most airships operated; this would take a good 40 minutes to achieve and with every passing thousand feet he would feel colder and colder.

When Slessor finally saw the giant airship it had been caught in the beams of the local searchlight batteries. Just as he was about to make his approach towards it, it disappeared into a cloud bank, and after much searching he decided he had lost it. His patrol had taken him two hours, and he was now running low on fuel. He returned to land back at Sutton's Farm, which had been lit up by ground staff, using old petrol cans filled with cotton waste material and soaked in petrol as a primitive flare path. Unfortunately, Slessor damaged his aircraft's undercarriage owing to a heavy landing and being somewhat blinded by a searchlight crew, who although well intentioned with the idea of illuminating his aircraft, actually hindered his approach. This had been Lieutenant Slessor's first operational flight; he was also the first British pilot to intercept an enemy airship over the United Kingdom.

The Zeppelin raids continued into 1916, with still no real success by the

Home Defence squadrons. One of the many problems was the right equipment to get the job done, especially the armament, which consisted of the Lewis machine gun, which in effect would spray the Zeppelin with .303in bullets. The airship could be easily patched up however, by some of the Zeppelin's crew who were sailmakers and repaired the damage by using quick sealing patches over the ruptured fabric.

The invention of the explosive bullet by an Australian, John Pomeroy, in August 1914, and also in Britain by Squadron Commander F.A. Brock, did help the RFC pilots in their battle against the airships. This new ammunition, which could blow large holes into fabric and then ignite the hydrogen gases, seemed the ideal solution to bring down the giant intruders.

By early 1916 the War Office proceeded to order the supply of one million rounds of the new ammunition for all .303-calibre machine guns to be used by the Home Defence squadrons.

Meanwhile further Zeppelin sightings by pilots stationed at Sutton's Farm continued. On 31st March 1916, Second Lieutenant E.W. Powell while on patrol sighted the Zeppelin L.15, the same machine that had evaded Lieutenant John Slessor a few months earlier; this could be seen at the height of around 8,500 feet.

This was commanded by Lieutenant Commander Joachim Breithaupt, who now was turning south-south-west on to the Thames, passing over Orsett, Essex. The time of the sighting was around 9 pm. Lieutenant Powell was unable to intercept, because he was too far away, but the airship was not destined to escape.

Lieutenant Claude Ridley, flying from Joyce Green airfield, was close enough to engage and fire into the L.15, before losing sight of it when the searchlight batteries swung away. It was not until the searchlight beams accidentally caught the L.15 between Erith, Purfleet and Dartford, that she was caught, with the ground defence batteries opening fire at Purfleet, Erith, Abbey Wood and Plumstead. Breithaupt now turned the Zeppelin northwards to avoid the accurate shooting of the gunners of the Purfleet battery, who eventually scored a hit that tore a gash in the airship's main structure. At 9.40 pm he dropped 20 high-explosive and 24 incendiary bombs in open fields near Wennington Road, Rainham, probably to lighten the load and gain extra height.

The L.15 was finally brought down by 2nd Lieutenant Alfred de Bathe Brandon, who had flown from the Hainault Farm airfield. He managed to fly above the Zeppelin and drop Rankin explosive darts, which although he could not see at the time, had inflicted serious damage causing the airship to lose height.

L.15 circled around Foulness Island, still losing hydrogen at an incredible rate. She continued out to sea, but finally ditched near the Kentish Knock Lighthouse, near Margate. Most of the crew were rescued by the armed trawler *Olivine* before the Zeppelin finally sank, after efforts to bring her back ashore failed. Breithaupt and his crew were landed at Chatham and sent to the Royal Navy Detention building, to spend the rest of the war as prisoners.

By 15th April 1916, it was decided that the various squadrons that were situated around London, should be formed into the 39th Home Defence Squadron, under the command of Major T.C.R. Higgins, who moved his headquarters from Hounslow to Woodford Green.

At Sutton's Farm, the conditions were improving rapidly, with timber hangars and brick buildings being constructed, making operational life more bearable. The arrival of new pilots and aircraft also helped to increase the morale, and by then the airfield had six serviceable aircraft. Among the new arrivals were William Leefe Robinson, who became flight commander of B flight; two young pilots, Lieutenants Frederick Sowrey and Wulstan Tempest, joined him in early June.

On 25th April, another Zeppelin alert was called and Lieutenant William Leefe Robinson was ordered to take off. He climbed to an altitude of 8,000 feet, when he sighted the Zeppelin LZ.97 some 2,000 feet above his position. He opened fire without success as his tracers fell short of the target and the airship began to outclimb him to safety. Lieutenant Robinson returned to the airfield somewhat disappointed with the outcome.

His luck was to change, however, five months later. On the night of 2nd/3rd September 1916, the German Army airship SL.11 left its base, to fly across the North Sea to make landfall at Foulness at 11.40 pm. The airship was not designated a Zeppelin, but a Schutte-Lanz, being made of a wooden frame, unlike the Zeppelins which were made of metal. Its commander, Captain Wilhelm Schramm, steered the airship on a new course to avoid the Thames defences, which were now well known.

He approached London from a northerly direction, travelling over Hertfordshire, and was to be seen over St.Albans at 1.10 am, finally dropping his bombs on London Colney, then at Enfield and Edmonton. Caught in the searchlight beams over Wood Green, the SL.11 was then engaged by the ground defence guns, which opened fire with no effect.

Earlier in the evening at 11.10 pm the telephone had rung at Leefe Robinson's bedside and he was ordered to 'Take air-raid action.' His aircraft, BE2c, serial No 2693, was wheeled out on to the field and made ready for take-off. Because Sutton's Farm was near the Thames, it was always dogged by fog and mist in late autumn and winter. That night was no exception, so mechanics and ground staff were busy lighting Money flares, which consisted of asbestos and paraffin, and burned for longer than the old method of buckets filled with petrol.

Leefe Robinson climbed into his cockpit, and checked his Lewis machine gun mounted above the top wing; the mechanic swung the propeller and the engine coughed into life. Robinson checked his instrument dials while the ground crew removed the blocks. He opened the throttle and the aircraft accelerated down the field and rose into the air. Meanwhile the SL.11 was making her way back home, crossing over the Thames, south-east of Woolwich, at about 1 am.

The following is the official report given by Lieutenant William Leefe Robinson on his engagement with SL.11 that evening and morning:

I have the honour to make the following report on night patrol, made by me on the night of the 2nd/3rd instant. I went up at 11.08 pm on the night of the 2nd, with instructions to patrol between Sutton's Farm and Joyce Green. I climbed to 10,000 feet in 53 minutes. I counted what I thought were ten sets of flares, there were clouds below me, but on the whole, it was a beautiful clear night.

I saw nothing until about 1.10 am, when two searchlights picked out a Zeppelin southeast of Woolwich. The clouds had collected in this quarter and the searchlights had some difficulty in keeping up with the aircraft. By this time I had managed to climb to 12,900 feet and I made in the direction of the Zeppelin, which was being fired on by a few anti-aircraft guns, hoping to cut it off on its way eastward.

I slowly gained on it for about ten minutes, I judged it to be about 200 feet below me and I sacrificed my speed in order to keep my height. It went behind some clouds, avoided the searchlights, and I lost sight of it. After about fifteen minutes of fruitless search I returned to my patrol.

I managed to pick up and distinguish my flares again. At about 1.50 am, I noticed a red glow in the northeast of London. Taking it to be an outbreak of fire I went in that direction. At about 2.05 am a Zeppelin was picked up by a searchlight over the north, northeast of London (as far as I could judge).

Remembering my last failure, I sacrificed height (I was still at 12,100 feet) for speed and made nose down for the Zeppelin. I saw shells bursting and night tracer shells flying around it. When I drew closer, I noticed that the anti-aircraft fire was too high or too low, also a good many rose 800 feet behind – a few tracers went right over. I could hear the bursts when about 3,000 feet from the Zeppelin.

I flew about 800 feet below it from bow to stern and distributed one drum along (alternate new Brock and Pomeroy) it seemed to have no effect. I then got behind it (by this time I was very close 500 feet or less below) and concentrated one drum on one part underneath.

I was then at a height of 11,500 feet, when attacking the Zeppelin. I had hardly finished the drum when I saw the part fired at glow. In a few seconds the whole rear part was blazing. When the third drum was fired there were no searchlights on the Zeppelin and no AA was firing. I quickly got out of the way of the falling blazing Zeppelin, and being very excited fired off a few red Very lights and dropped a parachute flare.

Having very little oil or petrol left I returned to Sutton's Farm, landing at 2.45 am. On landing I found that I had shot away the machine-gun wire guard, the rear part of the centre section and had pierced the rear main spar several times.

The falling blazing wreck of the SL.11 could be seen falling from the night sky from Staines to Southend. All over London people began cheering and crying out *'God save the King'* as the giant ball of flame continued its descent, finally crashing at Cuffley, just north of Enfield, behind the Plough public house in a beet field, where it burned on the ground for nearly two hours. Wilhelm Schramm and all his crew perished.

Once he had landed, Leefe Robinson who was totally exhausted and could hardly speak because of the cold, was met by Lieutenant Sowrey and taken to a small office, which had been made out of old aircraft packing casing. Here he was given a large cup of cocoa by a clerk, after which he wrote down his report and then went straight to his camp-bed in the hangar and immediately fell asleep. He was somewhat annoyed, when at dawn, he was awoken by Lieutenant Sowrey who said he would take him out to the scene of the crashed Zeppelin, Robinson shouted *For God's sake, can't a chap get some sleep on a Sunday morning?* Nevertheless he went to Cuffley and examined the remains of the SL.11, and was swamped with people wishing him all the best, shaking hands and patting him on the back. He stated later: *'My back is black and blue from all the thumps the crowds gave me'*.

The railways laid on special trains from King's Cross to carry an estimated 10,000 people to see the wreck at Cuffley. The bodies of the crew of SL.11 were initially placed under a tarpaulin, before being taken away and given a military funeral with Royal Flying Corp Officers carrying the coffin of Captain Schramm, at the village churchyard of Essendon. They were to stay there until they were exhumed in July 1966, and re-interred at Cannock Chase, Staffordshire, where the German dead of both World Wars now lie in the German Military Cemetery.

Leefe Robinson had become a national hero and on 5th September he was awarded the Victoria Cross, which was presented to him by King George V at Windsor Castle.

His photograph appeared in all the newspapers and magazines of the day, and he was recognised by crowds of people wherever he went. Even in his favourite restaurant in London, the Piccadilly Grill, where he would go to hear his favourite singer Violet Essex, he would not be left alone, drawing the attention of the audience from the singing star. Money too had also come his way. British businessmen had contributed large amounts of cash as rewards for the first airman to shoot down a Zeppelin over Britain; this amounted to £3,500.

At Sutton's Farm life would never be quite the same again, and the people of Hornchurch found new fame as they referred to 'our aerodrome'. There were frequent visits to the airfield by young single ladies, who were invited to take afternoon tea or a tour of the airfield by the young officers, including Robinson, who now had been promoted to captain.

Many Hornchurch villagers would often catch a glimpse of Robinson and Sowrey driving in a new Prince Henry Vauxhall car, which Robinson had purchased with some of his prize money.

On Saturday, 16th September, there was yet another airship alert. Again Leefe Robinson was the pilot on duty for that night, but whilst taking off down the field, his aircraft crashed into the boundary hedge. He escaped unhurt from the aircraft, which caught fire and was completely destroyed. This was the same aircraft, No 2693, that he had flown when shooting down the Zeppelin.

The following letter written by William Leefe Robinson to his parents and dated 22nd October 1916, perfectly sums up his attitude to the Zeppelin event and that of the British nation at the time:

October 22nd 1916.

My Darling Mother and Father

I do really feel ashamed for not writing to you darling old people before, but still, there it is – you know what I am.

Busy! Heavens for the last seven weeks I have done enough to last anyone a lifetime. It has been a wonderful time for me!

I won't say much about the 'Strafing' of Zepp L11 for two reasons, to begin with most of it is strictly secret and secondly I'm really tired of the subject and telling people about it, that I feel as if I never want to mention it again, so I will only say a very few words about it.

When the colossal thing actually burst into flames of course it was a glorious sight, wonderful ! It literally lit up all the sky around and me as well of course. I saw my machine as in the firelight and sat still half dazed staring at the wonderful sight before me, not realising to the least degree the wonderful thing that had happened!

My feelings? Can I describe my feelings? I hardly know how I felt. As I watched the huge mass gradually turn on end, and as it seemed to me slowly sink, one glowing, blazing mass, I gradually realised what I had done and grew wild with excitement. When I had cooled down a bit, I did what I think most people would not think to do, and that was thanked God with all my heart. You know darling old mother and father I'm not what is popularly known as a religious person, but on an occasion such as that one must realise a little how one does trust in providence. I felt an overpowering feeling of thankfulness, so was it strange that I should pause to think for a moment after the first 'Blast' of excitement as it were, was over and thank from the bottom of my heart, that supreme power that rules and guides our destinies.

When I reached the ground once more, I was greeted with 'was it you Robin' etc. etc. 'Yes, I've strafed the begger [sic] this time' I said, where upon the whole flight set up a yell and carried me out of my machine to the office cheering like mad.

Talking of cheering, they say it was wonderful to hear all London cheering.

People who have heard thousands of people cheering before, say they have heard nothing like it. When Sowrey and Tempest brought down their Zepps I had the opportunity of hearing something like it, although they say it wasn't as grand as mine, which could be heard twenty and even thirty miles outside London.

It swelled and sank, first one quarter of London, then another. Thousands one might say millions of throats giving vent to thousands of feelings.

I would give anything for you dear people to have heard it. A moment before dead silence (for the guns had ceased fire at it) then this outburst, the relief, the thanks, the gratitude of millions of people. All the sirens, hooters and whistles of steam engines, boats on the river, and munition and other works all joined in and literally filled the air, and the cause of it all, little me sitting in my little aeroplane above 13,000 feet of darkness!!, its wonderful!

And to think that I should be chosen to be the recipient of the thanks of all England! (For that's what it amounts to!)

Dear old 'G' who will be with you when you receive this will tell you something of the letters and telegrams I have received.

The day after I was awarded the V.C. I received thirty-seven telegrams, which includes one from my Colonel and one from General Henderson, who is of course the boss of the whole R.F.C.

I have had tons of interviews too; amongst which are those I have had with the Grand Duke Michael of Russia, Lord Curzon, General Sir David Henderson and heaps of others. When I went to Windsor to get the V.C. the King was awfully nice, asked me all about you dear people and grandfather etc, and showed me some awfully interesting photographs taken from the air over the German lines.

'G' will tell you all about the four days leave I had at Southbourne with her.

Oh, I could go on telling you what I have done and go on writing for a month of Sundays, but I must cut things short. I have, of course had hundreds of invitations most of which I have had to refuse owing to duty.

I went up to Newcastle for a day and was entertained by the Lord Mayor who gave a dinner in my honour, where I was presented with a cheque for two thousand pounds by Colonel Cowen of Newcastle. They wanted to make the whole thing a grand public function, but H.Q. wouldn't let them, for which I was very thankful. I've had endless other small presents; some of the nicest are paintings of the burning Zepp. By the by, about five artists have offered to paint my portrait for the R.A.

As I dare say you have seen in the papers, babies, flowers and hats have been named after me, also poems and prose have been dedicated to me, oh, it's too much!

I am recognised wherever I go about town now, whether in uniform or mufti, the City Police salute me, the waiters, hall porters and pages in hotels and restaurants bow and scrape, visitors turn around and stare. Oh it's too thick!

But the most glorious thing is that Sowrey, dear old boy, and Tempest, sweet soul, the two zepp strafers who have been awarded the D.S.O.'s are both in my flight!! Some flight – five officers, of which there are two D.S.O.'s and a V.C. and three zepps to our credit – some record!!

Well you darlings I'll close now or else I'll go babbling on all night and I'm really tired. I'll just tell you I'm not at present at Hornchurch, I'm somewhere in England on a secret mission but I'm going back to dear old Sutton's Farm again.

Well, do forgive me for not writing before.

Ever your loving son – Billy.

Sadly William Leefe Robinson would die of influenza on 31st December 1918, aged just 23 years. After leaving Sutton's Farm, he was sent to France. While flying with No.48 Squadron over the Western Front, he was shot down behind enemy lines on 5th April 1917 and became a prisoner of war. He returned home at the end of the war, suffering from ill health and exhaustion, brought on by the terrible conditions of the prisoner-of-war camp at Holzminden. He finally succumbed to the illness.

On the night of 23rd/24th September 1916, it was the turn of Lieutenant Frederick Sowrey to write himself into the history books, when he shot down one of two Super Zeppelins that were never to return to their home base.

The Zeppelins, L.32 commanded by Oberleutnant Werner Peterson and L.33 by Kapitanleutnant Alois Bocker, were two of 11 German naval airships sent out from Germany, to raid between the north of the Wash and as far as London.

At 4 pm on the 23rd, Leefe Robinson and Frederick Sowrey were taking afternoon tea, at the home of a Major Morton, along with his wife at Woodford. Major Morton was called to the telephone, and was asked to tell Robinson and Sowrey to return to Sutton's Farm immediately, as an alert had been received. It was not until 9 pm that both pilots received orders to stand ready; Sowrey was to take the first patrol.

Meanwhile the two Zeppelins had crossed the North Sea and had moved inland; L.32 reached Tunbridge Wells by 12.10 am on 24th September. He then turned northwards dropping a sighting flare at 12.30 am. At 12.50 am L.32 was caught in a searchlight beam over Swanley Junction; although the Zeppelin dropped bombs on the searchlight battery, it missed it. It continued over the town of Dartford and crossed the River Thames, east of

Purfleet, where it came under heavy fire from the gun positions situated between Beacon Hill and Tunnel Farm. The Zeppelin again answered by dropping nine high-explosive bombs, and six incendiaries, which all fell at Aveley.

At 11.25 pm, Lieutenant Sowrey had received his orders to patrol between Sutton's Farm and Joyce Green, and by 11.30 pm had taken off. By 1 am L.32 had dropped her bomb load and was now heading for home. The following account of what happened next is taken from Lieutenant Sowrey's report:

> The weather was fine and clear with a few thin clouds at 3,000 feet. At 4,000 feet, I passed another machine going in a northerly direction, I was then flying south. I continued climbing as hard as possible and at 12.10 am I noticed an enemy airship in a southerly direction. It appeared to be over Woolwich. I made for the airship at once, but before I reached it the searchlights lost it.
>
> I was at this time at 8,000 feet, there was a certain amount of gunfire, but it was not intense. I continued climbing and reached a height of 13,000 feet. At 12.45 am I noticed an enemy airship in an easterly direction. I at once made in this direction and manoeuvred into a position underneath it.
>
> The airship was now well lighted by searchlights, but there was no sign of gunfire. I could distinctly see the propellers revolving as the airship manoeuvred to avoid the searchlight beams. I fired at it. The first two drums of ammunition had apparently no effect, but the third caused the envelope to catch fire in several places, in the centre and front. All firing, was traversing fire along the envelope. Ammunition was loaded with a mixture of Brock, Pomeroy and tracer.
>
> I watched the burning airship strike the ground and then proceeded to find my flares. I landed back at Sutton's Farm.
>
> My machine was BE2c No 4112. After seeing the Zeppelin had caught fire, I fired a red Very light.

Lieutenant Sowrey's machine gun fire had in fact hit one of the cylinder petrol tanks stowed along the length of the Zeppelin's central walkway. In seconds it had engulfed the airship, sending it crashing down to fall at Snail's Hall Farm, Great Burstead, near Billericay, Essex. All the crew perished; Commander Werner Peterson's body was found some distance away from the wreckage. He had obviously jumped to his death, rather than being burnt alive.

After landing his aircraft back at Sutton's Farm at 1.40 am, Sowrey was met by Leefe Robinson and Captain Frederick Bowers, who congratulated him and gave him a hot drink. He then contacted Major Morton at Headquarters, Woodford Green, passing on his information and asking for permission to go to the crash site and inspect the remains of the airship.

This was granted, but not before he wrote out his report of the events.

Both Sowrey and Robinson, along with Captains Bowers and Stammers and Lieutenant Durstan, jumped into Robinson's Prince Henry Vauxhall, and began the journey to Great Burstead.

The people of Hornchurch, who had been watching the fall of the Zeppelin, cheered as the pilots passed through the village. By the time Sowrey and his group had arrived at the crash site, the area had been cordoned off by soldiers, to stop any members of the public from getting too near.

Heated words were in fact exchanged, when an army officer refused Sowrey entrance through, until he was told that this was the airman who had shot the airship down.

Again, as with Robinson's airship, thousands of people made the trip to view the downed airship, travelling by road and train, many picking up souvenirs of the Zeppelin's metal framework.

The public were even charged a fee of 2d to gain admission to the site; the proceeds went to the Red Cross Funds and about £80 was collected. Other people who inspected the site included high-ranking officials including David Lloyd George, shortly to become Prime Minister and Arthur Balfour who was with the Admiralty.

For his heroic actions Lieutenant Frederick Sowrey was awarded the Distinguished Service Order. The late Ronald Shelley, of Billericay, interviewed in 1994, at the age of 91, remembered:

> I was just 13 years old, when I saw both the Zeppelins come down in flames, the one at Cuffley and the one at Billericay. My father brought me over to see the remains of this one, the L.32. It was on a Saturday, I remember all the people. Anyone who had a car at the time was blowing their horns and cheering, the country lanes were completely clogged up with people, coming and going to the site. If it had fallen on the town, it would have burnt it to the ground.

Lieutenant Sowrey's son, Air Marshal Sir Frederick Sowrey, when interviewed in March 1997, recalled many of the memories that his father had of this time:

> He often spoke about the difficulties of night flying at that particular time; they were in fact the very first night fighters. There was no cockpit lighting for the instruments; he had a torch hanging around his neck on a lanyard with the battery tucked into his tunic pocket. He talked about the difficulties in finding the landing ground after a patrol, no aids as such, no radio, just visual, looking over the side trying to identify certain landmarks by moonlight if it was a clear night, or looking out for the flare path.
>
> Pilots was very much on their own. They operated at

altitudes, where these days you would use oxygen and the cold was very intense. For this, the pilot's pay was the princely sum of ten shillings a day.

He was elated when he had shot down the Zeppelin, as was his friend Bill Robinson, who had done the same earlier in the month. At twenty-three years of age, he was embodied with the spirit of emulating his fellow pilot. My father, Robinson and Tempest all belonged to the same flight in No 39 Squadron; in fact they broke the back of the German airship campaign. The effect of their better L. Class airships being shot down in flames, in sight and sound of the previously dispirited population of London, did two things; it lifted the morale of Londoners sky high, and it made the German Naval Airship Service think twice about the kind of losses it could sustain in a protracted campaign.

He was very appreciative of his ground crew, and insisted that when the photographs of himself were taken by his aircraft, the morning after the Zeppelin was shot down, the crew were in the photograph as well. They looked a bit embarrassed about being in the limelight, but he wanted them to share in some of the glory, which he had achieved, to rub off on them as well.

He often talked about his great friend Bill Robinson; relationships in the First War were very different to what they were later on. People didn't have the inhibitions in expressing their friendships, men would walk arm in arm, as some of the pictures of the time show, five or six Royal Flying Corps officers walking in a line. He received many hundreds of letters and poems from wellwishers thanking him for what he had done; he wisely kept all these for the future, and they are now kept at the RAF Museum, Hendon, where they can be seen by future historians.

Zeppelin L.33 had also been destroyed on 23rd/ 24th September; this was shot down by Lieutenant Alfred Brandon, who had flown from Hainault Farm airfield. Although Brandon failed to ignite it, the airship was losing its height and buoyancy owing to damage inflicted by anti-aircraft guns and his machine guns. The airship gradually came to earth and landed intact at Little Wigborough. Not wishing the Zeppelin to fall into British hands, the crew set light to it, and then proceeded to walk up the local country lane in regimental order to find the local or military authorities to surrender themselves. For his actions Lieutenant Brandon was awarded the DSO.

Another raid on Britain by Zeppelins took place on the night of 1st/2nd October 1916, when ten Zeppelins were sent to attack towns and cities in the Midlands, Norfolk, Lincolnshire and London. One of these Zeppelins was L.31, commanded by the famous airship commander Heinrich Mathy. As the airship approached London, it was intercepted by Lieutenant

Wulstan Tempest, also stationed at Sutton's Farm.

Tempest, who was a friend of Robinson and Sowrey's, had flown over to North Weald airfield earlier in the day, to meet with friends and stay for dinner in Epping. He was also on patrol duty for that evening and decided to begin this from North Weald. Told of the incoming Zeppelin, Tempest was ordered to begin his patrol at 11 pm.

By 11.45 he had climbed to an altitude of 14,000 feet and was over the south-west of London; below there was a heavy fog with the beams of searchlights penetrating up through the mist. Tempest turned his head north-east; where he could see the outline of Zeppelin L.31 against the illuminated sky. The ground defences had opened fire causing the Zeppelin to take evasive measures and start to climb, to avoid the barrage of exploding shells; Tempest continued to pursue at about 15,000 feet. He was about five miles behind the airship when his aircraft's fuel pressure pump decided to break down, causing the flow of petrol to his engine to dry up. Tempest had no option but to operate the hand pump to keep up the pressure in his petrol tank, while operating the rest of the aircraft's flying controls with the other hand. He was now becoming very exhausted as he finally came within firing range of the giant airship.

The gun batteries below had almost ceased firing, as L.31 moved out of their range. What happened next is drawn from Tempest's official report:

> As I drew up to the Zeppelin, to my relief I found that I was quite free of Anti-Aircraft fire, for the nearest shells were bursting some three miles away. The Zeppelin was nearly 12,700 feet high and climbing rapidly. I therefore started to dive at her, for though I felt I had a slight advantage in speed, she was climbing like a rocket and leaving me standing. I accordingly gave a tremendous pump at my petrol tank and dived straight at her, firing a burst into her as I came. I let her have another burst as I passed under her and then banking my machine over, sat on her tail, and flying along underneath, pumped lead into her for all I was worth. I could see tracer bullets flying from her in all directions, but I was too close under her for them to concentrate on me. As I was firing I noticed her begin to go red inside, like an enormous Chinese lantern, then a flame shot out of the front part of her, and I realized she was on fire. She then shot up about 200 feet, paused, and then came roaring straight down on me before I had time to get out of the way. I nose-dived for all I was worth, with the Zepp tearing after me, and I expected any minute to be engulfed in flames. I put my machine into a spin, and just managed to corkscrew out of the way in time as she shot past me, roaring like a furnace. I righted my machine and watched her hit the ground with a shower of sparks. I then proceeded to fire off dozens of green Very Lights, in the exuberance of my feelings.

I glanced at my watch and I saw it was about 12.10 am. I
then commenced to feel very sick, giddy and exhausted, and
had considerable difficulty in finding my way to the ground
through the fog; in landing I crashed and cut my head on my
machine gun.

For this outstanding action against the enemy and not withstanding other
difficulties, i.e., his aircraft's engine problem, Lieutenant Wulstan Tempest
was awarded the DSO. The Zeppelin L.31 crashed at Oakmere Farm,
Potters Bar; again there were no survivors.

Once again the newspapers and media were drawn to Sutton's Farm and
their three Zeppelin heroes. Photographs, postcards etc, showing the three
airmen's smiling faces adorned shops and houses across the land.

The people of Hornchurch, who were especially proud, contributed to a
collection, and on 14th October 1916, at the New Zealand Army Camp at
Grey Towers Mansion, Hornchurch, a presentation of three large silver
cups was made to William Leefe Robinson, Frederick Sowrey and Wulstan
Tempest, by the chairman of the Hornchurch Parish Council, W.H. Legg,
along with Thomas Gardiner JP.

The Germans tried one more raid in October 1917, but it was a complete
disaster, mainly due to bad weather conditions. A new menace however was
looming with the arrival of the German long-range bomber biplanes, the
LVG CII, a two-seater reconnaissance aircraft, converted to carry 20lb
bombs; this had a radius of 200 miles; while the twin-engined Gotha had a
crew of three, and carried a bomb load of great capacity.

The first aircraft raid carried out on London came on 28th November
1916. An LVG CII aircraft managed to elude the ground defences, and got
as far as the West End of London, dropping six 20lb bombs, causing only
minor damage; there were no fatalities, but ten people were injured. By the
time the Home Defence squadrons had been alerted, including Sutton's
Farm, who sent up Lieutenant Sowrey at 1 pm in his BE12 aeroplane, the
German aircraft was already making its return, being sighted near Hastings
and the Channel, with no hope of intercepting it.

These small raids continued during the first few months of 1917, until
towards the end of May, the Gothas of No.3 Kahgohl Staffel (Squadron),
who were based in enemy-held Belgium, began their first heavy raids. The
first on Folkestone on 25th May, killed 95 people; on 5th June, 22 Gothas
raided as far as Sheerness and Shoeburyness. On 13th June, 14 aircraft got
as far as London at 12.10 pm near Liverpool Street station, Aldgate East
and Fenchurch Street area. The Gothas dropped in total 72 100lb bombs,
inflicting 162 deaths and over 400 injured; among the fatalities were 18
children who died when their infant school was hit in Poplar.

Pilots from Sutton's Farm were alerted to the raid, and two BE12 aircraft
took off, piloted by Captain R. Stammers and Captain T. Gran, who sighted
the enemy at between 15,000 and 16,000 feet on their return from bombing
London. They began to chase the bombers from around 12,000 feet, firing
from below as they came within range. As they engaged the Gothas just

over Romford, Captain Stammers' aircraft engine began to give him problems and he had to break away from the attack and return to Sutton's Farm. Captain Gran continued his attack over the River Crouch, but the faster Gothas soon flew out of range, with the BE12's of the RFC totally out-matched by the speed and armament of the German aircraft.

By late June, the Home Defence squadrons were being allocated new aircraft in the form of the Sopwith Pup, a faster and more manoeuvrable aeroplane than the BE12, with better armament to deal with the Gotha threat. Six of the new aircraft were sent to No.39 Squadron, while their CO Major R.G. Murrey, was replaced by Major J.C. Halahan. On 7th July, Gothas flying at a height of 13,000 feet attacked London, dropping 26 bombs. Alerted to the raid Lieutenant E.S.Moulton-Barrett, flying from Sutton's Farm, took off in an SE5, another of the newly designed faster aircraft. In hot pursuit, he engaged three of the enemy aircraft, and emptied three drums of ammunition into one Gotha, with no result or effect showing on the enemy aircraft. Now out of ammunition, he followed the enemy formation as far as Shoeburyness, trying to push its course near to the anti-aircraft guns which were situated there.

Another squadron was ordered in to help repel the Gotha raids; this fell to No.46 Squadron, who had been withdrawn from the fighting in France. Led by its commanding officer Major Philip Babington, it arrived at Sutton's Farm with its Sopwith Pups on 10th July, 1917. This crack squadron had also gained the reputation of being airborne, from first news of an alert, in just five minutes. But by August 1917 the squadron was again re-assigned back to France.

On 8th August the flying ace Captain James McCudden paid a visit to members of No.46 Squadron. He was later (March 1918), given notice of his award of the Victoria Cross, for his outstanding service on the Western Front.

No.66 Squadron held the briefest of stays at the airfield. It had been carrying out ground attack sorties during the Battle of Messines during May. It was then sent to the northern coast of France to try and intercept Gotha raids on their way across to London. From here in July it was sent to Sutton's Farm. Led by its CO Major G.L.P. Henderson, it continued the same operations, but after three days was posted back to Belgium to prepare to take part in the Second Battle of Ypres and Menin Ridge.

In September, No.39 Squadron were posted to North Weald, and was replaced by No.78 Squadron. The squadron commander was Major C.W. Rowden, and it was equipped with the two-seater Sopwith $1^1/_2$ Strutter, which was soon to be replaced by the famous Sopwith Camel.

One of the squadron's first engagements with the enemy took place on the night of 25th September, when the squadron sent up Captain B.J. Bell on patrol. He was flying a course between the Thames and Joyce Green in Kent, at a height of 9,000 feet, when he was fired upon by a German Gotha aircraft. Captain Bell turned his aircraft to pursue the enemy aeroplane, following it eastwards for over 15 minutes, firing as he went, but lost sight of it over the Gravesend area.

Also during this month, was the first arrival of the women's service, the

Women's Legion Auxiliary. They were sent to Sutton's to work alongside the men as telephonists, clerical staff and drivers; some of them were billeted at the large country-house style building at Bretton's Farm, situated between the airfield and Dagenham.

It was during the beginning of 1918, that a young Ronald Shelley, as a boy used to spend some of his days visiting Sutton's Farm airfield. The following details are of events witnessed by him during his many visits:

> I used to get the steam train with my friends, down to Squirrels Heath station at Gidea Park, near Romford, and then walk down to Hornchurch village and Sutton's Farm. We got down there early one morning, but the sheds were closed, but we were sure that they would do some flying that day, so we hung on and hung on. We then decided to have our packed lunch, then go home as nothing was doing; all of a sudden the claxon sounded, the hangar doors opened and the machines were wheeled out on to the field. The mechanics warmed them up, and after a while they all took to the air, including Captain Armstrong in his red Sopwith Camel. It transpired that there was a 'Brass hat's meeting', and they were being given a show, Captain Armstrong did his stunting. I think he got into a bit of trouble because he did one or two really low dives at them, but to think we would have missed it, if we had gone home early.
>
> Another afternoon, we saw an RE8 spinning out of the sky. It crash-landed in an old beetroot field, next to the aerodrome, and my friend and I rushed over to where it was. Fortunately for the pilot, he had managed to pull the aircraft up in time to crash horizontally instead of nosing straight in. He was very dazed, and we tried to get him out. By that time however, the van had come over from the sheds, and they cut open the fuselage and carried him out, I picked up his goggles and helmet. They put him on a stretcher and I put his stuff on his chest, He said, 'What happened?'and then fainted. I later found out that his name was Jenkins.
>
> One day at Sutton's, we were sitting near the airfield hedge, when five Bristol fighters came into land, one after the other. By the time the fifth one got over the boundary hedge, he had sunk down a bit too low, and he caught his front wheel axle on a small tree stump as he came in; his aircraft nosed over smashing the prop to pieces. The chap got out with his nose bleeding. The mechanics came running over, and one took the broken prop blade and laid it in the undergrowth, saying, 'I'll come back for that later,' probably keeping it for a souvenir.
>
> I can remember another time, we walked up one of the roads, which had a gate at the end; this was close to the farm, next to the airfield, and very close to the hangar. A few

seconds later a couple of Sopwith Camels came racing low over our heads firing their machine guns at a target in the centre of the aerodrome. It was an exciting experience to see this, one could imagine what it was like with all the noise from the guns etc, and being on the Western Front, but also at the time it was very frightening.

At the beginning of March 1918, the RFC had a new aircraft, the Sopwith Snipe, which was intended to succeed the Sopwith Camel. This new aircraft, one of the prototypes, was given a flight demonstration at Sutton's Farm on 10th March in front of high-ranking Royal Flying Corps officers. It was left in the capable hands of Captain James McCudden VC, who proceeded to throw it around the sky with great manoeuvrability.

On 1st April 1918, the Royal Flying Corps became the Royal Air Force, and during this month, a new night training squadron, No.189, arrived at the airfield, to complement No.78.

The Germans mounted their last raid on London on 19th May 1918. One of the Gotha aeroplanes was intercepted by a Sopwith Camel from Sutton's, flown by Captain D.V. Armstrong of No.78 Squadron, who engaged the aircraft just north-west of Orsett, near Tilbury. He dived his machine at the intruder and fired bursts of machine gun fire, from above and below the enemy aeroplane, avoiding the return fire from the rear machine gunner. It had started to lose height, when it was also engaged by another aircraft, a Bristol two-seater fighter, from North Weald, belonging to Sutton's old squadron No.39. It was crewed by Lieutenant A.J. Arkell and gunner Air Mechanic A.T.C. Stagg, who now poured more deadly fire into the Gotha. After several minutes, the enemy aircraft burst into flames and headed down, crashing near the Royal Albert Dock, at Roman Road, East Ham.

By this time Sutton's Farm was now under No.49 Wing, whose headquarters were at RAF Upminster, Upminster Hall. The wing also controlled Hainault Farm and North Weald airfields; its commander was Colonel Malcolm G. Christie.

With no attacks being made by the German air forces, the airfield settled down to a quiet state of readiness, but during August and September there was little activity on the airfield. On Saturday, 3rd August 1918, a 'sports meeting' took place at the airfield at 3 pm, which was organized by No.78 and 189 Squadrons, with entertainment supplied by the New Zealand Hospital Band, who were billeted at the Gray Towers Mansion in Hornchurch. The sports programme included tug-o-war, three-legged race, one hundred yards race, football match, ladies' egg and spoon race, one-mile race and greasy pole; the judges for the day were Major Powell MC and Captain Gran MC.

Also about this time, an inter-squadron competition was organised by the RAF, titled 'Squadron in Arms', which included not only formation flying skills, but also ground maintenance, parade ground drill, and wireless telegraphy skills. The competition finals were held at Sutton's on 22nd

September 1918. The winner was No.141 Squadron from Biggin Hill, Kent, whose trophy was awarded to them by Lord Weir of Eastwood and General Ashmore, who commanded the London Air Defences.

On 11th November 1918, at 11 am, the First World War had come to an end, and with it Sutton's Farm's active role in it. What had started out as an experiment with just a small number of men, had ended with an airfield manned by 300 RAF officers and men, and 24 WRAFs; all of them could be proud of what they had achieved.

When the task of winding down the Home Defence airfields began, the War Office, lacking foresight, could not see any further use for the continuation of Sutton's Farm, and on 31st March 1919, No.189 (Night Training) Squadron were disbanded.

The last squadron to be posted to Sutton's Farm after hostilities had ceased, were No. 51 who arrived in May 1919, led by Major H.L.H. Owen. It was there for less than one month before being disbanded on 13th June. Finally on 31st December, No.78 Squadron, the last operational squadron at Sutton's Farm, were disbanded.

It is worth recording that during the whole of the night campaign from September 1916 to the end of May 1918, only three pilots were killed and one observer wounded, in all the thousands of flights carried out when raids were in progress. All the fatal casualties were due to crashes, with a single case of the observer being wounded in action on the night of 28th/29th January 1918. The observer was First Air Mechanic W. Merchant, who was flying with 2nd Lieutenant J.G. Goodyear in a Bristol Fighter of No.39 Squadron. The fatalities were 2nd Lieutenant S. Armstrong of No.37 Squadron killed on the night of 18th February 1918 and Captain A.B. Kynock, also of No.37 Squadron, killed on 7th March 1918, when in collision with another aircraft belonging to Captain H.C. Stroud of No.61 Squadron, who also died in the crash.

Most of the men and women who had played their part at the airfield were demobilised, and they tried to return back to their previous occupations and lives, as best they could. The airfield reverted to farmland, and was given back to Mr Tom Crawford, to continue his livelihood of growing farm produce. Most of the wooden buildings were torn down, but any of the brick ones that seemed suitable for farming use were left on site. The first part of this airfield's memorable story had come to a close.

CHAPTER 2

THE PHOENIX RISES
1920-1936

So it was, that after four years of world war, the peace and quiet of the countryside returned to Hornchurch village and Sutton's Farm. This tranquillity was only to last for another four years, however. In 1922, an RAF expansion programme was put forward by the Government of the day, under the scrutiny of a committee set up by the Secretary of State for Air, Sir Samuel Hoare, and including the Marquis of Salisbury and Lord Trenchard, the Chief of the Air Staff.

They were to look into the future role that the RAF would play alongside the other armed services, including its role in defence, should the need arise once more.

When the final report was submitted to the House of Commons in 1922, one of the main proposals was for the re-emergence of the Home Defence squadrons, for which the Government would allow concessions to provide for 14 bomber squadrons and 9 fighter squadrons. This was expanded, however, when the Prime Minister, Stanley Baldwin, announced on 20th June 1923 that the Defence Force would increase to 52 squadrons, comprised of 35 bomber and 17 fighter squadrons, with an estimated total of 394 bomber aircraft and 204 fighters. The squadrons were to include newly-formed auxiliary squadrons and special reserve units, whose staff and airmen were mainly weekend fliers who belonged to small flying clubs, although many trained 'on the job'.

With the increase of the RAF, it was clear new airfields would be needed for this expansion.

The Air Ministry sent teams to revisit the former airfields of World War One and designated the new sites, to gather information on their suitability. Sutton's Farm was visited by one such team on 24th November 1922. When they arrived, however, they found the former airfield almost unrecognisable, having been converted back to arable land. Apart from the few brick buildings, including the Guard Room and WRAF quarters there seemed little that could be used. However it was decided that the area could be re-developed into an airfield, because of its strategic importance, although it would have to be enlarged with more land further south.

In July 1923 the owners, New College, Oxford, signed the agreement of sale with the Treasury and Air Ministry for the proposed land, though the College did request that the new airfield boundary would be at least 300 yards from the Sutton's Farm house. Once again, however, farmer Tom Crawford had to relinquish most of his land.

The building of the new airfield did not start until the following year in May 1924. The design was of classic 1920s with all the brick buildings tall and strong, but basic, apart from the Officers' Mess which was built across the road from the main site, opposite the main gates. This stood in its own grounds, the entrance being dominated by the large Greek-like pillars. Inside were an ante-room for relaxing, a large dining room, and bedrooms. Adjacent to the Officers' Mess was the married quarters accommodation, which was the best accommodation that the RAF had for its officer-ranks at the time, and was quite exceptional.

On the main site there were three C-Type hangars and watch office, the main barrack blocks for enlisted men, the Sergeants' Mess, and of course a dining room and cookhouse; however it would take four more years of building and refinements before the airfield was completely ready.

The airfield was officially opened on 1st April 1928. It retained its name of RAF Sutton's Farm, but within two months it was decided to change it to RAF Hornchurch. The first commanding officer to take control of RAF Hornchurch was in fact the CO of the first squadron to be sent to the airfield. His name was Squadron Leader Keith Park, MC, DFC, who arrived with No.111 Squadron, which flew in from RAF Duxford equipped with Armstrong-Whitworth Siskin biplanes. Keith Park, a New Zealander, began the task of setting up the daily routines that the new airfield staff needed in the running of an efficient airfield. He would talk with the ground staff, as well as the pilots and airmen, about the problems they were experiencing. This kind of attitude would serve him well later, when as commander of No.11 Group during the Battle of Britain, he would be found visiting his airfields, talking to the battle-weary pilots (who held him in great respect) to find out their situation and needs. With Squadron Leader Park came three flight commanders, G.T. Richardson, A.J.E. Broomfield, DFC and H.J. Gemmel.

It was during April that Hornchurch received the first of many foreign pilots who were attached to the RAF for flying practice training during the 1930s. Lieutenant E. Reissar of the Estonian Air Force was assigned to No.111.

During the month of June, the station was forewarned that it was to play host to General Italo Balbo, who was commander-in-chief of the Regia Aeronautica (Italian Air Force). He had flown with 11 other aircraft from Rome to England, and Hornchurch would have the honour of escorting the Italian aircraft from the coast of Essex, up the Thames Estuary and to the final touch down at Hornchurch. They met the Italian aircraft with five Siskin aircraft of No.111 Squadron.

It was about this time that a young pilot officer joined No.111, who had just graduated from the RAF College at Cranwell, and was destined to change the course of aviation history by the mid 1940s; his name was Frank Whittle, and he would go on to design the first British jet engine.

By 1929, the airfield had settled down to a daily routine, and the squadron spent a lot of its time practising formation and set pieces for flying displays at the RAF Hendon Air Display. In March, a new commanding officer was assigned to the squadron, Squadron Leader F.O. Soden, who took over from Keith Park. During April and May, the aircrew were involved with army co-operation and anti-aircraft exercises. In June the first ever radio transmitter sets were issued to No.111 Squadron, whose CO commented at the time, 'this marked an epoch in the Squadron's progress, as we are now within the immediate control of the Sector and Group Commanders'. They were joined in July 1929, by two other squadrons on detachment to Hornchurch. These were No.19 Squadron from RAF Duxford, and No.23 Squadron who flew in from Kenley; they were flying Gloster Gamecocks.

John Gill was a schoolboy living in Dagenham at this time and remembers clearly the day trips he would take with friends to visit the airfield:

> We used to walk over from Dagenham, which was about a four mile walk; it would take us all day to get there and back. The area was so underdeveloped, it was all farmland. The two squadrons that were there were flying Bristol Bulldogs. They converted to Hawker Furys and later to Super Furys. Being youngsters, we would come up to the side of the aerodrome, and providing we all behaved ourselves we were allowed to sit just inside the railings of the boundary and watch the mechanics push out the Bulldogs to service them, and get them ready for the pilots to go off on their practice flights. We used to do that practically every summer holiday; even during term time we could see the planes flying around from our school in Dagenham.
>
> Occasionally we would walk past the main gates, where there would be a sentry on duty, and often see the Officers Mess across the road, which had tennis courts outside and a small croquet lawn. They would hold guest weekends there for people with families, who would come down with their children; some of the pilots of course were married and lived out in married quarters. One or two times I came over when they had air displays. They would improvise on different sports events, and they would have chariot races, where two pilots would pull a wooden contraption on wheels. Another pilot would stand on the seat of the chariot with a pair of reins, and they would have covered themselves in a chocolate sort of concoction they'd whipped up to make them look like Roman slaves. Then they'd have chariot races around the edge of the airfield, which provided quite a good alternative to watching aircraft all day.

Together the three squadrons participated in the Air Defence of Great

Britain Exercises, which took place in August, testing the skill and effectiveness of the squadrons in this role. By the end of August, Treble-One was sent away to Sutton Bridge gunnery camp for the annual firing practice. In September it was given its leave period, during which the station would seem almost deserted.

By October, Squadron Leader Soden had left and had been replaced by Squadron Leader Leonard H. Slatter, who was to be the first official Station Commander at RAF Hornchurch when the station headquarters were formed in January 1930. The weather in December 1929 was quite severe during 22 days of that month and it was impossible to fly because of thick fog.

On 15th January the station headquarters was officially opened under the Air Ministry Authority 909008/29, establishment No. HD/929. The station's strength was 27 officers, 243 aircrew and 28 civilian staff.

It was also on this same day that Hornchurch saw the arrival of another squadron, which in the next 11 years would distinguish itself many times while serving at the airfield. The squadron was No.54.

The squadron arrived at the airfield in their Siskin biplanes under the command of Wing Commander W.E. Bryant. By 4th April, Squadron Leader Slatter had been posted and the station commander's post had been filled by Wing Commander E.R. Manning. Four days later No.54 Squadron received their new aircraft, the Bristol Bulldog.

On 15th April 1930 Air Officer Commanding, Air Vice-Marshal Hugh C.T. Dowding, CB, CMG inspected the station for the first time.

Of the many visitors to Hornchurch, one of the most surprising at this time arrived from far across the Pacific to take part in a training course at the airfield. He was Lieutenant Y. Kobayashi, a member of the Imperial Japanese Naval Air Service. Unfortunately on 17th April, at about 3.30 pm while conducting an air exercise in a Siskin III aircraft, serial No.J8861, the aeroplane's engine suffered a failure and burst into flames. He managed to bale out, and the machine landed a short distance away from the aerodrome, burning itself out completely. Kobayashi was severely injured and suffered from superficial burns. On landing he was stretchered away, and taken to the Victoria Hospital in Romford.

The following letter was sent to Air Vice-Marshal C.L.N. Newall, Air Ministry, from the Japanese Naval Attaché in London regarding Lieutenant Kobayashi:

> Dear Air Vice-Marshal Newall,
> I greatly appreciate your letter of sympathy on the accident to Lieutenant Kobayashi the other day, and wish to take this opportunity of expressing to you personally and to all the officers concerned my grateful thanks for the care and attention shown to Lieutenant Kobayashi since the accident occurred.
>
> From the latest news I have received it appears that Lieutenant Kobayashi is making excellent progress and that he is well on the way to recovery.

It is extremely kind of you to offer further assistance, if this should be necessary I shall gladly avail myself of your good offers.

Yours Sincerely,
(Signed) SHIMADZU
Japanese Naval Attaché.

Another flying accident occurred on 29th April, when a Bristol Bulldog aircraft of No.54 Squadron, piloted by Flying Officer T.B. Byrne, crashed. During a routine flight in Bristol Bulldog K.1091, he had begun to put his aircraft into a dive, but once into the dive he noticed the wings starting to disintegrate. Without further hesitation he vacated his aircraft and landed by parachute unhurt, while his aircraft lay in pieces, smashed into the ground.

No.54 Squadron were sent to Sutton Bridge Camp for two weeks starting 28th July 1930, for air-to-air gunnery, ground strafing and bombing. Meanwhile back at Hornchurch, life continued at the same relaxed tempo, with No.111 participating in air displays and routine air and groundwork.

Hornchurch supplied three officers and eighteen airmen on 9th October for the Guard of Honour at Westminster Abbey, for the lying-in-state of the aircrew personnel killed in the R.101 airship tragedy. The airship had crashed at Beauvais, France while on route to Egypt. Among the 46 who perished were Lord Thomson, Secretary of State for Air, and Sir Sefton Brancker, Director of Civil Aviation.

By December 1930, No.111 had a new commander, Squadron Leader E.R. Openshaw, and in early 1931, the squadron replaced their old Siskin aircraft with the Bristol Bulldog. It was still heavily involved with experimentation on the new ground-to-air and air-to-air radio transmitting equipment, with squadron formations regularly practising using them. No.111 were also selected to test a new form of gun-sight. On 29th July 1931, a reflector sight was introduced and fitted to one of the squadron's aircraft for assessment. Trials were carried out at Sutton Bridge Practice Camp, and the results proved a great success. Also that year, the squadron was involved with tests of new high-pressure oxygen equipment, three new types of oxygen mask-microphones and new flying helmets; also a new type of Very light and a portable beacon.

In 1932, No.54 Squadron received a new CO, Squadron Leader S.L. Pope, who took over from Wing Commander Bryant and was later to become Chief of the Air Staff. One new arrival at the aerodrome was a young pilot officer, John Grandy, who was posted to No.54 Squadron from No.5 Flying Training School at Sealand; he arrived at Hornchurch on 29th August 1932. Also posted to Hornchurch at this time was a young New Zealander fresh from RAF Cranwell who would rise through the ranks to Air Marshal with a distinguished career, especially with Coastal Command, during the war; this was Charles 'Kiwi' Broughton. He was posted to No.111 Squadron before being sent to No.11 Squadron, flying Hawker Hart light bombers, based in Risalpur, India in 1933.

The routine at Hornchurch over the next couple of years was much the same as many other main RAF aerodromes, carrying out Air Defence Exercises, and preparing for air displays such as the annual Hendon Display.

RAF Hornchurch held an Empire Air Day Display on 24th May 1934, which attracted a large crowd of over 4,000 to marvel at the aerobatics of No.54 Squadron, and to look at the static display of aircraft stretched out over the airfield; £180 8s. 6d was raised and donated to the RAF Benevolent Fund.

The squadrons remained the same until 12th July 1934, when No.111 Squadron were sent to RAF Northolt and replaced by the newly re-formed No.65 Squadron. They arrived, flying Hawker Demons and led by Squadron Leader F.O. Soden. On 13th July, Hornchurch received a royal visitor, when His Royal Highness, Edward, Prince of Wales, arrived by aeroplane on a trip to visit the newly opened Ford Car Factory at Dagenham.

In early 1935, the aerodrome received two visits from VIPs, Air Vice-Marshal Sir Robert Brooke-Popham, Air Officer Commanding in Chief, Air Defence of Great Britain and Sir Philip Sassoon. It was also around this time that the new London Transport station at Elm Park, which was situated on the District Line, was now opened making visits to and from RAF Hornchurch much more accessible.

On 23rd March, 56 members from six Observer Corps posts affiliated to the station visited the airfield. Unfortunately owing to unfavourable weather it was impossible to demonstrate a series of flight attacks and aerobatics, but a Bulldog and Demon aircraft did manage to get airborne in the afternoon.

The Empire Air Day on 25th May 1935 was again a great success with an attendance of 4,503 and £163 11s. 6d. raised.

The Air Defence Exercises that year took place at RAF Kenley, with only No.54 Squadron taking part from Hornchurch. The exercises were formed with one attacking force of bombers (Southland), who had to try and break through a defending force of defensive fighters (Northland), who were directed on to their targets by ground controllers using radio-telephony. In December 1935, Hornchurch received a new Station Commander, Wing Commander Arthur Stanley Gould Lee; he had actually served as a lieutenant at Sutton's Farm during the First War with No.46 Squadron, flying Sopwith Pups.

Life continued much the same, except for the uneasy rumblings in Europe brought about by the powerful dictatorship of the new fascist Germany, which was causing many politicians to feel insecure about their country's defences.

The year of 1936 began with two significant events in January and February. The death of King George V on 20th January was a tragic loss to the nation. A Memorial Service was held at St Andrew's church, Hornchurch on 2nd February. This was attended by a contingent of 100 officers and airmen from the airfield, led by Flight Lieutenant G.W. Gay. A few weeks later RAF Hornchurch played host to the 1936 Air Defence of Great Britain Exercises. Over the week of the exercises various squadrons defended and attacked given targets, which included the Ford Motor Factory at Dagenham situated on the Thames, and also the Hornchurch airfield. The airfield's own squadrons were on the defending side along with other squadrons flown in; these included No.56 Squadron, flying Bristol Bulldogs, No.19 with Gloster Gauntlets and No.111, who were there to train for night interceptions.

Another of RAF Hornchurch's famous sons also arrived on the airfield that month, Pilot Officer Donald Osborne Finlay, posted from No.17 Squadron to No.54 Squadron, who presented himself to the squadron adjutant on 16th February. He was a fine athlete and became captain of the British Olympic team which participated in the Games held in Munich that year. He would have a greater role ahead in the Battle of Britain.

The Empire Air Day, held on 23rd May that year, recorded a new attendance level with 14,750 of the public coming through the gates, and many more watching for free outside. It was during this time that Hornchurch's squadrons started to convert from their Bristol Bulldog aircraft to the newer Gloster Gauntlet. The Gauntlet was a good 50 mph faster than the Bulldog and Demon aircraft, although the armament was still the same twin Vickers .303 machine guns; but the ceiling altitude was higher at 33,500 feet compared to 27,000 feet. The crowds were entertained from 2 pm till 7 pm including music by the band of the 28th Essex Anti-Aircraft Battalion Royal Engineers and the Dagenham Girl Pipers. Thirteen different types of aircraft, service and civilian, were exhibited in the aircraft park. A Short Scion aircraft gave passenger flights throughout the afternoon and 15 free flights were given as prizes in a height-judging contest.

In June 1936, airmen from Hornchurch won the Air Council Cup, and also the RAF Athletics Championship held at Uxbridge. Again Donald Finlay helped Hornchurch obtain victory by putting on an outstanding display of individual athletics to help his side through the event.

The continuing expansion of Hornchurch was more or less complete by June 1936, with the building of the Officers Mess extension, the Airmens Institute, the Warrant Officers and Sergeants Mess, and a watch office just beside a new third C-Type of hangar now all completed.

By July 1936, there were changes to RAF names. Instead of the Air Defence of Great Britain, the various commands would now be designated Fighter, Bomber, Coastal and Training Commands. The Air Officer Commanding Fighter Command was Air Chief Marshal Sir Hugh Dowding.

On Saturday 4th July 1936, two RAF officers and a sergeant pilot paid the first unofficial visit to the Aero 8 Club, Canute Air Park, Ashingdon. They were Flying Officer Bicknall of No.65 Squadron in a Hawker Demon, Pilot Officer Love in a Gloster Gauntlet and Sergeant Pilot Stringer flying a Bristol Bulldog. Various school parties visited the aerodrome to see the aircraft, before they took to the sky at 6 pm to perform an aerobatic display, diving in turn over the clubhouse as a salute.

During July, No.65 Squadron received several new pilots, one of whom was Flying Officer Gerald 'Sam' Saunders who arrived on 13th July 1936:

> I arrived at the airfield and No.65 Squadron, which consisted at the time of Flying Officer Horner 'A' Flight Commander, who was the Acting CO, and 'B' Flight Commander Flying Officer Bicknall. I can clearly remember the three large hangars and the grass flight path and how it was in very open country at this time. I was posted to 'B' Flight and Sergeant Boxall who had arrived with me went to 'A' Flight. I recall the squadron having four or five two-seater Hawker Demon aeroplanes, also a Hart Trainer, a Tiger Moth and a Puss Moth. The squadron went on a short holiday just before August and when I returned there were some more new pilots arriving. There was Bob Tuck, George Proudman and later on Adrian Hope-Boyd, and in 'A' Flight, Gordon Olive the Australian, Norman Jones the New Zealander; also Jack Kennedy and John Welford.

On the sporting front, on 16th July a swimming team of Flying Officer H.V. Horner, Corporal Warren and Corporal Clinton won the 150-yard open team race at the Valence Park, Dagenham, in the Marino Challenge Cup against other teams from the local companies of Ford's, Roneo and Brooks.

At the Olympic Games in Munich, Germany, Pilot Officer Donald Finlay of No.54 Squadron, finished second to the American athlete G. Towns in the 110 metre hurdles. Previously Finlay had set a new British record of 14.6 seconds for this event.

On 5th August 1936, No.65 Squadron acquired a new young pilot officer fresh from No.3 Flying Training School at Grantham in Lincolnshire; he was Robert Stanford Tuck and his name would become a legend in wartime aviation.

No.65 Squadron received a new CO on 7th August, Squadron Leader C.F. Grace, while No.54 Squadron were now led by Squadron Leader Cecil 'Boy' Bouchier, who had previously served in India. The late Air Vice-Marshal Cecil 'Boy' Bouchier remembered his posting to the aerodrome:

> I reported to the Air Ministry in London, and I was told I had been appointed to command No.54 (F) Squadron, based at Hornchurch in Essex, and if I wanted 'leave', I should first report to Hornchurch and take command of the squadron, then arrange for a short 'leave' with the Hornchurch Station Commander.
>
> To my delight, the latter turned out to be my good friend Wing Commander A.S.G. Lee, with whom I had served some 18 years before, as flight commanders and instructors at London Colney aerodrome in Hertfordshire, under the command of Squadron Leader Keith Park.

Once I had arrived, Lee told me there was a Squadron Leader's married 'quarter' available for me on the outskirts of Hornchurch town, about a mile from the aerodrome, which I gladly accepted. I then walked over to a huge new and beautifully built hangar on the aerodrome which housed No.54 Squadron. I took over command from Flight Lieutenant Rhys-Jones, who had been left temporarily in command.

Facing the aerodrome, No.54 Squadron had the centre hangar, with those of 65 and 74 Squadrons on the left and right respectively. Mine was the largest, most modern and well built of the three, with accommodation to spare to house comfortably the full complement of my twelve fighter aircraft in use, plus two additional aircraft per flight held in 'Immediate Reserve'. It also included a fine office for myself, and one for my two clerks, on the first floor, with windows looking out onto the aerodrome. The hangar also included offices on the ground floor for my three flight commanders, their flight sergeants and technical NCOs, large locker rooms fitted with cabinets in which the pilots kept their parachutes, 'sidcot' suits, flying overalls and other personal flying equipment.

'Boy' Bouchier was also credited with the design and finalising of the official No.54 Squadron crest, which was approved by King George VI, along with No.65 Squadron's new badge. He explained:

I did it with the kindly help and guidence of Mr Heaton-Armstrong, of the Chester Herald. It was he who suggested that as the squadron had fought both in Belgium and France in World War One, an appropriate and attractive heraldic crest might be a lion rampant, blue in colour, charged with a fleur-de-lys in gold on its body, to which suggestion I readily agreed. Thus, would be combined the Lion of Belgium and the Fleur-de-Lys of France. The squadron motto, 'Audax Omnia Perpeti,' was scrolled below the crest.

Having established the offical crest and motto for the squadron, I thought it would be nice to design an official 54 Squadron tie. I registered my design with a firm of tie-makers in Panton Street, off the Haymarket in London. Representing the blue of the Belgium lion and the gold of the fleur-de-lys, I chose an attractive shade of saxe-blue silk, with primrose coloured narrow diagonal stripes. I hope over the years, the tie has found favour with the squadron and is still worn with pride.

On 21st September, the famous World War One Squadron No.74 arrived at Hornchurch to take up their new posting. During the previous war this squadron had become the highest scoring unit in the Royal Flying Corps, with aces like Edward 'Mick' Mannock and Ira Jones; the squadron's nickname became 'the Tigers'.

Disbanded after the war, they re-formed in Malta in 1935, and now came to Hornchurch equipped with Hawker Demons.

Wing Commander Tom Rowland, then a new pilot officer, recalls joining No.74 Squadron at Hornchurch:

> I can remember it very clearly. After leaving Flying Training School at Sealand, I was posted to No.41 Squadron at Catterick who had Hawker Demons, and I arrived there the same day as another chap called Charlie Meares. We were met by Jack Boray who was the CO. He said, 'Our aircraft have only just come back from Aden, and half of them are all rusty, I don't know when we will have an aircraft for you to fly. In the meantime there's a request for two pilots to go down to 74 Squadron at Hornchurch, what about it, are you two interested?'. So we said yes, and we motored down from Catterick to Hornchurch on 10th November 1936. I remember it well because it was my birthday, and also the day that the Crystal Palace burnt down. We arrived at Hornchurch that evening and I remember the next day the whole of Hornchurch was taking to the air to fly down, and fly a left hand circuit around the burning remains of Crystal Palace.
>
> My first impression of the airfield was 'how terrific', three enormous hangars, a big camp; it all seemed to be ticking away in very good order, and we were very impressed.
>
> The commanding officer of No.74 Squadron was Squadron Leader Donald Brookes; he was a wonderful CO, and I can always remember paying my first visit to him. He said to me, 'Well now you've got to remember that we have got two-seater fighters, you have got a gunner in the back, so to let you know exactly what that poor gunner has to put up with, I intend to take you up, with you in the back and do a few aerobatics.' I can tell you that was one of the most terrifying flights I had ever been on, hanging on by my feet, with my toes under the ring on the fuselage floor; I found it very frightening.

As another year began to draw to a close at RAF Hornchurch, No.74 Squadron received another pilot officer who was to become one of the RAF's finest and most distinguished aviators; his name was Adolph Gysbert Malan. Better known as 'Sailor' Malan, because of his previous service in the Merchant Navy, he came from South Africa to join the RAF in January 1936.

He arrived at Hornchurch posted to No.74 Squadron on 20th December 1936, along with two other young pilot officers, Paddy Treacy and Vincent 'Paddy' Byrne. Tom Rowland recalls:

> I remember 'Sailor' Malan arriving, although he was on a

training course at Grantham, which ran parallel to the course I was on. His course finished three weeks to a month after ours did, so I was actually installed in No.74 Squadron before he arrived. I can remember being told he was a lot older than us, he was an ex-Merchant Navy officer who was experienced in navigation, and in fact a man of the world, and that we must treat him with due respect, which we did. At that particular time, apart from the CO, we were all pilot officers; there was not a flight lieutenant in the squadron. 'Sailor' Malan was made flight commander and everybody knows how he did in that line.

A visit by Air Chief Marshal Dowding to RAF Hornchurch in late 1936 saw the airfield raised to Sector Station 'D' Status in No.11 Group. He visited the operations room, newly installed in its underground block, with the then state of art ground-to-air control and the new primitive Radio Direction Finding (RDF) equipment being tested at that time.

CHAPTER 3

DARK CLOUDS ON THE HORIZON
1937-1939

The arrival of Air Vice-Marshal C.L.Gossage, the Air Officer Commanding No.11 Group on the 21st January 1937, saw the presentation of the new squadron badges to No.54 and No.65 Squadrons. Of a more serious nature, an outbreak of scarlet fever in the Officers' Mess on 20th February, found three junior officers and one waiter suffering from the complaint. The Mess was placed out of bounds until 1st March.

The unfortunate death of civilian Mr T. Gray, the temporary assistant groundsman of the W&B Department, on 9th April, who was killed by an aircraft of 65 Squadron whilst mowing the aerodrome, shocked all ranks and staff on duty that day.

April 1937 saw both No.65 and 54 Squadrons converting from their Gloster Gauntlet aircraft to the new Gloster Gladiator, the first RAF fighter in service with an enclosed cockpit. They were collected from the Gloster Aircraft Works on 27th April. Meanwhile No.74 Squadron converted from their two-seater Hawker Demons to Gauntlets, which meant that their aircrew gunners were surplus to the squadron's needs; so many of them were posted to other squadrons or were retrained as ground crews. New arrivals at this time to Hornchurch were Pilot Officers D.S. 'Sammy' Hoare and the Canadian Don Thom. 'Sammy' Hoare recalls his first impression of Hornchurch:

> I remember reporting to the squadron office, and there I was greeted by the squadron adjutant Tom Rowland who was very pleasant and began to tell me what a very good squadron I was about to join; he proceeded to show me around the place. It was all very very exciting for a youngster, but I was disappointed when reaching the hangars to see mostly Gauntlets, but also a few Demons. The Gauntlet was only slightly faster than the Hawker Fury which I had been training on at FTS. In fact some of the bomber squadrons' new aircraft like the Bristol Blenheim and Fairey Battles were faster. My disappointment was increased further when told that 54 and 65 Squadrons had Gladiators.
>
> Don Thom, who joined the squadron the same time as myself, was an accomplished gymnast and diver of

international standard. I can recall him spending time practising standing on his head or doing somersaults in a specially designed sandpit he had constructed; he even did handstands on the wings of Spitfires when they eventually arrived at Hornchurch.

Percy Morfill, posted as a sergeant pilot to Hornchurch in January 1937, remembers going to collect No.65 Squadron's new Gloster Gladiators in April:

> We went down to Glosters to pick up the new aircraft and I went down with 65's CO Squadron Leader C.F. Grace; I was flying on his left as his Number Three. On the way back to Hornchurch, he told us that he wanted us to do a formation landing. Coming into land he selected flaps and started to pump them by hand. This was the first time we had ever had an aircraft with flaps on it and of course the whole thing started tipping up. He said, 'bugger this new fangled bloody thing' so he came in without them. Another thing I remember about Squadron Leader Grace was that he had always flown open cockpits and he didn't like the Gladiator because of the sliding hood. He said, it was like sitting in a glass coffin, but he was a damn nice chap.

Hornchurch was graced by the unofficial visit on 4th May 1937 of the Maharajah of Nepal, accompanied by Commanding General Kaiser of the Nepalese Army; also Nagendra Mem Singh, the Prime Minister of Nepal. Air Commodore A.D. Cunningham and Mr Chaplin of the Foreign Office showed them around the airfield.

Tragedy struck 74 Squadron on 25th May, when Sergeant Boxall who was out on a practice flight was killed when his aircraft crashed into the ground at the Romford Flying Club at Maylands aerodrome, Harold Wood.

On the day of the coronation of King George VI, a contingent of NCOs and airmen, led by Flight Lieutenant J.H.S. Richards, was sent to line the procession route at Westminster Abbey. Later during the evening as part of the coronation day celebrations around Romford, three aircraft from Hornchurch displayed a mock night-attack made all the more effective with searchlights over Romford Stadium.

In June squadrons again participated in the Hendon Air Display, and the Empire Air Day at Hornchurch again attracted over 17,000 spectators. During this time Hornchurch received another change in Station Commander with the arrival of Group Captain M.B. 'Bunty' Frew.

Between 6th and 8th September, No.65 Squadron co-operated with Metro-Goldwyn-Mayer Film Co Ltd, in the making of a film entitled *The Shadow of the Wing*. On the 6th, Squadron Leader Grace led the squadron during the filming of flying sequences, while on the two following days it was led by Flight Lieutenant L.C. Bicknall. The co-operation consisted of a series of attacks, on an Anson aircraft over London, the Anson carrying the film camera crew.

On 23rd October, Hornchurch played host to a visiting German delegation of high-ranking Luftwaffe officers, including Generals Erhard Milch and Ernst Udet, and the German Air Attaché Major Polte.

They were to be shown around the airfield by Air Vice-Marshal Sir Victor Goddard and to inspect the squadrons' aircraft and pilots. There was also to be a flying display, but this was called off due to bad weather.

It was about this time that the RAF had just brought into service the latest reflector gun sight for their fighter aircraft. The pilots at Hornchurch had been given strict instructions that if any of the visiting German officials asked about the device, they were not to reveal its operation. One of No.65 Squadron pilots, Bob Stanford Tuck, recalls the inspection:

> Station Commander Group Captain 'Bunty' Frew had said to me: 'You can answer any questions but ones regarding tactics, operations or the new gun sight; if they do, say that you have not learnt how to use it yet.' Our Gladiators were lined up with their pilots standing beside for the inspection, when the German General Milch and his interpreter came up to my aircraft and decided to inspect the cockpit. He asked in English how did the gun sight work. I replied in the prescribed way I had been told, when suddenly Air Vice-Marshal Goddard interrupted and proceeded to give him the full details. I was quite appalled.

During November, the Armistice church parades were again attended by airmen from Hornchurch. Squadron Leader Cecil Bouchier led 100 airmen to services held at St Andrew's Church and also at the Towers Cinema for a second Remembrance Service.

On 27th November, No.54 Squadron received another new pilot officer into their ranks. His name was James Anthony Leathart, and he would later lead 54 Squadron with great distinction. He recalls:

> My main impression of the station was that I was greatly surprised when shown the Officers Mess, and how it was situated separately across the road from the main camp, as I thought it would have been together on the main site. Once I had got into the routine of things at Hornchurch, I was given the job as an Orderly Officer. An Orderly Officer had to go around the camp checking on various appliances etc, one duty being to dip and check the level of the petrol tank which ran the fire pumps. On one occasion I dipped the stick which was in the tank and this completely disappeared, which seemed rather extraordinary. I then realised that the airman in charge of this had been pinching the petrol and cutting the amount pinched off the bottom of the dipstick.

James Leathart would soon affectionately be nicknamed 'Prof', because of his academic background and his invention of the Oxometer, a measuring instrument of non-existence, with which every new pilot posted to the squadron was tricked. Each pilot would be sent around the camp to collect the Oxometer; when reaching the said place, they would be told, 'No we don't have it, go try over there'. And so the joke carried on, until one bright pilot officer with the help of the station workshops actually built an unusual, but impressive gadget and named this the Oxometer.

They would fill one end of the gadget with soot, and when the unfortunate new pilot who was tasked to find the Oxometer, eventually came across it, he was of course asked to check the instrument by blowing down one end.

Many a black mouthed pilot officer was seen running, much to the amusement of other pilots and personnel, to wash off the embarrassing soot mark around his mouth.

Between 5th and 18th December, the Searchlight and Sound Locater Co-Operation Unit, the 339 Coy-RE (T), held their winter camp at the station for searchlight exercises; 59 other ranks were accommodated.

James Leathart made his first flight at Hornchurch with passenger Pilot Officer Warcup on 8th December 1937 in Hawker Hart (K6484) doing circuits and landings. Eight days later, on the 16th, he flew his first flight in a Gloster Gladiator (K7926).

The year 1938 started badly at Hornchurch with a flying accident involving two No.65 Squadron Gladiators. On 18th January, Flying Officers Robert Stanford Tuck and Adrian Hope-Boyd with Sergeant Geoffrey Gaskell were practising formation flying when disaster struck over the fields of Uckfield in Sussex. The aircraft had moved into line-astern formation with Flying Officer Hope-Boyd leading, followed by Gaskell and Tuck. Suddenly the aircraft were hit by rough air turbulence causing Gaskell's aircraft to edge over to the left and fall back; Tuck's aircraft was slightly above and behind Gaskell's. Tuck saw what was happening and was easing off the throttle to allow for Gaskell's position, when Gaskell's aircraft suddenly hauled up on its tail and banked to the right directly in front of Tuck. There was no way to avoid the aircraft from colliding. Tuck's aircraft propeller sheared through the fuselage of Gaskell's plane just behind the cockpit and killed the unfortunate pilot.

Both aircraft started to fall from the sky; Tuck fought to free himself from his cockpit which had been damaged by the debris from Gaskell's Gladiator. He smashed at the canopy with his fists, but still it would not budge; he even tried with his whole body pushed up against it, with his feet firmly pressed against the seat and instrument panel. All the while the aircraft was spinning down with the centrifugal force pushing him down into the cockpit. Finally after an eternity he freed himself and was shot out of the cockpit by the extreme forces.

His parachute opened and he began to float down to safety, when he suddenly noticed that his white flying suit was covered in blood; he discovered that spurts of blood were shooting out from his throat. With a new emergency at hand, he tore the silk scarf from around his neck to try and stop the bleeding. Panic was beginning to take over when, with his hand, he found that part of his right cheek seemed to be hanging away from his face. Just at that moment he landed on terra firma with an almighty thump, twisting one ankle. He tried to stand up, but because of his loss of blood he decided it was better to stay seated. He managed to ease the flow of blood with his scarf and was happy to see the sight of some farm workmen coming to his aid.

His wound to the face was probably caused by a piece of loose aircraft wire strutting which had caught him like a whiplash when he baled out; it had cut his cheek wide open from the top of his ear down to the chin. This would leave him scarred for the rest of his life.

Feeling very lucky to have survived, he remained in hospital for a week. The following Court of Enquiry found Tuck totally blameless for the accident and death of Sergeant Gaskell. Undaunted by the accident Tuck continued to fly with the No.65 Squadron aerobatic team. Sergeant Percy Morfill who flew in the team remembers:

> It was quite interesting, everybody had a go at this flight aerobatics. No.74 didn't do very well, neither did 54 Squadron, so 65 Squadron were the only aerobatic team at Hornchurch. It was a bit of a job compared to modern days as we just didn't have the power really. Loops were easy, but barrel rolls were a bit of a job and used up quite a bit of space; but at the bottom of a formation loop we used to come down to about 200 feet which was a little bit frightening at the time.

Another royal foreign visitor to the airfield came on 31st March. The Sultan of Muscat and Oman arrived with the AOC of No.11 Group, and was duly given an inspection of No.74 Squadron aircraft, which were lined up on the tarmac apron in front of the hangars. After lunch, the Sultan was given a display of flight drill carried out by four of No.74's aircraft.

Another air collision occurred in April, again involving Robert Stanford Tuck, as he practised aerobatics over Great Warley, Essex, ready for the Hendon Air Display.

Tuck, Leslie Bicknall and Percy Morfill were at 6,000 feet when another formation of Gladiators appeared out of a cloudbank very close to them. Bicknall was forced to bank sharply and go into a steep climbing turn to the left. Tuck tried to do the same, but in doing so struck the rudder and tailplane of Bicknall's which broke off; Bicknall's aircraft went into a flat spin, but he managed to get out of it and parachuted down. Tuck's aircraft, although damaged, was still flyable; he set course for Hornchurch hoping that the aircraft would hold together and wondering if the undercarriage had been damaged in any way. Keeping the aircraft just above the stalling speed of 80 mph he arrived back at Hornchurch to make a perfect landing. It was not till later that while he was giving his report on the sequence of events, he was told that when the ground crew had taken the damaged aircraft into one of the hangers, a piece of the wing had fallen to the ground. Percy Morfill recalls the collision:

> Bicknall was the flight commander, Tuck was on the right and I was on the left of the formation. We were above cloud and using cloud base as height, so you could say height at 200 feet above cloud base as a safety net. We were working on this system, and were flying along when all of a sudden these aircraft came out of the clouds, dead ahead of us. Bicknall did an avoiding action by turning sharply to the left, I pulled up and disappeared up above somewhere, but was around in time to see Bicknall's aircraft tailplane hit by Tuck's wing. I hadn't gone into cloud then, but I did see the thing spinning down with no tail on at the time, but I didn't know what had happened to Tuck. I went down through the cloud and was in time to see Bicknall coming down on his parachute; he landed right on the edge of the Southend Road. I saw him coming down and I thought I hope the traffic doesn't hit him or anything like that. So I proceeded to fly low over the road and beat the traffic up to try and slow them down until they realised something was happening. He was lucky that he landed clear of the road, just on the grass; a car stopped and he was picked up. I then looked around for Tuck, but he'd managed to get back with a bent wingtip and what have you.

On 2nd May, No.74 Squadron said farewell to their CO Squadron Leader Brookes; he was posted to HQ Coastal Command, prior to posting to HMS *Ark Royal*. His replacement was Squadron Leader George Edward Sampson. Known as 'Sammy', he had as his new Adjutant 'Sammy' Hoare, so they were known around the squadron as 'Sammy One' and 'Sammy Two.'

One of the most famous woman aviators of the day arrived during Hornchurch's Empire Air Day on 28th May 1938. Jean Batten, a New Zealander, appeared to meet the public and sign autographs. On view was the aircraft she had flown solo non-stop halfway around the world, the Percival Gull monoplane. During her stay she was presented with a bouquet of flowers by six children dressed in aviation clothing.

It was also during this event that many of the public caught their first glimpse of the first new RAF monoplane fighter, the Hawker Hurricane. Attendance was a record-breaking 7,967 adults, 3,263 children, 926 cars and 437 motorcycles.

On 9th June Hornchurch played host for the No.11 Group mobilisation exercise, to study the effects that would arise from a fighter station on full war alert. This included tests on dispersal of aircraft, supplies of fuel and armament, plans for gas attack and air raids and anything else an enemy might try to throw at the airfield. The exercise was to last till 16th June and was of such importance that the AOC in C of Fighter Command was present along with AOC No.11 Group; also representatives from the Air

Ministry as well as station commanders from Biggin Hill, Northolt, North Weald and Duxford. During the exercise Bomber Command 'raided' London and the south-east using Bristol Blenheims and Fairey Battles.

No.74 Squadron were sent up to intercept with their Gauntlet aircraft, but although they could see their attackers they could never engage because they could never catch the bombers because of their speed. Sighting was considered a success for the purposes of the exercise at this time however as there was no radar or ground control operation to help. Tom Rowland remembers the exercise:

> I can remember them very well, every window in the entire camp was papered over with dark paper and different parts of the station were exercised on different days. Various officers from No.11 Group checked how fast and efficient the ground crews were at re-arming and re-fuelling aircraft. One of the odd things I remember was that they had put all these square shaped pieces of metal painted yellow all over the camp. We asked what they were and we were told they were gas detectors; 'Well, how do they work?' we asked and we were told that if gas gets on it they turn red. Well, there were airmen dressed up like men from Mars in anti-gas kit; they were there all day marching up and down looking at these yellow gas things.
>
> So Vincent Byrne and I got together and decided we should do something about this, so after they had inspected the yellow plate next to where we were situated and, once the airman was out of sight, we went out with a bottle of red ink and poured it onto the plate; we then proceeded to view the situation from around the corner.
>
> The airman then returned and looked down at the plate, then looked again, bent down and looked, then got up and rushed off down the tarmac ringing his bell and it was too late to stop him. Anyway the gas alarm sounded all around the camp, and the station came to a complete standstill. The Station Commander, 'Bunty' Frew, was in the Operations Room at the time conducting the exercises and had one of the No.11 Group inspectors with him. He said, 'That's a fine thing to thrust on us, you should have given us a bit of warning about this one'. The poor Station Commander hadn't even got his gas mask with him. They said, 'Its nothing to do with us'. Well anyway, an appeal was sent out and of course I had to own up to it and received a mild rocket from the Station Commander.

On 16th June, aircraft of No.54 and No.74 Squadrons proceeded to Leysdown Ranges, Isle of Sheppey, for air firing practice. During the morning Sergeant Pilot R.M. Marsh of No.54 was killed in a flying accident. He was given a service funeral at RAF Station, Eastchurch, and buried at Leysdown on 21st June.

A total of 190 Observer Corps members from the six posts in each of No.17, 18, and 19 Observer Groups visited the station and were entertained to lunch and tea. Owing to the great increase in numbers over previous years, meals were served in No.54 Squadron's hangar and the catering was undertaken by the NAAFI. Transport to bring Observer Corps members from Church End, Pitsea and Canvey had to be borrowed from Northolt and North Weald, since the M.T. Section could not meet the requirements.

After lunch the visitors were able to visit various buildings, and during the afternoon a height judging competition was held, two small prizes being awarded for the nearest estimates. Passenger flights were made available in an Anson of No.217 Squadron, a Fairey Battle of No.105 Squadron, and a Harrow from RAF Marham.

On 30th July, Pilot Officer Charles Brian Fabris Kingcome arrived from Cranwell to take up his post with No.65 Squadron. He had fond memories of this time:

> I was so delighted to get to a fighter station, because there was always a lot of competition to get into fighters, always has been in the Air Force, only a man brave beyond belief would ever want to go into bombers; us cards all went into fighters.
>
> One of the main advantages of the fighter squadron was we had Gladiators, which then were the best front line aeroplane, and also that we were only half-an-hour from the centre of London, which was the greatest flesh spot in Europe, so it was an ideal posting.
>
> The quarters in the Officers' Mess were marvellous, they were luxurious beyond belief. We led this very civilized life, we dined in the Mess in full officers dress every Thursday and the food was superb; you had your own batman and quarters. There was no bar in those days so you did all your drinking in the ante-room with steward service.
>
> The gardens outside the Mess were beautifully kept with pristine lawns and flowerbeds. We were paid fourteen shillings a day, which was about seventy pence, too much some people thought.
>
> There were sport facilities available I remember. I was a great squash fanatic in those days and used to play most evenings. There were also tennis courts; basically I concentrated on squash as you only needed one other person to get all the exercise you needed.
>
> I remember my old friend Bob Tuck with great affection. He was a brilliant pilot, not everybody's friend as he was a bit flamboyant and thought by some not enough stiff upper lip; too much the Clark Gable with the thin pencil moustache which was illegal according to RAF regulations. His scars from his crash were still livid on his face, which he was very proud of. He used to try and pass them off as sabre scars

received in duelling in Austria, because he loved all that sabre stuff and bits of histrionic flourishes. I'd have thought it was more glamorous in those days to have had your face cut open from bracing wires while baling out of an aircraft.

It was during this period at the airfield, that Wing Commander Frank Dowling, OBE, then a corporal in charge of the operations room crew of two clerks and sixteen aircrafthands, was given the job of helping select local civilians who were interested in joining the Royal Air Force Volunteer Reserve to train for operations room duties. He remembers:

> The Operations officer, 'Charles' Meares (ex 74 Squadron – later Squadron Leader) and I interviewed about 200 applicants, from whom we selected our quota of 30 for enrolement.
>
> We had a nice mixture of people from all walks of life; banks, insurance, self-employed etc; we even had a tanner whose hands were permanently dyed from all his hide work. Later our first WAAF airwomen reinforcements included a House of Commons clerk and a qualified pilot; the latter left eventually to become an ATA ferry pilot.
>
> Our war establishment was three crews – to provide 24-hour coverage of plotting, recording and teleprinting – each in the charge of a corporal. As senior corporal I was in overall charge. Shortly before my commissioning, the overall establishment was increased to flight sergeant in overall charge, and a sergeant in charge of each crew – all ranks to be remustered to a new trade of clerk special duties.
>
> 'Charles' Meares suggested that I should remuster to clerk special duties and become the flight sergeant. I demurred on the ground that I was an ex-Ruislip apprentice, and preferred to remain a corporal clerk general duties.
>
> I became Assistant Station Adjutant in May 1940 and one of my first pleasant duties, in concert with Squadron Leader Meares, was to arrange the requisite promotions and remusterings of my former colleagues.

In August 1938, another Home Defence Exercise was held under even more realistic conditions, owing to the ever increasing international crisis on mainland Europe, and the ever strengthening German armament programme continuing to go unabated.

During the exercises No.65 Squadron carried out what would be later called Air Support Strikes, when they co-operated with the 1st and 2nd Divisions of the Aldershot Command, in which they carried out low-flying mock attacks on infantry, tanks and ground defences. This role was usually carried out by Army Co-Operation squadrons. Also in August, on a more peaceful day, No.54 Squadron, led by Flight Lieutenant P.E. Warcup, won the Aerobatic Cup at a competition at Northolt.

In September, a young pilot officer from Wanganui, New Zealand, arrived at Elm Park railway station to take up his position with No.54 Squadron; this was Alan Christopher Deere:

> I arrived with another young pilot, a Canadian named Art Charrett. We got out at the railway station, and walked the half-mile or so to the main entrance at Hornchurch. I was quite surprised at how built up the area was, with the amount of houses in the vicinity of the airfield.
>
> When we arrived we were told that the squadron were now on leave and that perhaps we could take a couple of more days out, until they got back. But after declaring our state of finances or the lack of them, we were then told we could be temporarily posted to No.74 Squadron. With 74 Squadron, I was allowed to fly in one of their Gloster Gauntlets when the time permitted. I was attached to 'A' Flight, their commander being 'Sailor' Malan; we were to become very good friends as the years went by.
>
> When they returned from leave, I was introduced to the commanding officer of No.54 Squadron, Squadron Leader Toby Pearson, and my flight commander R.C. 'Bubbles' Love. I spent my first week with the squadron learning various jobs, such as officer in charge of clothing and pay, the navigation inventory and reading the daily orders; but also on the more interesting side learning about the aircraft.

By 23rd of September, the situation on the continent had reached a crisis point, which became known as the Munich Crisis. Prime Minister Neville Chamberlain flew to Munich to meet Herr Hitler on the 29th and 30th to discuss proposals to avert another conflict, after Hitler laid claim to the Sudeten region in Czechoslavakia. An agreement was approved by all parties to the Czechoslovakian problem, by which the Sudetenland was ceded to Germany. This seemed to stop Hitler's further moves on German expansion.

At this time RAF Hornchurch had been put on full war alert. All personnel on leave were called to duty, the Operations Room was manned on a 24-hour watch, and all squadrons were called to immediate readiness, with a small number of pilots required to sleep at night in the crew-rooms. The daily inspection parades and dining nights in the Mess were now cancelled, although the Station Commander's parade every week was maintained for discipline.

It was also during the crisis that the squadrons at Hornchurch were for the first time ordered to camouflage their aircraft. Group Captain 'Sammy' Hoare reflects:

> We camouflaged No.74 Squadron's aircraft at the time of the Munich Crisis; up until then we'd had our Gauntlets all nicely

silver painted with the squadron badge and the Tiger stripes painted along the fuselage. We were suddenly brought back from Sutton Bridge Practice Camp, when we were then told to camouflage all the aircraft. This was fine except we did not have the required materials to do the job. We had various coloured paints and dopes but we hadn't enough green; we mixed blue and yellow together. Not enough brown, so we mixed red and black; all sorts of mixtures to achieve or resemble green or brown camouflage. Nor did we have enough brushes, these nasty mixtures of paint were spread all over the wings and fuselage using brooms, brushes and odd bits of rag. The aircraft looked terrible and they stayed this way for two or three weeks until we received the right amount of proper green and brown paints; with the help of the riggers the job was then done properly. Of course after we got rid of our Gauntlets we received Spitfires, but these were already camouflaged.

James Leathart of No.54 Squadron also remembers:

We completely ran dry of paint, so groups of airmen were sent out to all the local shops in Hornchurch and nearby Romford, to see if they could muster any more to finish the job.

The return from Germany by Prime Minister Chamberlain waving the signed peace declaration by Adolf Hitler and the promise of 'Peace for our Time', gave false hope that war had been averted.

On the night of 10th October, Flying Officer Gerald 'Sam' Saunders of No.65 Squadron took off on a night flight, but on his return owing to very bad mist which had covered the airfield, he misjudged his landing approach and caught the undercarriage of his Gladiator aircraft on one of the barn roofs just outside the airfield, ploughing across the field and stopping against a brick wall of a farm outbuilding. He climbed out of the smashed aircraft unhurt, not even a scratch, but on running clear of the aircraft sprained his ankle on one of the bricks from the wall.

On 25th November, No.74 Squadron's team of pilots won the Sir Philip Sassoon Challenge Trophy with a spectacular victory. The finals were held at RAF Northolt and consisted of various categories of manoeuvres and attacks.

The 'A' Flight team consisted of 'Sailor' Malan, Flying Officer Tom Rowland, Pilot Officer 'Charlie' Meares, Gordon Haywood and Sergeants Ian Hawken and John 'Polly' Flinders. They had been flying together as a team for nearly two years. 'Sammy' Hoare remembers the competition:

The Sassoon Trophy involved a flight of six aircraft doing the various standardized Fighter Command forms of attack. In the case of 74 Squadron, this comprised only 'A' Flight; 'B' Flight had taken part in the preliminary rounds, but 'A' Flight had been chosen. Other squadrons from the various other airfields took part; they were flying mainly Gladiators and some Hurricanes. However 'Sailor' Malan, leading 'A' Flight who were still flying their old Gauntlets, walked away with the trophy, which was a very notable achievement in those days.

Also in December, the airfield received a brand new piece of technology in the shape of a Link Trainer; this was fitted with an instrument panel as used in the new Spitfire fighter aircraft. The Link Trainer was the original flight simulator.

As 1939 dawned, there was great expectation among the squadrons at Hornchurch with the promise of being re-equipped with one of the RAF's new monoplane fighters, the Supermarine Spitfire.

On 26th January 1939, No. 54 Squadron suffered the loss of Pilot Officer T.R.T. Carr-Ellison, when his aircraft, Gladiator K.7930, crashed into high ground at Weston near Baldock, Hertfordshire, owing to adverse weather conditions.

The first squadron to receive the new Spitfire aircraft at Hornchurch was to be No.74, and it was flown into Hornchurch on 13th February 1939. The aircraft, a Spitfire Mk1 Serial No.K9860, was delivered by Squadron Leader D.S. Brookes, 74 Squadron's old CO, who had flown the aircraft up from Eastleigh, Hampshire. Brookes was now the RAF Overseer to Vickers Supermarine, liaising between the RAF and the firm.

Flight Lieutenant James Leathart went down to the Supermarine Works at Eastleigh and received No.54 Squadron's first Spitfire K9880 on 3rd March, while No.65 Squadron were the last to receive their Spitfires; their first Spitfire was collected by Flight Lieutenant A.N. Jones on 21st March 1939. Also flown into the airfield were a Fairey Battle and a Miles Magister, which were used for Blind-Flying instruction and training the pilots to convert to monoplanes. Brian Kingcome, with No.65 Squadron, remembers his first flights in the Spitfire:

We were extremely lucky and we re-equipped in the March, several months before the war, so come the war we had quite a lot of Spitfire flying hours under our belts, which was a huge advantage. One thing I always remember was, I could never work out what kept the 'bloody' wings from falling off; I was the sort of chap that liked to see what was holding me together. With the old biplanes you had the rigging wires and the flying wires which gave you a lot of security; here you are in a Spitfire with these thin wings. The first time I took off I thought, 'Christ they are going to fall off, they are never going to stay on.'

But finally you get used to the idea of the cantilever construction; after a few trips it was the most enjoyable experience. One was expecting it to be difficult, but it wasn't, the Spitfire always gave one great confidence. It was a totally docile aircraft, and was very pilot friendly; it didn't have any vices at all, it wouldn't stall unexpectedly or do anything without letting you know first. It was all round perfection for its time.

In early March, RAF Hornchurch played host to 22 officers from the 2nd Army Division who had been invited as guests for the day. They arrived at the airfield in an Imperial Airways Liner Hannibal aircraft, and after lunching at the Officers' Mess they were treated to watch a tactical flying display showing off the new Spitfire fighters. No. 74 Squadron were given the task of doing the demonstration. 'Sammy' Hoare remembers:

A few of our pilots had been up giving the Army VIPs a short display of loops, turns and low passes. Paddy Treacy had just completed his first-class demonstration and was coming into land. He pumped down his undercarriage, but the wheels had not locked in the fully down position, so as he landed and taxied to the hangars, his undercarriage began to retract slowly into the wings with the Spitfire sinking into the ground. The Army bods thought this was all part of the show.

One was heard to say, 'What a beautifully controlled manoeuvre to finish off such a fine display.'

As the situation in Europe began to worsen once more, the squadrons kept busy with practising fighter tactics and mock dogfights. They were also receiving a lot of new pilots into their ranks, many who would make names for themselves at Hornchurch during the forthcoming conflict; such as George Gribble, John Mungo-Park, Johnny Allen, Harbourne Mackay Stephen, Jock Norwell and John Freeborn, as well as many others.

The final Empire Air Day display took place on 20th May, and attracted a huge crowd of 45,000. During the day, famous air racing aviator Alex Henshaw arrived in his record breaking Mew Gull aircraft and signed autographs. He would later during the war years, become one of Supermarine's main test pilots for the Spitfire. From the event a total of £1,850 was donated to the Air League.

In the middle of June, the new Station Commander, Wing Commander C.T. Walkington presented the air raid wardens of 'E' Group, Hornchurch, with their new official badges. Presenting them, Wing Commander Walkington stated that the work of the air raid wardens would be of great national importance and also their 'behind the scenes' work was essential should the enemy attack. Also present at the ceremony were Mr V.H. Field, the Chief Warden, Mr H.S. Curtis, Head Warden and Mr C.C. Mussett, Deputy Warden.

The ceremony took place at the Sutton's Senior School, where afterwards the audience were entertained by the Geoffrey Tucker Dance

Band and Mr Macy's Trio. There were also two stage-acting sketches performed by the Hornchurch Youth Centre, and a conjuring display by Mr A. Goddenkent, the stage manager.

On the sporting front, Hornchurch could muster a very good rugby team at this time, and a few of the pilots also played for some first class clubs. Alan Deere of 54 Squadron played for the RAF and Norman Pooler of 74 Squadron played for Rosslyn Park. Had not the war intervened the team would have been even better as Pilot Officer Don Cobden arrived in 74 Squadron in November 1939 – he had played for the New Zealand 'All Blacks'.

It was the same Norman Pooler, whose death on 26th June shocked the entire station. His friend D.S. 'Sammy' Hoare explains:

> We had been out of the camp and had been drinking at one of the local pubs. I got back to the Officers' Mess at around 10.30 pm, and there were a few chaps still around in the Mess, who had not gone to bed. I decided with a couple of others to have one more drink, when my friend Norman Pooler walked in, started having a chat and shaking hands and shouting, 'Well I'm off now, cheerio chaps'; he said the same to me, and I said, 'Now don't be stupid, where are you going?' He then produced a gun. We all had a service revolver at this time.
>
> We didn't quite know what to do about this, so we grabbed him and escorted him back to his room and said, 'Go to bed, old chap, and sleep it off.' We didn't think any more of it apart from that. However, the next morning, he didn't turn up as usual at the flights and a couple of hours later, the gardener who was attending the flower beds in front of the Mess, came across Norman Pooler with a bullet straight through his forehead.
>
> Just what time this happened, nobody really knows. Obviously, in a depressed state of mind he had gone out after the party in the Mess, laid on the lawn and finished things off. There was a Court of Enquiry of course afterwards, but I didn't hear what the result was, a clear-cut case of suicide one presumed. We never found out why he did it, although I knew he had a bit of financial and girlfriend trouble.
>
> The funeral was a private one and the squadron was not represented. Afterwards, an urn containing his ashes was delivered to the squadron office, with a request from his family that Pooler's ashes be scattered over the airfield.
>
> Norman Pooler had been a very capable and popular pilot; he was also a fine rugby player and had excelled in the sport, playing for the RAF in many competitions. He was a great loss to the squadron.

Soon afterwards, there was a report of Pooler's ghost being sighted around the airfield, especially around the hangar and in the direction of the crew room, where it would disappear. So real was the sighting, that one of his ground crew suffered a nervous breakdown soon afterwards.

John Gill, who as a boy had visited Hornchurch many times, later joined the RAF on reaching his eighteenth birthday. After his training he was posted to Hornchurch as a flight rigger with No.74 Squadron. He remembers his first days there:

I arrived and was taken to the Orderly Room which looked out onto the perimeter of the airfield. From there I was introduced to the flight sergeant of 'B' Flight, Flight Sergeant Etteridge, who said he had no Spitfire or pilot for me at this time, as they were fully up to standard with crews, but they did have an aircraft in the hangar and needed someone to look after it. As I went into the hangar with him, he said, 'This one will do for you', and this was a Gloster Gauntlet, the only one left on the station. This was JH-L, with the old squadron code-letters, before they changed them just before the war broke out. I eventually got used to maintaining the Gauntlet after a few weeks, and I got a regular pilot who would use it mainly at the weekends; this was Flight Lieutenant Malan. He would come in and see the flight sergeant to make sure the aircraft was alright to be used, take-off in it for about half-an-hour towards the Grays area, then indulge in some aerobatics, just to keep his hand in.

Eventually the aircraft was taken away off the strength of the squadron. By then I'd been allocated to a Spitfire, whose pilot was Pilot Officer Derek Hugh Dowding; his father was chief of Fighter Command. From there I was passed over to another, Flying Officer Mainwaring, who had joined in the early thirties.

Derek Dowding was regarded by the squadron as a most delightful and intelligent chap, but as regards his attire he was somewhat untidy, not what you would have expected from the son of an Air Chief Marshal. His father, because of his serious temperament, was nicknamed 'Stuffy' Dowding, so it was decided because of his untidiness to nickname the young Dowding 'Scruffy'.

On 10th July, No.74 Squadron flew to Le Bourget Airport, near Paris, France, to take part in an air display to mark the Bastille Day Celebrations; there they flew alongside other squadrons of the French Air Force.

On 1st August, a mass flight of 32 RAF aircraft carried 250 public schoolboys from Tangmere Aerodrome to RAF Hornchurch, as part of the annual training of the Officers Training Corp Air Section, who were camped at Selsey Bill in Sussex. The cadets were shown around parts of the station and showed keen interest when given the chance to view the cockpits of the Spitfires on show.

Although war looked an extreme possibility by August, there was still every opportunity at Hornchurch for the pilots to enjoy themselves, relaxing and spending evenings drinking with friends from the other squadrons at the Officers' Mess. James Leathart remembers one amusing incident.

> We were sitting outside the Officers' Mess, it was a beautiful evening, and we were having a few drinks about 8 pm when we received an invitation to go to the Sergeants' Mess for drinks at around 9 pm. The party eventually broke up and we went to get our hats and coats to walk from the Mess to the Sergeants' Mess across the road. As we got ready to go, the Station Commander couldn't find his hat. We all helped him to look for it, but nowhere in the Mess could we find it, and no way could he walk through the guardroom without his hat on; so we sent for his car. He sat in the back and so we went to the party at the other Mess.
>
> But what had happened was that Pilot Officer Dowding had stolen the Group Captain's hat, and had started to walk towards the Sergeants' Mess; when he got to the guard room gate the guard saluted the Group Captain's hat. It was starting to get dark by then, and as the guard stood there saluting, Dowding had a rotten apple with him, which he proceeded to throw at the guard. We didn't know any of this had happened at the time. Anyway when we arrived, we noticed the most extraordinary thing; the Group Captain's hat was hanging on one of the cloakroom pegs. We didn't know how it had got there, but anyway, he was happy enough to get his hat back.
>
> After we had finished, and it was time to come back, he didn't bother to send for his car; he just put his hat on and decided he would walk back to the Mess. He got as far as the guardroom and this time the guard had a rotten apple ready which he hurled at the Station Commander; that's a true story!

The last Air Defence Exercise before the war was undertaken on 11th August, which included a trial of the new radio location signal. This was a signal, transmitted by a friendly aircraft, which could be recognised by the ground radar operators; this was later known as IFF (Identification Friend or Foe).

Apart from the home-based squadrons taking part, Bristol Blenheim light bombers of No.25 Squadron flew in from Tangmere for the exercise. The opposing forces were named 'Eastland' (hostile) and 'Westland' (friendly).

Also featured during the exercise at Hornchurch was the newly installed 'Tannoy' loud speaker system, which had been set up at various points around the airfield, such as crew rooms, hangars and dispersal. This enabled the operations controllers to pass on instructions to pilots and ground crews right across the airfield.

On 11th August 1939, Spitfires of No.54 Squadron flew down to Rochford from Hornchurch led by Squadron Leader 'Toby' Pearson, to carry out flights over the east coast.

By 22nd August, RAF Hornchurch along with many other airfields was put on immediate war footing. The following extract from the Station Diary shows how Hornchurch was brought to readiness just before war with Germany was declared on 3rd September 1939.

22nd August:	Instructions were received to recall all officers above the rank of Flight Lieutenant from leave; none were away.
23rd August:	All regular personnel recalled from leave.
24th August:	The Station Defence scheme put into operation and all aircraft of squadrons to take up positions at dispersal points. Camouflage of all buildings begun by Works and Buildings Dept. The Operations Room to be manned continuously with a skeleton crew.
25th August:	Fifteen officers arrived on posting for war appointments.
26th August:	Certain war vehicles collected from Wembley.
27th August:	Class E and Volunteer Reserve personnel begin to arrive.
28th August:	One officer and forty-four men of the National Defence Guard arrived to augment station personnel on guard duties.
31st August:	Splinter-proof boxes placed in position in hangar windows by Works and Buildings Dept.
1st September:	Operations Room manned continuously with complete staff.
2nd September:	General Mobilisation of the R.A.F including the Auxiliary Air Force and Reserves.

Tragedy was to strike No.74 Squadron again on Wednesday, 30th August, at around 11 am when a newly posted sergeant pilot, the 24-year-old Cyril Gower, who hailed from Coventry, was killed. His Spitfire K9881, coded JH-G, crashed on to the ground of the playing fields of John Henry Burrows Intermediate School (now the Grays School).

He had taken off with two other aircraft to practise formation flying. While over the Grays area his aircraft was seen to be in trouble, probably through engine failure; he took evasive action to avoid the other two aircraft. An eyewitness report stated that:

> He attempted to guide his Spitfire away from a housing estate, narrowly missing the rooftops in Lodge Lane, hoping to find an open space to carry out a wheels-up landing; the aircraft stalled, dipped a wing and crashed into the playing field. The aircraft was immediately surrounded by young children who had to be quickly taken away; one child was seen rushing away with an armful of live ammunition which had spilled from the wreckage of the wings.

Another witness to the event was Bob Ballard. Aged twelve years at the time, he recalls:

> Back at home in Bradleigh Avenue, Grays, I fearfully saw my first Spitfire crash. It was during the school holidays, otherwise I would not have seen the incident.
>
> Three Spitfires, flying in Vic formation were coming across the northern district of Grays from the direction of Hornchurch, going east towards Southend.
>
> Suddenly the one on the port side pulled up slightly banking away from the other two, turning towards my position, the propeller milling slowly, the aircraft clearly in trouble. It was coming down!
>
> The pilot looked like he was going to do a forced-landing in the only reasonable open space available, which was the sports playing field of the local Intermediate School, situated at the Lodge Lane end of Hathaway Road. Now quite low, the Spitfire crossed over Lodge Lane, when without warning the starboard wing dipped, stalling the machine which plunged in a dive into the edge of the school field, just inside the iron railings.
>
> I saw the crumpled wreck on the edge of the field with a wing lying some distance away, but did not get as near as one of the lads who succeeded in getting a souvenir, which from memory probably came from the carburettor, as it was varnished cork attached to an alloy bracket.

One of the first men to arrive from RAF Hornchurch to the scene of the crash was J. Gylander, who remembers:

> At the time I was a flight mechanic with 'B' Flight, No.74
> Squadron. I was detailed to go to the scene of the crash in
> Grays with two other airmen.
>
> At that time the squadron were living in 'Bell tents' at the
> dispersal point away from the hangars and billets.
>
> On the day of the crash, Sergeant Gower, Flight Lieutenant
> Treacy and another pilot went up to practise fighting tactics
> and also to get flying hours in on Spitfires.
>
> When the flight commander landed and gave us the news of
> Gower's crash, a small group of us were detailed to go to the
> crash site. In the group was myself, Bill Williams, a flight
> rigger, also Corporal Felstead who was in charge of our flight;
> there was also a sergeant and one officer.
>
> When we arrived at the crash scene, we found the aircraft in
> a small field, where on one side was a school, also bungalows.
> The nose of the Spitfire had buried itself about six feet into the
> roots of some fruit trees, which were in the back garden of one
> of the bungalows (No.173 Lodge Lane).
>
> The police and fire service were also at the site. Sergeant
> Gower's body was still in the cockpit. Corporal Felstead, Bill
> Williams and myself managed to cut away the door flap and
> part of the fuselage; we then lifted out his body and laid him
> on a blanket.
>
> As you can imagine there was quite a lot of activity. The
> local doctor and eventually an RAF doctor arrived, and the
> body was then taken away. There was a lot of wreckage to be
> cleared up. Three of us stayed at the scene to guard the Spitfire
> for two days until the RAF recovery team arrived.

Flight Rigger John Gill:

> Yes I remember young Gower who came to the squadron in
> the August of '39; he was a Volunteer Reserve pilot. The first
> time he took up a Spitfire from here just to get acquainted with
> it for flying control; it was the aircraft I was flight rigger on.
>
> Sergeant Gower took the aircraft off; he was supposed to be
> gone for about half-an-hour doing circuits and bumps, just to
> get to know the area and the various landmarks. But he found
> considerable trouble in getting his approach right for landing,
> he just couldn't get the aircraft down. This went on for about
> an hour or so, and was getting very near the end of the
> aircraft's flight endurance. After many circuits, it was Flying
> Officer Mainwaring who contacted him on his R/T and talked
> him down.
>
> He made a reasonable landing eventually, but it seemed he

was going to need quite a lot more flying experience with circuits and bumps. Unfortunately he was killed when flying with 'B' Flight while over the Grays area; I believe they were doing some attack and diving manoeuvres in formation. He was only here for a few weeks, and on the same day he was killed, in the afternoon he was supposed to be meeting his girlfriend outside the main gates of the aerodrome, to take her out for the evening. So somebody had to go and meet her and tell her what had happened.

I think his funeral was carried out in his home town, with representatives from the squadron going there. As became usual later in the war, his personal possessions were given back to his family, while the rest of his belongings like flying kit, boots etc were taken to the Flight Office and auctioned off. Everybody paid so much for a certain article and the money raised was then sent to his family.

On 1st September, despite numerous warnings, Germany invaded Poland. Two days later, at 11.15 am, Britain would again be at war.

CHAPTER 4

THE BALLOON GOES UP
September 1939 – May 1940

As the day started to dawn on Sunday, 3rd September 1939, many of the ground crews and station personnel were already up and about their business. Many of the Hornchurch squadrons' aircraft were already dispersed around certain areas of the airfield, and were being attended to by their ground crews and checked for the morning flights.

The Spitfires were now standing in sandbagged protective pens, which had taken the pilots and men many weeks to fill up and erect. For the past couple of weeks the groundcrews and some of the pilots had been living out on dispersal in bell tents; because of the warm nights, some ground crew had even slept under the wings of the aircraft, and some pilots in their cockpits.

After war had been declared, the eating arrangements were organised so that a certain amount of men would be released at various times from dispersal, to come over to the dinning mess, which was on the edge of the parade ground. There they could get a quick meal; they were allowed about half-an-hour before other crews would come over and take their meals. The Sergeants' Mess was catered for as normal, as were the officers. The pilots at readiness would make do with a snack lunch brought over to their bell tents at dispersal.

By this time, the squadrons had also changed their squadron aircraft recognition codes, as a measure against German Intelligence, who had probably recorded various squadron code identities. No.74 Squadron changed from JH to ZP, No.54 from DL to KL and No.65 from FZ to YT.

Later in the morning, it was announced that the Prime Minister Neville Chamberlain would make a speech to the nation at 11.15 am. At Hornchurch many of the squadrons listened in on portable radios, which they had out at dispersal as well as in the Officers' Mess.

Brian Kingcome remembers the speech which entered Great Britain into war with Germany:

> I can remember when war was declared, and I can remember we all went into the commanding officer's Flight Office, down in the hangar for an important announcement at 11.15. At that exact time the Prime Minister came on and we listened to his rather dreary boring voice coming out over the radio, telling

us that a state of war now existed. It was all very flat somehow; there was no drama or tension or call to arms, just this sorrowful defeated voice going on. I looked around at my fellow companions and remember thinking to myself, probably the whole lot of us will be dead in three weeks, if statistics from the First World War are to be followed. As I looked at all these chaps I thought, its bad luck on them, we are all going to be dead. No sooner had Chamberlain finished his speech on the radio, than we expected to hear the murmur of hordes of German bombers approaching, and that became the norm at dispersal for a while.

Security around the airfield at the outbreak of war was undertaken by the members of the Local Defence Volunteers, later to be called the Home Guard. Flight Rigger John Gill No. 74 Squadron:

There was nothing here at all in the beginning, nothing at all. There was the LDV and just ourselves with rifles, taking it in turns to do regular patrols and that's as far as the defence went here. Later on they brought in an Ack-Ack gun unit, set up on the edge of Rainham; but the air raids didn't start till much later.

The Local Defence Volunteers were mainly old ex-servicemen from the First World War, but some had served previous to that, so they all had stirring stories to tell us about the old days; they used to keep us well amused with their tales.

They stayed here with us for quite a while, but nobody had any weapons at all; they just had a stick or stave. They weren't allowed to carry weapons; it was just a question of doing a patrol around the airfield. However we were issued with our rifles and a few bullets, which we had to account for every day in case someone had lost any.

We did have one incident, when one of our fitters was on aerodrome guard one evening. He was walking around the airfield doing his patrol with his rigger when he heard what he thought was a suspicious noise, and he called out, 'Who's there?'; he heard a noise back and without thinking put the rifle up to his shoulder and fired a shot.

The next morning the farmer whose ground bordered the airfield, came round looking very, very disturbed that someone had shot one of his cows. The fitter who had done the shooting maintained that it had been a suspicious person lurking there.

The RAF then had to pay the farmer for the loss of one cow; we didn't get the meat to keep either, that went to the local butchers.

The first operational patrol undertaken at Hornchurch was on 4th September at 2.50 am, when a report came through that German night bombers had been picked up by radar. Official papers record that No.74 Squadron were notified by the control room, and Red Section, led by Flight Lieutenant Malan, took off, followed shortly afterwards by Yellow Section, led by Paddy Byrne. The suspect enemy raid was in fact RAF bombers returning from one of the first raids of the war, on the Kiel Canal. All the Spitfires were recorded as having returned to Hornchurch after a wasted trip, landing at just after 4 am. It has, however, been reported by one of the squadron pilots that only Flight Lieutenant 'Sailor' Malan took off and carried out the patrol. This is much more likely as night patrols were always made by single aircraft. A section of Spitfires would not have been viable in night conditions, certainly on the second day of the war.

However on 6th September, there was to occur an incident that would sour the long history of No. 74 'Tiger' Squadron. This episode would become known in RAF circles as the 'Battle of Barking Creek'. 'Sammy' Hoare of No. 74 Squadron explains:

> I was flying that day, as were the other Hornchurch squadrons. A false plot had been spotted over on the Essex coast; there was a fault I think in the RDF station there at Canewdon, or otherwise they had not been notified of aircraft returning from over the North Sea. This aircraft was reported as unidentified and initially three Hurricane fighter aircraft were sent off from North Weald aerodrome to investigate. Well this started the ball rolling, the three Hurricanes were then unidentified by the RDF station, I suppose through lack of communication or something. The RDF station then had one unidentified aircraft plus a formation of three, so the controller at No.11 Group decided he should send off a flight of aircraft to investigate further; so six aircraft went off to investigate the three.
>
> It is a very involved story, but one can see that from then on, since the RDF station wasn't working as it should have been through lack of experience and communication, plus not keeping up with the situation, every time a formation was sent off it confused the situation even more. Eventually flights and sections from Hornchurch and North Weald were being directed all around the sky, chasing after each other and, in some cases, even chasing after themselves. Of course there were no enemy aircraft anywhere in sight. It all arose after the misidentification of one aircraft.
>
> I might add that in our sector, which included the Thames estuary, the Naval guns at Chatham started firing at us. The Navy at that time would fire at anything with wings, because they couldn't tell one from the other. The whole thing deteriorated into an absolute farce and no one knew what was going on.

I was flying in 'B' Flight. It was a beautiful morning, absolute cloudless sky, you could see for miles and we could see other formations of aircraft, but we didn't bother to chase them or anything. But 'A' Flight, led by 'Sailor' Malan with Paddy Byrne leading the second section, presumably thought they saw something of which they were suspicious. I don't know whether they were being directed on to it or if it was a casual sighting. Anyway Paddy Byrne led his section towards two aircraft flying from North Weald. Whether or not Byrne had been instructed to do so by 'Sailor' Malan or by the controller I do not know. Nor did I know if any attempt at positive identification was made or who gave the order to attack. But anyway they came up behind the two North Weald Hurricanes and shot them down. It was about the same time as the original aircraft that had caused all the fuss in the first place, a Blenheim returned from a reconnaissance patrol over the North Sea; this was then shot down by our Ack-Ack. So we had a Blenheim and two Hurricanes shot down for no reason at all.

What the subsequent Court of Inquiry discovered I do not know, it was never published; we were never told what really happened. As far as the squadron was concerned, we felt unhappy about it really, because the Hurricane had been flying in service for quite a long time by then. We all knew what a Hurricane looked like, so how were two Hurricanes mistaken for enemy aircraft? I think the squadron as a whole felt a little upset about the whole thing; there was no official comment from the squadron commander and the whole thing passed off quietly.

The Hurricanes that had been shot down were from No.56 Squadron; one of the pilots, Pilot Officer Halton-Harrop, was unfortunately killed, while Pilot Officer Rose was injured. Now, for the first time, one of the pilots involved in this incident, Wing Commander John Connell Freeborn, recalls his own memories of the events that led to the tragic error on 6th September 1939 and also the aftermath:

From what I can remember, it was a very clear morning up above, but on the airfield there was a thick layer of about ten feet of mist. There was a call to scramble and 'A' Flight led by Flight Lieutenant Malan took off, leading the first three aircraft of Red Section with Paddy Byrne following with the second three of Yellow Section. I was flying with Paddy Byrne.

We were quite a bit away behind the first section of aircraft and were trying to catch them up, when Malan sounded the 'Tally Ho' over the R/T, seeing these supposedly enemy aircraft.

The sad thing about it was, as squadron adjutant I had to take the squadron order book around to the pilots, which was signed that under no circumstances were we to attack any single-engined aircraft. At that stage of the war the German fighters could not get to us, their aircraft's range was unable to carry them that great distance.

Anyway the attack was sounded and our section went in and we shot down the two unidentified aircraft which turned out to be Hurricanes.

It was after that, that I headed back to Hornchurch with John Flinders who was a sergeant pilot. When we landed we looked for Malan, but he was nowhere to be seen; instead I was met by the squadron CO Squadron Leader Sampson, who told me I was to be placed under close arrest with Paddy Byrne. From that time on Byrne and I were separated from contact with one another. A Summary of Evidence was taken at Hornchurch.

Before the subsequent hearing, I was quite worried, only being a youngster. But our commanding officer was a hell of a nice chap and he said 'Sir Patrick Hastings is Intelligence Officer at Fighter Command Headquarters. Go and see him.'

Sampson released me from close arrest to open arrest so that I could go and see Sir Patrick. When we got there he was very kind and said that he would act as our defence barrister.

He then asked us to go to Biggin Hill and see Roger Bushell, who was CO of No.601 Squadron; he too was a pre-war barrister. Sir Patrick Hastings wanted Bushell to act as his No.2 on the case, and Bushell agreed.

Eventually we were sent to Fighter Command Headquarters at Bentley Priory to stand before a General Field Court Martial.

After much deliberation on the evidence provided by the concerned parties relating to the events that had taken place, Sir Patrick Hastings in his summing up, turned around to the court and said, 'This young man should not be condemned for his actions, he should not be here facing a Court Martial.' Soon after that the case was dismissed; both Byrne and I were acquitted on 7th October 1939. But from that day on, Malan and I never got on very well together.

John Freeborn returned to No.74 Squadron and resumed his RAF career. Fighting over Dunkirk and during the Battle of Britain, he was to claim many enemy victories, becoming an ace. He was awarded the Distinguished Flying Cross on 18th August 1940. By the end of October 1940, he had flown more operational hours and sorties than any other pilot in Fighter Command during the Battle of Britain. He was released from the RAF as wing commander in 1954.

On that day also, No.65 Squadron had been on patrol. Two of their pilots recall what happened. Firstly Brian Kingcome:

> No. 65 Squadron were on patrol at 5,000 feet. We were being
> led by Gerald Saunders and we were told to orbit over the
> Thames. Half our orbit took us over the Isle of Sheppey, the
> other over the Estuary; every time we got over Sheppey the
> anti-aircraft guns would all open up. We kept orbiting, didn't
> move, you know, 'England expects every man' and so on; this
> was all done by radar control.
>
> When we landed back at Hornchurch, Gerald Saunders
> managed to get hold of the battery commander whose unit had
> been doing this shooting. He said, he was very sorry indeed,
> but they badly needed a bit of target practice, they hadn't had
> any practice and the war had been on for nearly a week.

Wing Commander Gerald 'Sam' Saunders:

> We were on patrol in the Medway area passing over Chatham
> and Sheppey. Our aircraft at that time had been painted black
> and white underneath for easy identification from the ground,
> but our anti-aircraft guns opened fire on us. I sent a signal to
> the controller telling him to inform the defences that we were
> not hostile, but when we turned around over the coast again,
> they opened up again on us in spite of the fact that we had
> contacted headquarters. A hole suddenly appeared on my
> starboard wing and some shrapnel went through the fuselage,
> rattling around the back of my seat, which I was not too happy
> about.

At about this time, Hornchurch also played host to the London Film
Company, who wanted to shoot footage of Spitfires for a forthcoming film,
The Lion has Wings. Directed by Alexander Korda and starring Ralph
Richardson and Merle Oberon, the film was a semi-documentary and told
the story of the RAF's new Bomber and Fighter Command squadrons.

'B' Flight of No.74 Squadron was tasked with undertaking the flying
sequences and the many take-offs and landings that the film unit required
for their footage. 'Sammy' Hoare was one of the pilots who was involved
with this filming:

> The whole business was looked down upon somewhat by 'A'
> Flight, who weren't involved at all; it was only 'B' Flight who
> were doing the flying for *The Lion has Wings*. For about a
> week we had the film crew on the airfield who were taking
> lots and lots of shots of the tents we lived in, the aircraft pens,
> and a few take-offs and landings. We were still wearing our
> smart white flying suits at the time, and it was a very
> entertaining week. We had lots of beer flowing and we joined

in with the film crew. It was all rather amusing, but it was all rather frowned on by 'A' Flight who were seriously concentrating on their training at that time, while we were just flying around for the fun of it. I didn't get to see the film myself when it was finally released, but I don't think they used too much of the footage, although we flew quite a number of sorties.

As the days rolled into weeks, the anti-climax of having no real contact with the enemy began to develop into boredom; patrols were sent up to investigate sightings and unidentified plots.

During this period, which would be labelled the 'Phoney War', the pilots practised their dogfight skills and tactics.

No.600 'City of London' Auxiliary Squadron arrived at Hornchurch on 2nd October, flying Bristol Blenheim aircraft and led by Squadron Leader The Viscount Carlow. The Station Commander, Wing Commander Walkington was posted away and replaced by Group Captain C.H. Nicholas DFC AFC on 4th October.

On 22nd October, No.74 Squadron were ordered down to Hornchurch's satellite airfield at Rochford, where the conditions were very basic with only the Southend Flying Services Clubhouse, one wooden hangar and re-fuelling pumps. Rochford was to see the coming and changing over of many of the Hornchurch-based squadrons during this period.

The death of Flying Officer A.A. Vickers was recorded on 16th November, killed while carrying out night flying practice in a Blenheim of No.600 Squadron.

On 20th November, No.74 'Tiger' Squadron recorded their first enemy aircraft victory of the war, when a Heinkel He111 was intercepted by Flying Officer W.E.G. Measures, Pilot Officer Temple-Harris and Sergeant Flinders over the Thames estuary, near Southend.

It was also on this date that Pilot Officer Colin Falkland Gray, a New Zealander, arrived to take up his new position with No.54 Squadron. Very soon after arriving he had the misfortune to damage his Spitfire on landing whilst the Air Officer Commanding No.11 Group, Air Vice-Marshal Keith Park, was visiting the airfield, and saw what happened. Pilot Officer Colin Gray:

> I had only just arrived at Hornchurch and the squadron was involved with flying convoy patrols up and down the coast. I had taken my Spitfire up on a flight and was preparing to come into land. Around this time the airfield had some newly constructed blast shelters around the airfield, which reduced the flight path area somewhat. Unfortunately I had misjudged my approach, which was too low, and I proceeded to tear off my undercarriage on one of the new shelters. After the aircraft careered across the ground on its belly and came to a grinding halt, I clambered out, a little shaken but otherwise unhurt. I

was met and told to clean up and report to the Station Commander. I thought 'I'm definitely for it now'. I was brought before the Station Commander, who was furious about the whole thing, but my squadron commander, 'Toby' Pearson, had a few quiet words with him and calmed the situation, and I was lucky enough to be given another chance.

The next day, three aircraft out on patrol over the Cherbourg area were forced to land because of shortage of fuel. One of the 74 Squadron aircraft was written off on landing; the pilot Don Thom was uninjured and made his way back across the Channel by ship. The other two pilots, Treacy and Bushell, refuelled and returned to Hornchurch. Although it was not a completely wasted trip for when Paddy Treacy landed at base and taxied to dispersal, he recovered from his aircraft three bottles of French champagne, which were taken to the crewroom and shared around.

On 20th December, the Station Commander Group Captain C.H. Nicholas was posted from Hornchurch and was replaced by Group Captain Cecil A. Bouchier, who had previously commanded No.54 Squadron from 1936 to 1938. He started his command at Hornchurch by trying to tidy up the station and give the main camp more pleasant surroundings, as will be referred to later. But he also noticed a change of mood in the pilots. Air Vice-Marshal Cecil Bouchier remembers:

> My first impression after taking over command of the sector from my old friend Group Captain Nicholas was that there was, understandably, more tension here in 11 Group, particularly amongst my squadron commanders and pilots. They had already seen how Austria, Czechoslovakia and Poland had collapsed before the onslaught or threat of the German Luftwaffe. They were also about to see how Norway, Holland, Belgium and France in little over five weeks, would all collapse before the Nazi war machine.
>
> Talking to my squadron commanders and pilots in the ante-room of the Officers' Mess over a drink before supper, they all seemed strangely quiet and apprehensive. Even the lion-hearted 'Sailor' Malan told me he was worried as to how he would shape up to the Luftwaffe when the time came.

The entertainment at Hornchurch during the Christmas period of 1939 consisted of the station cinema, where they would show films at the weekend. No.601 Blenheim Squadron arrived at the aerodrome for a couple of days. During this time, Max Aitkin was commanding officer; he was known to have very good connections with show business society. He managed to get the entire cast of the Windmill Theatre to come down from the West End, and give a show. The Windmill Girls were the hit of the evening obviously, because they danced around very exotically, very scantily dressed. They were encored again and again. This didn't please

some of the young WAAFs watching the show, who could not see the
entertainment value of this performance; they all got up from their seats
and left.

Christmas eve and Christmas day were both very misty days, and so all
flying was cancelled.

There was much activity on the aerodrome in January 1940. Station
Commander Bouchier recalls:

> During my first weeks at Hornchurch, there was a good deal
> to be organised on the ground, and at my two forward airfields
> at Rochford (Southend), and at Manston.
>
> This included the siting of large oblong wooden dispersal
> huts, two per squadron, adjacent to concrete perimeter tracks
> encircling the airfields. Furnishing them with a few easy
> chairs, a table, and a direct telephone line to the controller in
> my Operations Room. These huts were for the use of pilots
> throughout daylight hours when the squadrons were placed at
> a state of 'readiness' (off the ground inside five minutes), or,
> off the ground inside 15 minutes when at 'available'. When
> squadrons in times of inactivity were placed at 30 or 45
> minutes 'available', pilots were permitted to take their meals
> in the Officers' Mess, with motor transport standing by to rush
> them instantly back to their aircraft, should things start to 'boil
> up' and the Controller had ordered the squadron or squadrons
> concerned back to a state of five minutes 'readiness'.
>
> I also arranged for half-filled sandbags to be laid in small
> piles of six every fifty yards alongside every road and path
> within the whole area of the Hornchurch Station.
>
> These loosely filled sandbags were for use by all personnel
> in the 'smothering' of incendiary bombs, should these be
> dropped by the enemy on the aerodrome in great numbers,
> either by day or night. Thus if anyone was near a blazing
> incendiary bomb, all he or she had to do was take the sandbag
> and place it gently on top of the bomb, which would be
> rendered harmless by the loose sand. I also had placed at
> various points around the perimeter of the flightpath, large
> dumps of hardcore which I arranged with the Air Ministry's
> 'Works and Bricks' Department to bring to the airfield. The
> hardcore was to be used to fill in quickly any bomb craters on
> the airfield after an enemy attack.

On 25th February, No.74 Squadron received Squadron Leader Francis
Lawrence White into their ranks as a supernumerary, before his actual
appointment as the commanding officer of the squadron on 1st March
1940.

The Station Diary recorded two aircraft accidents during this month. A
Blenheim of No.600 Squadron crash-landed while operating from Manston

on the 11th, killing an Army observer. Then on the 15th, Pilot Officer R.E. West was killed and his passenger Sergeant Rawes injured when their Miles Magister aircraft crashed at Upminster.

One incident that happened on the airfield at this time, which could have ended in tragedy, was seen by Flight Rigger John Gill:

> I recall I was in working in one of the hangars doing some painting on an aircraft, when one of the armourers who was working on another Spitfire, walked into the hangar with a friend from the cookhouse. He was showing him around the aircraft as he'd promised; he sat the chap from the cook-house in the cockpit and explained all the various controls. When it came to the control column, he said, 'Now this button is the one that fires the guns, the pilot turns this over from safety to fire.' So this is what his friend did, and all at once the eight Browning machine guns went off very loudly indeed. I had walked passed the aircraft and had just cleared it by then; I dived to the floor with bullets ricocheting all over the place, Flight Sergeant Etteridge, who was sitting in his office having five minutes shut-eye, also dived for cover, with bullets going through the windows, smashing all his geranium flowers off the window sill; this covered the flight sergeant with mould and earth. He was not a happy man that afternoon.
>
> The armourer and the cook were marched off to the guardroom to await charges and were given a few days inside for the incident.

Flying Officer John Mungo-Park had joined No.74 Squadron in September 1939. He had transferred from the Fleet Air Arm as a lieutenant, and took a commission with the RAF. He was a descendant of Alexander Mungo-Park who was an eighteenth-century adventurer and explorer.

He was a very get-up-and-go pilot, and for the time he was with the squadron he was always in the thick of things. He was also the one who organised a low-flying competition one afternoon at Rochford airfield, with the other pilots he had talked into flying with him. The pilots all put a half-a-crown into a kitty; whoever flew the lowest would collect the winnings. Flight Rigger John Gill remembers:

> So every pilot flew a low pass across the airfield, much to the disgust of the Flight Sergeant, who didn't want any damaged aircraft, but the flying went ahead and the winner was Mungo-Park himself. He had actually touched the ground with his propeller tips. We had seen clogs of earth fly up as he flew across a very shallow depression on the airfield, where he more or less went out of sight. We thought he'd gone in, but he appeared again; he managed to land safely and when he taxied in, we could see that the tips of his prop blades were bent.

He was full of apologies to the flight sergeant who was pretty annoyed about it. The next thing was we had to get busy with blocks of wood and hard-faced hammers, to hammer the blades straight, so there was no evidence if anybody came back to find out what had been going on. All the winnings were actually used to buy beer for the lads who had put the damage right on his aircraft.

As mentioned previously, Group Captain Bouchier, the Station Commander, had decided to try and tidy up the look of the airfield. A special entry in the Station Diary for 30th April, 1940 reads:

> During the last month, a determined drive has been made by the station commander to make the station a pleasanter and more attractive place. Roads and paths were cleared up and edges whitewashed, grass verges and lawns were cut. A number of bulbs, plants and rose trees were planted, and every squadron and section given tools to cultivate their own part of the camp.
>
> In consequence, the main road to headquarters and the ground around the hangars and workshops are gay with spring flowers and should be gayer still when the summer comes.

Finally on 10th May, 1940, the German army made its move. Hitler sent his Panzers pouring through Holland and Belgium, sweeping all opposition before them; five days later he sent a second thrust through the Ardennes Forest towards Sedan to pierce the Maginot Line, which ran from Luxembourg to Switzerland, and had been thought to be impregnable by the Allied Command.

As the situation worsened, the armies of France and Belgium, and the British Expeditionary Force were all in retreat from the lightning advance of the Germans, who were using the new aircraft-ground support tactics to good effect. Blitzkrieg was the new terror weapon, pushing armies and civilians aside.

On the afternoon of 15th May, the pilots at Hornchurch were told that there would be a briefing that evening in the Officers' Mess games room. That evening Station Commander 'Boy' Bouchier informed the pilots of the very serious situation that had developed over in France and Belgium.

CHAPTER 5

DUNKIRK AND THE FALL OF FRANCE
16th May – June 1940

The first patrols by squadrons from Hornchurch were sent to fly over Ostend, on the Belgium coast. This was undertaken on 16th May, when 12 aircraft of No.74 Squadron took off at 8 am, and 12 aircraft of No.54 led by Squadron Leader Douglas-Jones, left at 10.35 am hours, and cruised up and down the patrol line for about thirty minutes; no enemy aircraft were encountered.

On the 17th, No.65 Squadron claimed a Junkers Ju88 bomber shot down over Flushing by Flying Officer J.H. Welford at about 8 am; this patrol was led by Squadron Leader Desmond Cooke.

On the 20th May, Vice-Admiral Sir Bertram Ramsay, a Flag Officer Commanding Dover, was charged with the task of organising a possible evacuation of the BEF under the code-name Dynamo, as the army retreated towards the Channel ports. Operation Dynamo was implemented between 6 pm and 7 pm on Sunday the 26th, when every available ship and boat was ordered to head for the Dunkirk area. During the preceding week many men had already been evacuated from Boulogne and Calais, where fierce fighting took place between the 19th and 26th.

Hornchurch was now in the forefront of the action, with the squadrons maintaining air cover over the beaches that were now under constant attack by the Luftwaffe. While on patrol on the morning of 21st May, Pilot Officer Johnny Allen of No.54 Squadron was ordered to investigate an unidentified plot over the Channel; this turned out to be a force of 20 Junkers Ju88 bombers. Despite the overwhelming numbers, he dived into the attack under heavy fire from the formation of enemy aircraft; he managed to destroy one of the enemy before his ammunition ran out. This was No.54 Squadron's first confirmed victory.

About 12 midday, 'A' Flight of No.74 Squadron was scrambled to patrol the Dover area. The visibility was not very good and the cloud base was down to 800 feet. Climbing out of the clouds near Calais at an altitude of 17,000 feet, Flight Lieutenant Malan came across a Heinkel He111 bomber which was so close that he almost collided with it. He pulled his aircraft into a tight turn and he then engaged the bomber. With bullets hitting the German aircraft, black smoke began pouring from the port engine, and one of the undercarriage legs dropped out. It was unlikely that the German would make it home.

While Malan tried to reform his section over the radio, he spotted another aircraft, this time a Junkers Ju88. He pursued the bomber and opened fire on it from astern from a range of 500 yards, but to no real effect. He came at the aircraft again from another position and saw his bullets strike home from a range of 150 yards, the Junkers went into a dive, flames pouring from the aircraft as it went down. 'Sailor' Malan claimed both aircraft as destroyed.

From the same engagement, after shooting down a Ju88 and damaging a Heinkel 111, Pilot Officer Bertie Aubert was reported missing, but it was later found out that he had made a forced-landing near Calais, after running low on fuel. He managed to get a flight back to England in a Bristol Blenheim aircraft on 23rd May. Pilot Officer Johnny Freeborn also claimed a Ju88 destroyed, and Pilot Officer Measures, a Heinkel 111. Back at base No.74 Squadron claimed for six enemy aircraft.

At 8.30 am on 22nd May, No.65 Squadron's 'A' Flight, led by Flight Lieutenant Gerald 'Sammy' Saunders, patrolled over the Dunkirk and Calais area; it was to be an uneventful patrol. One of the Spitfires developed an engine problem, however, and was forced to make a belly-landing at North Foreland. Pilot Officer Ken Hart was uninjured in the landing, but his aircraft (K9920) was a complete write-off.

In the afternoon 65 Squadron flew another sortie, this time over Calais and Boulogne and engaged a lone Junkers 88. Pilot Officer Smart, in his attack, put the rear gunner out of action and damaged the starboard engine before losing sight of the aircraft in clouds.

The day started early for the men of No.74 Squadron on 23rd May. They flew their first sortie at 6 am patrolling between Boulogne and Calais, at a height of 2,000 feet. Flying that morning was Squadron Leader Francis 'Drogo' White, who noticed a small German observation aircraft at low level and decided to investigate. The aircraft was a Henschel 126, which upon sighting the Spitfires above started to take evasive action. Squadron Leader White dived into attack, giving the German aircraft bursts from his machine guns, which hit the wings and fuselage. White's diving speed was so fast that he overshot the Henschel; however the enemy aircraft was finished off by the following Spitfire flown by Flying Officer W.E.G. Measures. During the attack, the German gunner had managed to fire off some shots and one of these had hit White's Spitfire in the radiator causing his engine to overheat; he had no option but to find somewhere to land before his engine seized up. He decided to land at Calais-Marck airfield. On return to Hornchurch, the Station Commander, Cecil Bouchier, was told of Squadron Leader White's position, and it was decided to mount a rescue attempt.

The mission was given clearance from Group Headquarters and members of No.54 Squadron were given the job. Flight Lieutenant James 'Prof' Leathart was told by Cecil Bouchier to take the squadron's two-seater Miles Master aircraft over to Calais-Marck, and to pick two pilots to go as escort with him. James Leathart recalls the events before and during the rescue:

I was feeling rather pleased with myself, having just shot down a Messerschmitt 110 over Dunkirk, when I saw a Spitfire streaming glycol. It was clear that he would not get back across the Channel, so I stayed with him until he landed on a very small flying club airfield at Calais-Marck. I waggled my wings, to show the pilot that I knew he was safe. I then returned to Hornchurch for breakfast. It was during my meal that I was informed that the CO of No.74 Squadron had not returned.

It therefore seemed quite reasonable to me to go back to Calais-Marck and rescue Squadron Leader White. It so happened that my squadron (54) had just been equipped with the first Miles Master dual-control aircraft for blind flying instrument training. It was a comparatively light aircraft compared with the Spitfire and having a Rolls-Royce Kestrel engine of some 800 hp, it had a very useful performance [not far short of current fighters] (Miles Master Serial No. N7681).

Talking with my two flight commanders, Al Deere and Johnny Allen, I asked them if they would escort me. They said 'yes', so 'Daddy' Bouchier went and got permission from Group, and off we went.

We flew low across the Channel to Calais-Marck. I landed and waited for Squadron Leader White to come and jump into the back; after about ten minutes, my engine began to overheat so I decided to take off again, without a passenger. However I had scarcely got my wheels up, when tracer bullets came racing past me; I was being attacked! So I broke the seal on the throttle, to allow extra power from the engine, and did the steepest turn in my life. Two Messerschmitt 109s flashed past me pursued by my escort. I dropped the Master back on the airfield and jumped out, running for the nearest ditch, and landing right on top of Squadron Leader White who had been hiding there, watching the aerial battle overhead.

We stayed there for sometime watching the battle and seeing two Me 109s being shot down by Al Deere.

During all this time the German tanks and lorries were going along the road at the edge of the airfield towards Dunkirk. Why they never put a shell through the bright yellow painted Master, I will never know.

After about an hour, things looked all right to go back, but it was only then that I realised that we had no battery starting trolley. We had only had the Master a few days and I did not know if it could be started by hand; however searching through all the likely places we found two starting handles, one fitted on each side of the engine. We cranked furiously with one eye on the German traffic along the road. Eventually, it started and we jumped in with great relief; however, I'd

forgotten that the safety seal on the throttle was broken.
Giving it full throttle for take-off, the aircraft went up and, to
my great surprise, climbed almost vertically. Nevertheless we
got home safely and were not shot down by the Navy, when
flying at nought feet back across the Channel. We stopped at
Manston for fuel and landed at Hornchurch in time for lunch.

The engagement with the German fighters above Calais-Marck was tackled
by Johnny Allen and Alan Deere, who had been circling above the airfield;
Allen at 8,000 feet above cloud, and Deere at a lower altitude. Alan Deere:

> The first time I knew something was up, was when Johnny
> Allen screamed over the R/T: 'Al, they're here, Huns, a dozen
> or so just below and heading towards the airfield. I'm going in
> after them.' I told Johnny to keep me informed. I thought I'd
> better try and somehow warn 'Prof' Leathart, but as the Master
> carried no radio, perhaps waggling my wings might draw his
> attention to the danger. Just at that moment a Messerschmitt
> 109 came zooming out of the clouds, firing at the Miles Master,
> which he fortunately missed. I managed to turn inside the 109,
> who tried to avoid my fire by pulling up vertically, presenting
> me with a perfect target. I fired a burst and smoke began to
> pour from his aircraft, which stalled and then dived straight
> into the water's edge from a height of about 3,000 feet.

While this had all been going on Johnny Allen had been engaged with
fighting Me109s above, with Alan Deere hearing Allen's voice calling over
the R/T, 'Red One I'm surrounded. Can you help me.' Flying up through
the clouds to assist his comrade, Deere then encountered two Me109s who
were seen to be heading inland. Going after them, he soon came within
range, giving a long burst of fire to the Number Two aircraft, which after
being hit rolled onto its back and careered down.

The other German tried every manoeuvre to shake the Spitfire off, but
eventually Deere had to break off because he had run out of ammunition.
The German continued flying inland and escaped.

Johnny Allen had survived, although his aircraft had been slightly
damaged. He and Deere met up over mid-Channel, Allen landing back at
Hornchurch accompanied by Alan Deere doing a victory roll over the
airfield.

This was also according to official records, the first combat victory by a
Spitfire against the Messerschmitt Me109. Pilot Officer Alan Deere's
combat report was sent to the Air Ministry for analysis regarding the
performance of the Spitfire's comparative strengths and weaknesses against
the 109s. The report was rejected, since it was deemed not acceptable,
given the already published figures on the fighter's performance.

However Deere's facts were soon to be proved right as the war
progressed.

Back at Hornchurch, Group Captain Bouchier received a signal from Air Vice-Marshal Keith Park, to No.54 Squadron; it read:

> Air Officer Commanding sends his congratulations to No.54 Squadron on the magnificent fight put up by Flying Officers Deere and Allen, who so severely punished superior numbers this morning.

Later that day, a Blenheim from No.600 (City of London) Squadron was sent over to Calais-Marck with two fitters, Corporal Higginbottom and Leading Aircraftman Cressay, a new radiator, and a supply of glycol, in an attempt to salvage Squadron Leader White's aircraft.

Another 74 Squadron pilot shot down that day was Flying Officer 'Paddy' Byrne, who was hit by ground fire while on patrol over Clairmarais Wood. He survived but was wounded in the leg; he was captured and spent the rest of the war in Stalag Luft 3 prisoner of war camp.

Other squadrons were now also using RAF Hornchurch as their base, during the Dunkirk emergency. No.92 Squadron flew in from Northolt on the morning of 23rd May. Their Commanding Officer was Squadron Leader Roger Bushell, who had come to Britain from South Africa and was a very good sportsman and champion skier, who had coached the British Winter Olympic Team in 1936. Also in the squadron at this time was Robert Stanford Tuck, who had recently been posted from No.65.

The squadron took off on its patrol that morning of the 23rd at 8.30 am. While patrolling the beaches they encountered six enemy Me109s and claimed all the aircraft destroyed. Sadly Pilot Officer Pat Learmond was shot down almost immediately during the dogfight; his aircraft was hit, exploded almost at once, and went down in a ball of flame.

The squadron flew another sortie at 13.45 pm. This time they engaged a formation of Heinkel 111s, with an escort of over 20 Me110 fighter-bombers, and above them Messerschmitt 109s. In the ensuing dogfight, Roger Bushell's aircraft was hit and he had to crash-land. Flying Officer John Gillies also was shot down, but survived; Sergeant Paul Klipsch was killed. Flight Lieutenant 'Paddy' Green was hit in the thigh by a piece of armour-piercing shrapnel, but managed to fly his aircraft, although vomiting and feeling faint. He stuck his thumb into the wound and pressed hard hoping to stop the flow of blood. He landed at Hawkinge aerodrome, his cockpit awash with blood. He was hospitalised immediately, the surgeon saving the leg, but he would be out of the war for some time.

Roger Bushell and John Gillies were both captured and became prisoners of war; Bob Tuck took over as acting commander of No.92 Squadron. The next day, 24th May, Flight Lieutenant Brian Kingcome transferred from No.65 Squadron to become a flight commander for No.92. The following signal was sent from AOC to No. 92 Squadron:

> Air Officer Commanding sends congratulations to No.92 Squadron in their magnificent fighting and successes in the

first day of war operations and sincerely hopes that the
Squadron Commander and the other two missing pilots will
turn up later, as many others have in the past fortnight.

The number of German aircraft claimed shot down by No.92 Squadron that
day was 23, for the loss of four Spitfires and another seven badly shot up,
with the loss of four pilots and one wounded.

Early in the morning of 24th May, on their first patrol, a section of No.74
Squadron led by Flight Lieutenant 'Paddy' Treacy, shot down a German
Hs126 observation aircraft. They lost Flying Officer D.S. 'Sammy' Hoare,
whose aircraft was damaged by enemy fire, and was forced to make an
emergency landing at Calais-Marck airfield. 'Sammy' Hoare recounts the
events:

> We had on that occasion seen a Henschel 126, a German
> reconnaissance aircraft. Although our instructions were to
> patrol just the Channel coastline, we were told that we could
> go inland, if we were investigating any aircraft, or for some
> other reason; in this case we had seen this other aircraft. Paddy
> Treacy had seen it, and I was leading the second section. We
> must have been somewhere around St Omer, about 15 miles
> inland. The Henschel was flying very low down, and in fact by
> the time I went into attack it with my section, it was down to
> about treetop height. It was in flames and just as I pulled away,
> I saw it crash and go up in a pall of smoke. Anyway I managed
> to collect a bullet from somewhere; it may have been a
> German infantryman or light flack. It may have been from our
> own troops on the ground, or even the Henschel we'd just shot
> down. Nevertheless I reformed and intended to go back to
> base, when Mungo-Park called me up and said I was
> streaming glycol; so I thought the sensible thing to do was
> what Squadron Leader White had done the previous day, and
> go into Calais-Marck airfield.
>
> I knew the previous day that we had sent two groundcrew
> over to the airfield to service his aircraft and repair it. I
> thought if I can get in here, perhaps they can do a quick patch
> up and then I can get home. But it didn't work out that way,
> and I was too late.
>
> At that time the military intelligence just could not keep up
> with the speed of the German advance westwards. We were
> not told the disposition of British and French forces nor where
> the front line was (did anyone know!) and there was never any
> mention of an evacuation. In fact Calais had been reinforced
> only the previous day with a British armoured unit.
>
> When I landed on the airfield Corporal Higginbottom and
> Aircraftman Cressay came out, and were beside the aircraft
> immediately; I told them what had happened. They saw a hole

on the side of the engine cowling; they undid the cowling and some panels. We found quite a large hole in the pipe leading from the header tank to the engine. I'd obviously been hit by something, and lost all my glycol; the engine was boiling.

At that time we had no idea how long a Merlin engine would last without any glycol. Before I had landed my radiator temperature gauge, my oil temperature and pressure gauges were all registering well above the limits; and after I landed the engine kept running even after I had switched off and left the cockpit. So things were getting hot. With hindsight of course, I might have taken a chance to get across the Channel, but in the circumstances, not knowing what the position was, I just landed; it seemed the sensible thing to do. The alternative of course was to get halfway across the Channel and bale out, or go on a bit further and hope to reach Manston, or let the engine blow up in my face. Those were the alternatives, but I took the wrong one.

In the adjacent fields German tanks were arriving on the scene. Before Hoare and the other two aircraftmen could destroy the Spitfire, small-arms fire began whistling around their bodies. They hit the deck and began to crawl away into the long grass to escape the oncoming troops. In the confussion Cressay lost contact with the other two but was later captured. Hoare and Higginbottom reached the boundary of the airfield and headed north to the coast, stealing a couple of bicycles on the way.

For the next 36 hours they spent a lot of time trying, unsuccessfully, to get some small boats from the sand dunes into the water. They also cycled east and west hoping to make contact with some friendly forces, but none were found. There was no obvious solution to their predicament. They were eventually captured together with some army evacuees from Calais by members of an SS Panzer unit, who were spraying the beaches with machine guns to deter would-be escapers. By that time German forces had reached the entire coastline of northwest France apart from the Dunkirk enclave, and Calais which held out for another twenty-four hours.

Earlier that morning at 8.30 am, No.92 Squadron, now led by Flight Lieutenant Tuck, took off with the eight aircraft that were still serviceable. Over the French coast, they encountered various enemy aircraft, claiming in this action seven aircraft shot down. During the battle, Bob Tuck shot down two Dornier 17 bombers, but was himself hit by return enemy fire. He was wounded on the inside of his thigh.

Almost out of ammunition and fuel, he headed for home back across the Channel at about 500 feet. He found that his thigh was sticky with blood and he did his best to staunch it with a handkerchief. By the time he landed back at Hornchurch, his leg had stiffened. He noticed a small tear near his right trouser pocket, and feeling inside he took out some of the loose change he had been carrying. Upon inspection, he noticed that one coin had stopped a bullet, but another must have embedded itself into the back of his thigh.

He was taken to the Romford General Hospital, and there was examined by the hospital surgeon. After probing the wound for a couple of minutes, the surgeon removed a small piece of metal. It wasn't a bullet, but a small duralumin nut from the rudder pedal! It had been shot off by a bullet with such force that it had embedded itself into Tuck's leg. The surgeon was heard to joke afterwards 'A few inches higher, and they'd have had to transfer you to the WAAF.'

On this sortie No.92 Squadron lost Flying Officer Peter Casanove, whose Spitfire P9374 was hit and he was forced to crash-land on sand dunes at Dunkirk; he too was eventually taken prisoner.

No.74 Squadron were up again in the afternoon over Calais and Boulogne. They attacked a formation of three Heinkels; Malan destroyed one, Sergeant Bill Skinner damaged another and Johnny Freeborn got an Me109 probably destroyed.

However they lost Pilot Officer Aubert, who that very morning had just returned from France, after being shot down earlier. Paddy Treacy was seen baling out, as was Sergeant Tony Mould. Both of them managed to get aboard ships at Dunkirk and reached England safely.

Both No.65 and 54 Squadrons had seen action in the morning. At 12.30 pm, No.54 were involved with their first really big formation of enemy aircraft when over Calais at 12,000 feet, they attacked Heinkels, escorted by Me109s and 110s. They claimed nine aircraft destroyed and four probables.

In the following interview given to *Life Magazine* in 1940, James 'Prof' Leathart gave an insight of what the fighting over Dunkirk was like:

> Over Dunkirk at around 10,000 feet, we ran into a whole flock of Messerschmitts which came charging down out of the clouds. They had obviously been sitting upstairs guarding some of the bombers hidden in the smoke below. They nearly caught us. I saw tracers going past my ears and actually heard the rattle of guns from the one on my tail, and then he was gone. I followed him down, banging the throttle open and leaning on my stick, but in the smoke clouds hanging over Dunkirk I lost him.
>
> Up again I saw the rest of the squadron at about 6,000 feet. They were in a hell of a mix-up with Hun fighters and some Junkers 88's; I climbed up to join them.
>
> My radio was open and as I climbed, I could hear the stream of occasional comic backchat passing between some of the members of the Squadron, punctuated with bursts of gunfire as they were popping off at the Huns. Once, for instance, I heard a New Zealander calling and saying calmly, 'There's a Messerschmitt on your tail', and the reply 'Okay pal'; and then I was in it too.
>
> Again there was that lovely feeling of the gluey controls

and the target being slowly hauled into the gunsite. Then thumb down on the trigger again and the smooth shuddering of the machine as the eight-gun blast let go. His tail folded back on his wings and there was a great flash of smoke and flames as he went down.

No.54 Squadron lost two pilots that day: Flying Officer T.N. Linley who was killed in Spitfire P9455, and Sergeant J.W.B. Phillips who was shot down after strafing a lorry convoy; he baled out and was captured.

On 25th May, No.92 Squadron flew a number of patrols before being told that they would be going up to RAF Duxford that following afternoon, to rest and be re-equipped, as well as to receive a new commanding officer; this was to be Squadron Leader P.J. Sanders.

No.54 Squadron were again back in action, when they were chosen to escort a Fleet Air Arm squadron of Fairey Swordfish biplanes on a bombing raid. Pilot Officer Colin Gray, the New Zealander, was one of the pilots picked to be an escort, and recalled:

> We'd been sent on a mission to escort some Fairey Swordfish from Detling Airport in Kent, across the Channel to dive-bomb Gravelines. Now this took quite sometime, because they only cruised at about 90 knots, and it took almost an hour before they finished the job.
>
> Since we were already over the other side, 'Prof' Leathart decided to carry on and patrol inland. After a couple of minutes we sighted about 24 109s and 110s. We dived to attack this lot, and I was watching one of the 109s I'd been shooting at bale out. I thought now, this is good, when suddenly my aircraft was hit from behind by a hail of bullets and a couple of cannon shells. One of the cannon shells hit the inspection hatch, just behind the cockpit and blew out the air-bottle and hydraulic control, which meant I couldn't work my undercarriage, flaps or fire my guns. The other cannon shell went over my head and into the port aileron and jammed it in the up position; this threw me into a spiral dive which was a far better escape manoeuvre than I could have devised, because I never saw the enemy aircraft again. I eventually got the aileron free and set course for home and mother.
>
> The subsequent landing at Hornchurch was a little difficult because I had no airspeed indicator; the shell that had gone into the aileron had also taken off the pitot head. I also had no flaps or brakes. Judging the landing speed was a little difficult and I made a mess of my first attempt but I got it in the second time.

Also during this dogfight, Flight Lieutenant Max Pearson claimed an Me110, while Johnny Allen destroyed two Me110s, before being hit himself; his engine caught fire and he was obliged to bale out. He came down in the Channel quite near to a Royal Navy destroyer and was picked up. James Leathart recalls:

> During the combat, Johnny Allen called up over the R/T, 'Oh hell, my engine's packed up', then he shouted, 'I'm on fire,' then 'Yippee there's a destroyer downstairs, I'm baling out.' He turned up in the Mess three days later wearing a Naval sub-lieutenant's jacket and a pair of bell-bottomed trousers.

Also shot down and forced to crash-land on the beach near Dunkirk was Pilot Officer George Gribble. He managed to get aboard a ship, still carrying his aircraft radio, which he felt was still 'secret' and should not fall into enemy hands. Unfortunately No.54 also lost Sergeant Buckland who failed to return.

Another squadron, No.19, flew down from Duxford on the 25th. Their Commanding Officer, Squadron Leader G.D. Stephenson, led 12 Spitfires into Hornchurch to start operations the next day.

On Sunday the 26th, 54 Squadron were once more up early on dawn patrol. The Form F below is the Fighter Command Combat Report for that patrol:

F.C.C.R/63/ 40   FORM "F".   SECRET.

FIGHTER COMMAND COMBAT REPORT

To: Fighter Command.

From: No.11 Group.

Composite report.

54 Sqdn patrolling Calais-Dunkirk 0505-0645 at 15,000 feet sighted two Me.110's above. These were attacked, one being shot down. The Squadron were then ordered to rendezvous Calais at 10,000 feet; a destroyer was being bombed by two lone Ju 88's whilst a formation of 20 E/A (14,000 ft) appeared in the distance. 1 Ju88 was shot down and the Sqdn by now split up attacked the Me110's, which formed into a circle making it difficult for our a/c to attack, whilst a number of our a/c found 2 E/A on their tails when attacking a Me110 . . . i.e. once again the enemy rely upon local superiority of at least 2-3 to one, and whilst a number of fighters are lost, the bombers are able to carry out their task with little interference from the air. Towards the end of the combat 12 Me.109s appeared in a line astern circling above Dunkirk.

Only one of our pilots encountered these (no result). It

would appear that reinforcements had been called up although one Squadron of our aircraft could not have accounted for the large numbers of a/c present and the Me's themselves made no attempt to take the offensive.

Enemy Casualties.

1 Ju.88 shot down in the sea by F/Lt. Leathart (confirmed by P/O Deere)
2 Me.110 (one in flames) by F/Lt. Leathart (confirmed by F/S Tew)

1 Me.110 certain by McMullen
2 Me.110 certain by P/O Deere
1 Me 110 possible F/Lt Pearson
1 Me.110 possible F/S Tew
1 Me.110 possible P/O Way

Several further E/A were attacked without known results. All our A/C returned safely, one damaged (but serviceable), by cannon fire – which E/A shot from both front and rear guns.

Evasive tactics of E/A during combats were to dive and turn.
1 Me.110 was chased to Lille by F/Lt Pearson before he left (it) in a distressed condition.
R. 1123 26.5.40.

No.19 Squadron flew two patrols on the 26th. On the first patrol in the morning they met up with 21 Ju87 Stuka dive-bombers who were escorted by 30 Me109s. In the combat that followed, ten enemy aircraft were shot down but the squadron's CO Squadron Leader Stephenson was shot down, as was Pilot Officer Watson.

Flying Officer Ball was wounded in the head and arm. Later it was confirmed that Geoffrey Stephenson had survived a forced-landing and had been taken prisoner, but Pilot Officer Watson was posted as missing. Flying Officer Ball returned to Hornchurch; a bullet had passed through the top of his helmet and hair, leaving a small wound.

The second sortie that day was led by Flight Lieutenant Brian Lane. His combat report of the following action reads:

At 1600 hours I was leading three sections of the squadron on a patrol over Dunkirk area at 8,000 feet, when the rear section reported eight Me109s at 1,000 feet above. The E/A dived in ragged formation to the attack and the squadron broke formation to escape. I saw an E/A diving to attack P/O Sinclair who escaped into cloud. The E/A pulled out of the dive just above the cloud and headed for France. I chased it and delivered a climbing attack from astern firing a burst of 4-5 seconds at about 300-200 yards range. The E/A lurched onto its side and fell in a vertical dive. I followed it down and pulled out at 2,500 feet, when the E/A was well below me.

During this operation Sergeant C.A. Irwin was shot down and killed over the Channel; his body was never recovered. Pilot Officer Michael Lyne was wounded in the leg while in combat with Me109s. He managed to get back across the Channel, but was forced to land his aircraft (L1031) on Walmer beach, near Deal.

No.74 Squadron claimed a Henschel 126 on their first patrol which was shared by Pilot Officer H.M. Stephen, Warrant Officer E. Mayne and Pilot Officer D. Cobden.

By Monday 27th May, Dynamo was in full operation and the scores of Little Ships were to make trips across the Channel each day. The armies on the beaches continued to bravely endure the Luftwaffe bombing, while patiently awaiting their turn in the long queues to get aboard a ship and home to safety.

No.54 Squadron were airborne at 4.30 am. They encountered a Ju88 at 20,000 feet. Flight Lieutenant Max Pearson went into the attack and followed the bomber into the smoke clouds over Dunkirk. That was the last anyone saw of Max Pearson; he was presumably shot down by the enemy aircraft or ground fire. The general report of the action read:

Nine a/c of 54 Sqdn were patrolling Calais-Dunkirk at 16,000 feet to 21,000 feet. S.E. of Dunkirk a Ju.88 was sighted at 20,000 ft and engaged first by one section of 3 a/c in line astern and then by a second section in the same line formation. Both sections used No.1 attack and while getting back into position, fired several bursts into the e/a's flanks.

The e/a must have been heavily armoured for it kept on its course in spite of intense firing from our fighters. No cannon was noticed but both rear guns were firing incendiary bullets. The e/a used no evasive tactics beyond the usual tack of changing speed and harassing our fighters by intense fire.

When last seen the e/a's starboard engine was smoking badly and he was being chased inland by one of our fighters, F/Lt Pearson.

Pilots in order of attack:

F/Lt. Leathart	rounds fired	2,393
P/O. Deere	,, ,,	1,993
P/O. Allen	,, ,,	2,720
P/O. Couzens	,, ,,	1,940
Sgt. Norwell	,, ,,	1,498

F/L. Pearson   missing, last seen chasing the Ju.88
                                     towards Dunkirk.

FC/S 17570/INT   (signed) P. Shallard F/O
                                     Intelligence Officer,
                                     54 Squadron.

At 5.45 am No.19 Squadron took off for France, while at 6.30 am No.17 Squadron flew into Hornchurch to await orders. At 7.50 am, No.74 Squadron were airborne from Rochford, and at 8.50 am were patrolling south of Dunkirk. They encountered several Me109s flying above. During the combat Flying Officer Johnny Freeborn, Pilot Officer P.C.F. Stevenson, Warrant Officer 'Tubby' Mayne and Flight Lieutenant 'Sailor' Malan claimed five Me109s and two probably destroyed.

On the return journey, Malan and Stevenson engaged a gaggle of Dorniers. Picking on one, they managed to damage it, but during the attack Stevenson's Spitfire was hit in the radiator. Switching off his engine, he managed to glide down towards Dunkirk to make a wheels-up landing; he avoided capture and had returned to the Squadron by 31st May.

During the afternoon, Alan Deere, Johnny Allen and James Leathart spotted several Ju88 bombers attacking what appeared to be a white hospital ship just off Calais. After the combat, 54 Squadron's tally had increased by two.

No.74 lost Flight Lieutenant Paddy Treacy in the afternoon, when the squadron was engaged with enemy bombers over Gravelines. Treacy mistook Calais for Dunkirk and crash-landed; he was captured by German troops, but managed to escape from his captors.

He found a rowing boat, and tried to make it back across the Channel. He was spotted by two Messerschmitt 110s and a German motorboat was sent after him and he was recaptured. He was to escape again later, this time getting back to England by route of France, Spain and passage on a ship to Eire. He arrived back in early 1941.

The day's tally for Hornchurch squadrons came to 19 aircraft. At the end of the day's operations, No.74 were ordered to prepare to fly to Leconfield, to take a well-earned rest. The Tigers' score stood at 15 confirmed enemy aircraft, 11 probable, and four damaged. They were replaced by No.616, who flew down to Rochford, Hornchurch's satellite airfield.

On 28th May, RAF Fighter Command Headquarters decided to try using the squadrons over Dunkirk in larger formations, which might have more impact against the big German formations of escort fighters. At Hornchurch, this was tried, at 4.30 am when No.19, 54 and 65 Squadrons took off as a Wing. Unfortunately due to the thundery cloud conditions and poor visibility, the squadrons soon lost contact with one another.

No.54 Squadron did spot a single Dornier Do215 and Alan Deere led his section into the attack. Deere pressed the firing button on his control column and watched the bursts from his guns strike the Dornier's port engine. He was about to give it another shot, when his aircraft was hit by return fire from the Dornier's rear-gunner. Alan Deere remembers the encounter:

At Dunkirk, I regret to say, I was shot down by the rear-gunner of a Dornier, which eventually came down itself. It was fairly cloudy and this Dornier had just appeared out of the clouds over the bridgehead; I had my flight with me and we chased him. I got onto his tail and was firing a burst at him, I could see return fire from the rear-gunner and suddenly I felt a juddering sort of thing. I think I was fairly lucky; a bullet from the gunner went into my glycol tank, which meant my coolant system was gone.

I had to come down and I crash-landed on the beach between Dunkirk and Ostend. The Dornier came down over me, smoking, and glided away inland. I think he must have landed somewhere further inland.

I wasn't injured until I landed. Then I hit my head on the front of the cockpit and cut it, and it knocked me out momentarily; it cut a gash on my forehead. I had landed wheels-up of course, right on the edge of the water; the tide happened to be coming in when I came to. I scrambled out of the thing, got my parachute out and walked up the beach towards a cafe I saw. By that time the tide was gradually coming up over the Spitfire and it was never recovered, so I imagine it sank into the sand.

So anyway, I had this bad cut on my forehead, and it was there in this small cafe on the coast, that a woman there said that I was bleeding rather badly. She stuck it together with plaster and put a bandage around it.

I knew they were evacuating from Dunkirk, so I set off for there. I expect it took me around two or three hours because there was a lot of refugee traffic. Eventually I found a bicycle, which I saw lying unattended and got onto it and rode off. I was originally going to go to Ostend, but I met a couple of British Army tommies inland. I said to them, 'Where are you going?' They said, 'You tell us.' I said, 'Aren't you evacuating?' They replied that they were staying put until they had met up with some of their particular company, but they were eventually heading for Dunkirk. So that's where I went with the soldiers.

When I arrived there it was pretty hectic, with the strafing and the bombing; we were on the beach taking cover. There was an organisation to get off the beach run by the Army; you got into a sort of line. At the time I got out, they were still able to get the ships alongside the jetty at Dunkirk; a destroyer had come in and I'd been able to get on it. But there were other people swimming out to the boats and other things.

The conditions aboard the destroyer were very cramped; we were crowded out with soldiers, 'stuffed to the gills' in fact. We were bombed near to pulling off, the cloud fortunately was fairly low, which made the German's accuracy poor and we didn't get hit.

The soldiers aboard gave me a very rough time; they were very anti-RAF. They said where the hell had we been, and I who had been flying ten days non-stop until the time I was shot down, flying two or three sorties a day, was feeling pretty tired.

I answered in no mean manner and said, 'We were there, perhaps you didn't see us.' They weren't very pleased with me, I was the only airman on board of course. They were pretty unpleasant I suppose, but one couldn't blame them really, they were rather worn out, you know.

Another 'Wing' was ordered up from Hornchurch at 9 am, consisting of No.19, 65 and 616 Squadrons, led by 65's CO Desmond Cooke. All the squadrons were heavily engaged with enemy fighters and bombers over the French coast.

The cost to the Luftwaffe was four Me109s and two Dornier 17s destroyed, and two Me109 probables. Although No.65 Squadron lost Pilot Officer 'Tommy' Smart who force-landed on the beach, he got back to 'Blighty' two days later.

Squadron Leader M. Robinson of No.616 Squadron managed to get his damaged aircraft back as far as Manston, where he crash-landed. Another pilot of the same squadron, Sergeant M. Ridley, was wounded. No.54 Squadron received orders on the 28th, to move up to Catterick in Yorkshire for a well-earned rest; they would be replaced by No.41 Squadron.

That day another squadron arrived to take up their place at Hornchurch; this was No.222 Squadron, which had flown down from Kirton-in-Lindsey, Lincolnshire. They were led by their commanding officer Squadron Leader H.W. 'Tubby' Mermagan; also arriving with them was 'A' Flight's commander by the name of Douglas Bader.

On 29th May, patrols were mounted at dawn by the Hornchurch squadrons. They took to the air at about 4.15 am, and Squadrons No.19, 41, 222 and 616 reached the beaches of Dunkirk at 4.45 am. But it was an uneventful patrol and no enemy formations were seen in the vicinity. The weather forecast that day was for overcast and lots of low cloud. As the weather deteriorated No.41 Squadron were forced to land at Biggin Hill on the return leg.

One of 222 Squadron pilots, Pilot Officer John Broadhurst, failed to find Hornchurch, ran out of fuel and had to make a landing with wheels-up; he returned to the squadron a little embarrassed.

The weather continued to be very poor during Thursday, 30th May, and no sorties were flown by Hornchurch squadrons that day. Only Rochford sent up one aircraft on a weather test that morning; the Spitfire on returning to the airfield suffered undercarriage failure on landing and collapsed. The pilot, Flying Officer Denys Gillam, was uninjured.

By 31st May, over 194,600 British troops had been taken off the beaches, which was a miracle in itself. German artillery, which had been moved up, was now targeted on the beachhead. The weather in the Channel was starting to blow up, with increasing heavy winds, but the weather for flying was overcast with cloud base at 10,000 feet. No.41 and 222 Squadrons flew the first patrols of the day at about 4.30 am.

Over Dunkirk, 222 Squadron encountered anti-aircraft gunfire from the mainland. One of their aircraft was damaged, and the pilot, Pilot Officer G.G.A. Davies, had to land his aircraft on the beach, which he did with his undercarriage down; he reported being fired at on the way down by a French 75 mm gun located at Fort West, Mardyke.

He was met on landing by French soldiers. Speaking French, he was able to find out the best route to the harbour at Dunkirk. After setting fire to his Spitfire, he made his way to the evacuation point and managed to get aboard a paddle-steamer and returned to Ramsgate in the early hours of 1st June, eventually arriving back at Hornchurch at teatime the same day.

The same two squadrons were again in action later in the morning, claiming a Heinkel 111 destroyed by Pilot Officer Tony Lovell and Flight Lieutenant J.T. Webster of No.41 Squadron; Webster also destroyed an Me109. Pilot Officer Tim Vigors of No.222 Squadron claimed a probable on a Heinkel 111.

On 1st June 1940, the pilots were up very early, taking an early bite to eat around 4 am, before the four squadrons were ordered off on their first patrols of the day at 4.30 am. The weather forecast for the early morning was for fair to good visibility. They made landfall over France at 5 am, and after patrolling for over 30 minutes, No.19 Squadron spotted a dozen or so Me110s at about 4,500 feet. The squadron led by Flight Lieutenant Brian 'Sandy' Lane, went into the attack; upon seeing the Spitfires, the Me110s went into a defensive formation circle.

Messerschmitt 109s, noticing their comrades below being attacked, now peeled off and went diving down on to No.19 Squadron's aircraft. Meanwhile No.222 had also joined in the affray. The sky was now a mass of twisting and turning aircraft, and during the dogfighting No.19 claimed a number of successes. Pilot Officer Henry Collingham Baker destroyed an Me110, and also claimed a probable; Flight Lieutenant Wilf Clouston claimed an Me109 destroyed. Sergeant Bernard Jennings claimed two Me110s destroyed, Pilot Officer Gordon Sinclair two Me110s destroyed, as well as single Me109s claimed by Flight Sergeant Steere, and Pilot Officer Haines, and single Me110s by Flight Sergeant Unwin and Flight Lieutenant Lane. Unfortunately, there was one casualty. Sergeant Jack Potter was shot down while engaged with an Me110; another enemy aircraft's fire hit his aircraft, and he had to ditch his aircraft into the sea. He was unhurt and managed to return by ship.

No.222 Squadron's encounter with the enemy was none the less dramatic, engaged mainly with the enemy fighters. Pilot Officer Hilary

Edridge claimed a probable Me109, at which he fired as it flew into his sights. CO 'Tubby' Mermagen destroyed an Me110, as did Flight Lieutenant A.I. Robinson, Pilot Officer T. Vigors and Sergeant S. Baxter. Flight Lieutenant Douglas Bader who had been posted to 222, claimed his first victory of the war during this combat; flying Spitfire P9443, he shot down an Me109. No.222 lost three pilots that day. Pilot Officer Roy Morant force-landed on the beaches, but escaped later by channel steamer. Pilot Officer H. Falkust was shot down, baled out and was captured; Sergeant L.J. White was killed in action.

The Hornchurch squadrons, having returned home, were quickly turned around by the ground crews, who went to work refuelling and reloading fresh ammunition into the wings, ready for the next scheduled sortie. During this time the pilots would have enough time to get themselves something to eat and drink.

At around 8.25 am the squadrons took off once again. Over Dunkirk, the Luftwaffe was making life hell for the ships and troops, with the Ju87s, 88s and Heinkels having a field day, because of the lack of RAF air cover.

No.19, 41, 222 and 616 were again involved with heavy clashes with the German bombers and the final tally for the sorties was as follows:

No.19 Squadron:
1 Heinkel 111 – destroyed.   3 Heinkel 111 – probable.
                                    2 Dornier 215 – probable.

No.41 Squadron:
1 Heinkel 111 – destroyed.   1 Dornier 215 – probable.

No.222 Squadron:
                                    1 Heinkel 111 – probable.

No.616 Squadron:
1 Junkers 88 – destroyed.   3 Heinkel 111 – probable.
                                    4 Junkers 88 – probable.

However during the engagement, No.41 Squadron had lost Pilot Officer Bill Stapleton and Flying Officer W.E. Legard. Legard was killed during the action, but Stapleton crash-landed and survived. He remembers the following events:

We came down to Hornchurch from Catterick between 27th and 28th May, having been told in the Mess one morning at Catterick that we would be flying south that day. We loaded up what little things we could take, into bundles wrapped in newspaper, then stuffed them into the flare-tubes and flew down.

Our commanding officer was Squadron Leader H.R.L. 'Robin' Hood, and my flight commander was Terry Webster.

We had standing patrols of 36 aircraft over Dunkirk, and as we left another 36 would arrive. We were told to stay seaward of the coast so that if the German aircraft turned inland, as they always did, we were not to follow them. The day I was shot down I had actually followed an '88, which was my mistake! The minute they saw us they would drop their bombs and make off, straight for home. When I first encountered the enemy I couldn't believe it; it was like watching a film and I couldn't believe this was all happening. I was 19 years old.

I wasn't that well trained and I hadn't fired my eight guns until I opened up on an enemy aircraft.

I was shot down by flak on my second trip of the morning. We were very short of fuel and I was in the arse-end charlie section, which had to keep an eye on the rear of the squadron. As we were turning for home, I looked back and saw '88s coming out of cloud, heading straight for the ships. I called out, '88s and, like one man, 36 aircraft went for them and I found myself chasing this one guy I was determined to get; but I didn't.

I turned for home when Pilot Officer 'Wally' Wallens, my section leader, called me up and said 'get back'. I wasn't quite sure at that time where I was, so I called up Hornchurch and managed to get a bearing. I turned on course and saw an airfield below me, absolutely packed with Heinkel 111s; they were not even dispersed around the airfield, they were tightly packed together. I just prayed I had some ammunition left and went into a strafing attack. I hadn't any ammunition left, but it wouldn't have taken more than a hundred rounds to set the lot alight; all I could see were German ground crews leaping off the wings to take cover. I pulled up, realising I couldn't do much, and I headed out towards the sea; as I got over the coast the German flak opened up on me.

The 40 mm flak got my tailplane, it was that close. The aeroplane was controllable but not the way one would have liked it. I was only at 800 feet, so I could not bale out, and I came down in the sea. I got out, I don't know how, and was shot at for about two minutes with machine guns and rifles; then they stopped firing. My legs were buggered, they were hit rather badly and I couldn't move them. Two of the Germans swam out from the shore, flak-artillery guys, and they could not have been more helpful or kinder in getting me back to shore. That was it. I ended up eventually at Stalag Luft 3.

Back at Hornchurch, that evening the station was visited by the Secretary of State for Air, Sir Archibald Sinclair, who had come down from London to get first-hand accounts of the air-fighting situation and in turn congratulate the men for their work.

This day also saw the award of the Distinguished Flying Cross to Acting Flight Lieutenant A.G. 'Sailor' Malan, for his outstanding leadership over Dunkirk and engagements against the enemy.

This was to be the last day that squadrons from RAF Hornchurch would be involved in the evacuation. However on the 2nd June, the Hornchurch Sector received an unexpected visitor from the Dunkirk beaches. Pilot Officer Peter Brown of No.611 Squadron, while operating from Martlesham Heath airfield, was bounced by Me109s on his first combat patrol and was badly shot up. He set off for home, in poor visibility, hoping that nothing vital had been hit. After a 70 mile flight over the North Sea, he made landfall at Foulness Point, but was dangerously low on fuel.

Within a few minutes he was over Rochford airfield, and landed with great care. Now he was safe, or nearly. As the wheels touched down the aircraft swung dangerously to the left; one of the German bullets had burst a tyre. He managed to keep the aircraft under control and made a safe landing. At dispersal the flight sergeant started to count the bullet holes, but gave up after 30; fortunately none of the bullets had struck a vital part of the Spitfire. Pilot Officer Brown had been very lucky indeed to survive that day and he remembered Rochford with gratitude.

The operation continued, however, till 4th June, when the last ships left Dunkirk at about 3.40 am. Shortly afterwards the town and beaches fell to the Germans. Hornchurch, which had played its part in the air cover over most of the withdrawal, had lost 23 pilots, killed or captured.

The amount of Allied troops rescued from Dunkirk between the dates of 26th May and 4th June, stood at 338,226. It was a miracle rescue, which came out of defeat, and in which all the services played such a great part.

The following message was sent to RAF Hornchurch, as well as other airfields:

Signal from Headquarters, No.11 Group

To Hornchurch, A291.

Air Officer Commanding sends following message to pilots and all personnel of the Fighter Stations, Sector Stations and Forward Airfields:

The Admiralty reports that the Dunkirk operations were completed this morning.

During the last two weeks our Fighter Squadrons operating over France have shot down a total of 527 German bombers and fighters, 371 of which have been confirmed as destroyed, for a loss of 80 of our pilots. By their successes in air combat our squadrons have protected the Army during retreat, have enabled the Navy to embark the Army from Dunkirk and the beaches, and also protect our bombers and reconnaissance aircraft and established moral ascendancy over the German bombers and fighters. The Air Officer Commanding congratulates the pilots on their magnificent fighting and highly commends the technical and administrative personnel whose work made it possible for the pilots to succeed.

It is hoped that we shall now be given a short respite in which to organise refit and train new pilots in order to inflict yet heavier casualties on the German fighters and bombers when they attack this country and coastwise shipping.

On 4th June, No.54 Squadron returned to Hornchurch from Catterick to take over from No.41 Squadron. No.74 Squadron also returned from Leconfield. No.222 Squadron flew back up to Kirton-in-Lindsey. No.19 Squadron returned to Duxford on 5th June, and No.616 back to Leconfield on the 6th.

The main duties carried out now by the squadrons were to be convoy and reconnaissance patrols. The squadrons had been re-equipped and new pilots and aircraft brought up to strength, each with 16 aircraft.

It was around this time that the question of gun harmonization was introduced to RAF commanders. No.74 Squadron's 'Sailor' Malan, who was a very good combat marksman, was very keen on having guns harmonized at 250 yards to achieve maximum effectiveness. There was also the introduction of various ammunitions for the guns.

Many of the pilots were keen on the De Wilde bullet shells, which when hitting a target would cause a flash, so the pilot would know without a doubt that he was hitting the enemy. James 'Prof' Leathart was so impressed with the De Wilde, that he made a report and sent it on with recommendation to Fighter Command Headquarters. In their wisdom they sent the Command Armament Officer down to Hornchurch who, after meeting with the pilots, was impressed enough to take action with the manufacturers. Supplies of the De Wilde steadily increased.

It was at this time that Alan Deere of 54 was informed of his award of the Distinguished Flying Cross and was promoted to flight lieutenant.

On 10th June, while on patrol, Pilot Officer Ben Draper of 74 Squadron encountered an Me109, which he damaged, and also a Dornier 17.

By 10th June, Britain had another enemy to contend with, when Mussolini brought Italy into the war. Prime Minister Winston Churchill, speaking in the House of Commons on 18th June, declared in his speech:

What General Weygand called the Battle of France is over.
I expect that the Battle of Britain is about to begin.

Although it was relatively quiet during the daylight hours, the Germans did send a number of night bomber raiders over to Britain during this period. On 18th/19th June 1940, just such a raid was spotted by searchlight batteries over the Southend area of Essex. At that time No.74 Squadron were on detachment down at Rochford. Having seen the searchlights picking out the enemy bombers, Flight Lieutenant Malan was keen to have a go at the raiders and asked permission from his CO to take off. It was a clear night with a full moon, but the chances of picking up an enemy bomber in those days was very slim, unless the searchlight batteries could hold the enemy in their beams long enough for an aircraft to engage. Luckily the raider was caught in a beam flying at around 8,000 feet. Malan, who had taken off from Rochford a few minutes earlier at 00.20 am, soon caught up with the Heinkel 111. Closing in from astern, Malan opened fire from a range of 200 yards and saw his bullet hits flash when striking the bomber which now started to spin to the ground. As he looked ahead he noticed another aircraft caught in searchlights. He flew towards this aircraft, another Heinkel, and opened fire. It began to burn and thick smoke belched from it as it started to dive down. This aircraft crashed at Chelmsford, impacting in the Bishop of Chelmsford's garden and Springfield Road.

Malan landed back at Rochford at 1.30 am. This was a unique combat, as it was the first time that a fighter pilot had managed to intercept and shoot down two enemy aircraft in one night.

For No.74 Squadron it was quite a celebration, although Flight Lieutenant 'Sailor' Malan had recently had his own personal celebration, after his wife Lynda had given birth to a son; she was in a nursing home at Westcliffe-on-Sea, near Southend.

No.54 Squadron was sent down to operate from Rochford airfield on the 25th. The daily routine consisted of flight or squadron patrols over occupied territory, convoy protection and training up the new boys; also long boring spells at readiness.

It was while at Rochford that three members of the squadron were called to return to Hornchurch. Flight Lieutenant Alan Deere on returning from a training flight, was met by fellow pilot Johnny Allen and told that they were required to go back to Hornchurch as the Station Adjutant had said that a VIP would be visiting the station, and they would be required to meet him. The two pilots travelled back to Hornchurch in the Miles Magister two-seater trainer. Also invited was James Leathart, who had already left for home base.

Once they had arrived, they noticed that the airfield was alive with anticipation. The VIP was none other than King George VI, along with Air Chief Marshal Hugh Dowding, accompanied by Air Vice-Marshal Nicol and Air Commodore Fielden. The King was there to present awards to five of Hornchurch's most notable officers. The ceremony was held on the hard-standing between two of the large hangars. A square was made up of NCOs, airmen and WAAFs whom the King inspected, speaking to some of them. Station Commander Cecil Bouchier remembers the royal visit:

> The morning of the King's visit arrived and the royal cavalcade of cars drove up to my Headquarters at Hornchurch, and I stood, alone, outside to receive His Majesty King George VI. The King got out of the Royal Daimler followed by the C.in.C Fighter Command, Sir Hugh Dowding.
> The C.in.C presented me to the King as Group Captain

Bouchier. After shaking hands, the King in the uniform of a Marshal of the Royal Air Force, said, 'Well Bouchier, what would you like me to do?' I said, 'I have just received the first decorations to be won by my pilots, and it would be nice, Sir, if you would graciously be pleased to present them.' 'Splendid' and in turning to the C.in.C, the King said, 'Dowding, I'd like Bouchier to ride with me.'

It was a warm, sunny morning, as the King and I stepped down from the royal car and walked slowly towards a plain trestle table set in front of the parade, now standing to 'Attention'. Upon the bare table top rested a small black velvet cushion piped with gold braid around its edges, which my WAAF driver, Townley, had hastily stitched together overnight for the occasion.

It was while the King was chatting, that somebody had noticed that Bob Stanford Tuck had forgotten to have sewn onto his tunic the small metal hook on which the medal would be hung. He ran off hurriedly to the orderly room and explained the situation. A WAAF typist quickly went to the washroom and returned, blushing slightly, having taken a hook from her underwear. Then with shaking hands she sewed it into position on the tunic. He raced back to take his position.

The officers about to receive the awards were lined up, and the citations were read out to the following as they stepped forward to receive their awards from His Majesty the King.

Pilot Officer John Allen, 54 Squadron, the DFC; Flight Lieutenant Alan Deere, 54 Squadron, the DFC; Flight Lieutenant Adolph Malan, 74 Squadron, the DFC; Squadron Leader James Leathart, 54 Squadron, the DSO; and Flight Lieutenant Robert Stanford Tuck, 65 Squadron, the DFC. To conclude Group Captain Bouchier called for 'Three Cheers for His Majesty the King,' which echoed across the parade ground. Cecil Bouchier continues:

With the medal ceremony over, the King and I walked away from the parade. I then proceeded to show the King some of the pilots and aircraft out on dispersal.

We reached the first dispersal hut on the perimeter of the aerodrome, and I followed His Majesty. We walked over to where the No.54 Squadron pilots in their 'Mae Wests' were sprawled out on the grass. I introduced an amazed 'A' Flight Commander to the King and, at my request, he, in turn, introduced the equally astonished, but delighted members of his flight to his majesty.

Afterwards I took His Majesty to the Officers' Mess for lunch, where later the King had more informal talks with the pilots over coffee in the ante-room. With his departure time now long overdue, the King turned to me and said, 'Good-bye,

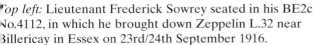

Top left: Lieutenant Frederick Sowrey seated in his BE2c No.4112, in which he brought down Zeppelin L.32 near Billericay in Essex on 23rd/24th September 1916.

(Author via R. Shelley)

Top right: Lieutenant John Cotesworth Slessor was one of the first airmen to fly from Sutton's Farm. He arrived on 13th October 1915 and that same evening would encounter Zeppelin L.15 over London. Although the airship escaped, Lieutenant Slessor could claim to be the first pilot to intercept an enemy aircraft over Great Britain.

(Author's collection)

Middle: Lieutenants Sowrey and Robinson chat with a well wisher in Sutton's Lane, Hornchurch, after Robinson had shot down the German Schutte-Lanz Airship SL.11 at Cuffley. *(F. Sowrey collection)*

Bottom right: Francis H. Maskell served at Sutton's Farm as Lt Leefe-Robinson's mechanic. He was initially transferred from the Somerset Light Infantry.

(W. Barnard)

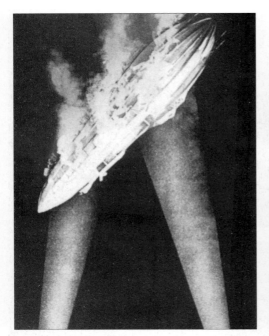

Top left: The morale of the citizens of London was lifted with the sight of the giant Zeppelins being brought down by pilots flying from Sutton's Farm. Before these events the Zeppelins had free reign in the skies over London.

(Author's collection)

Top right: The presentation of silver cups to the three Zeppelin heroes, Robinson, Sowrey and Tempest. Given by Councillors representing the Parish of Hornchurch.

(Luff collection)

Middle right: Lined up for the camera (left to right), Lt F. Sowrey, Lt W. Leefe-Robinson, Capt Stammers and Lt W. Tempest, 1916.

(F. Sowrey collection)

Bottom left: The graves at Great Burstead, Billericay of the German commander and crew of Zeppelin L.32. They were later re-interred at the German Military Cemetery at Cannock Chase. *(Author via R. Shelley)*

Bottom right: The SE.5 aircraft Serial No. A8941, flown by Captain James Ivor Mackay of No.39 Squadron, 1917.

(J.M Bruce/ S. Leslie collection)

Top left: Ronald Shelley aged 13 years. He witnessed the Zeppelins SL.11 and L.32 fall from the sky in September 1916. He was also a frequent visitor to Sutton's Farm to watch the aircraft take to the air.

(Author via R. Shelley)

Top right: An FE.2d Serial No. 1883 of No. 78 Squadron; note the wooden hangars in the background, 1917

(J.M. Bruce/ S. Leslie collection)

Bottom left: The ladies of the Women's Legion Auxiliary outside one of the wooden buildings at Sutton's 1917/18. Miss Grace Hewitson is pictured centre. *(Mrs. M. Crabtree)*

Middle right: A Sopwith Pup, Serial No.305 of No.189 Night Training Squadron at Sutton's Farm 1918. *(J.M. Bruce/ S. Leslie collection)*

Bottom right: A Sopwith Snipe, Serial No. E8076 used by No. 78 Squadron while stationed at Sutton's Farm 1918.

(J.M. Bruce/ S. Leslie collection)

Top left: The entrance to RAF Hornchurch just after its re-opening in April 1928.

(Luff collection)

Top right: Officers of No.111 Squadron relax outside the Watch Office at Hornchurch. Pilot Officer Frank Whittle, who later developed the British jet engine, is seated third from right in this picture. *(Author's collection)*

Middle: Armstrong-Whitworth Siskin J-9198, flying with No.111, with Squadron Leader Keith Park in the rear cockpit.

(Air Historical Branch)

Bottom left: Hawker Demon aircraft of No.65 Squadron prepare for flight outside a hangar and Watch Office, 1936. *(Author's collection)*

Bottom right: A view of the Officers' Mess with its splendid lawn and flower beds and also a wonderful collection of various motor cars, 1937. *(Author via D.S. Hoare)*

Top left: A Gloster Gauntlet Serial No. K7863 of 74 'Tiger' Squadron stands in front of the main hangar at Hornchurch, 1937. *(Author via D.S. Hoare)*

Top right: Carefree days at Hornchurch as men and dogs relax, 1937. Left to right: P/O Boyd, P/O Tuck, F/O Saunders and P/O Giddings.

(Author via G. Saunders)

Middle: S/Ldr Cecil Bouchier, CO of No.54 Squadron, stands with his personal Gloster Gladiator, 1937. *(Author via D.Bouchier)*

Left: The Three Amigos. Sergeant Pilots at Hornchurch (left to right): Philip Tew, No.54, and William Franklin and Percy Morfill of No.65. Both Franklin and Morfill would later achieve 'ace' status during WWII. *(Author via P. Morfill)*

Top left: Flying Officer Gerald Saunders sits among the wreckage of his Gloster Gladiator, after the wreckage was collected and laid out in a hangar.
(Author via G. Saunders)

Top right: Sergeant John Flinders of No.74 Squadron is presented to The Sultan of Muscat by Squadron Leader D.S Brookes who is pictured wearing his white flying suit.
(Author via D. S. Hoare)

Middle left: Time to relax and have a beer, outside the Officers' Mess block, summer 1938. Left to right: P/O Mainwaring, P/O Hayward, F/O Malan, P/O Rowland with beer, all from No. 74, F/O Saunders and P/O Tuck of No. 65.
(Author via T. Rowland)

Middle right: Brian Kingcome, who started his RAF career at Hornchurch in 1938. This portrait by Cuthbert Orde was sketched later in the war.
(Author via L. Kingcome)

Right: Sergeant Pilot Percy Morfill of No.65 Squadron tries out the Spitfire cockpit for size. The first Spitfire aircraft started to arrive at Hornchurch in February/March 1939.
(Author via P. Morfill)

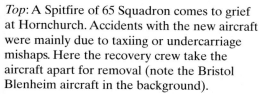

Top: A Spitfire of 65 Squadron comes to grief at Hornchurch. Accidents with the new aircraft were mainly due to taxiing or undercarriage mishaps. Here the recovery crew take the aircraft apart for removal (note the Bristol Blenheim aircraft in the background).

(Author via P.Morfill)

Middle left: Spitfires of No.54 on show in 1939 during Hornchurch's last Empire Air Day before the outbreak of war. *(Author's collection)*

Above right: A wonderful study of a fighter pilot. Flying Officer Tom Rowland poses for the camera in mid 1939. *(Author via T. Rowland)*

Bottom left: Wing Walkers? Don Thom, pictured on the right, of No. 74 Squadron was a Canadian and an outstanding gymnast. Here he is practising headstands on the wing of one of the Squadron Spitfires with fellow pilot 'Sammy' Hoare, who is still trying to get the hang of it. Also of interest is the aircraft's two-colour painted underside. This was black and white for identification, used in the early stage of the war, in order that the Ground Defences, Royal Navy etc, did not fire on friendly RAF aeroplanes.

(Author via D.S. Hoare)

Top left: 'B' Flight, No. 74 Squadron, out on dispersal at Hornchurch listening to the Prime Minister's declaration of war speech on 3rd September 1939. (Note the portable wireless on top of the car roof.) Flight Sgt Ernie 'Tubby' Mayne is leaning against the car door

(Author via D.S. Hoare)

Top right: In a party mood, Officer Pilots of No.74 Squadron, left to right: F/O Mainwaring, F/O Mungo-Park, F/O Hoare, P/O Browne, P/O Dowding (crouching), F/O Thom with dogs. *(Author via D.S. Hoare)*

Middle left: A Blenheim of No.600 'City of London' Squadron comes into land at

Hornchurch, October 1939. Below is the dispersal area of No.74 Squadron.

(Author via D.S. Hoare)

Bottom left: F/Lt Adolph 'Sailor' Malan of No.74 stands with his aircraft. He would become one of the RAF's outstanding Fighter Command leaders of WWII.

(Author via D.S. Hoare)

Bottom right: John Connell Freeborn was with No.74 'Tiger' Squadron and flew more operational hours during the Battle of Britain than any other pilot in Fighter Command.

(Author via J.Freeborn)

Top left: This photograph shows members of 'A' Flight, No.54 Squadron prior to Dunkirk, May 1940. Left to right (back): Deere, Pearson, Blake; left to right (front): Norwell, Gribble, Way, Mackenzie. *(Deere family)*

Top right: Flight Lieutenant James 'Prof' Leathart of No.54 receives his DSO award from His Majesty King George VI at Hornchurch on June 27th 1940, for his rescue at Calais-Marck of Squadron Leader Francis White.

(Author via J.Leathart)

Middle left: Pilot Officer Alan Deere of No.54, who hailed from New Zealand, is seen here with his Spitfire 'Kiwi'1, May 1940. *(Deere family)*

Bottom left: Engine fitter G.F 'Ricky' Richardson of No.54 Squadron was Alan Deere's mechanic. They became friends and kept in touch until Deere died in 1995.

(Author via Richardson)

Bottom right: Pilots of No.65 receive their presentation tankards from Sir Edmund Benthall of the East India Trading Company. Left to right: G/Capt Cecil Bouchier, F/Lt Saunders, F/O Olive, F/O Nicholas, F/O Smart (receiving tankard), Sgt MacPherson, P/O Kilner. *(Author via G. Saunders)*

"Scramble" — '40

Top left: No. 54 Squadron prior to the Battle of Britain; of the 17 pilots pictured here only 8 would survive the battle. Back row, left to right: Sgt W. Lawrence, Sgt G. Collett, unknown, P/O D. McMullen, P/O P.Howes, P/O A. Finnie, P/O D. Turley-George, P/O H. Matthews, F/Sgt Tew, P/O C. Gray. Middle row: P/O J. Allen, F/Lt A. Deere, S/Ldr J. Leathart, F/Lt B. Way, P/O G. Gribble. Front row: Sgt J. Norwell, P/O E. Coleman, P. Shallard (Intelligence Officer), P/O W. Hopkins.
(Author via Deere family)

Top right: Pilot Officer Eric Barwell who served with No.264 'Madras Presidency' Squadron flying the Boulton-Paul Defiant aircraft. He would become an 'ace' and successful night-fighter pilot. *(E.Barwell)*

Middle left: One of RAF Manston's hangars which was destroyed when the Germans bombed the airfield on August 12th 1940. This photograph was taken a couple of days later, when workmen were trying to shore up the building structure with wooden beams.
(D. Glaser)

Bottom left: Sergeant Fred Barker and his pilot Sergeant Edward Thorn (left) of No.264 Defiant Squadron. They became the top scoring Defiant crew with 13 confirmed victories during the period of Dunkirk and the Battle of Britain. Note the teddy bear mascot. *(Author via Barker)*

Bottom right: Pilot Officer Percy Prune scrambles off on another mishap with his loyal dog Raff. *(G.F.Richardson)*

Top left: Boulton-Paul Defiant aircraft of No.264 Squadron. They were to suffer terrible casualties while flying operations from Hornchurch in August 1940. *(IWM)*

Top right: Pilot Officer John Mackenzie of No.41 Squadron steps from his Spitfire, August 1940. *(Author via F. Mileham)*

Middle left: Pilots of No.65, August 1940. Left to right: Sgt H. Orchard, F/O R. Wigg, F/O L. Pyman and F/Lt G. Olive. F/O Pyman failed to return from action over the Channel on 16th August, while Sgt Orchard was killed in action in 1941. Note the wireless technician checking the aircraft's radio. *(D. Glaser)*

Middle right: An Eagle has landed? The Luftwaffe Major who was captured after his aircraft was brought down near the airfield. He was entertained at the Officers' Mess during the evening. This photograph was taken outside the Mess by Assistant Station Adjutant Frank Dowling, August 1940. *(Author via F. Dowling)*

Left: A 19-year-old Pilot Officer, E.D. 'Dave' Glaser of No.65 Squadron, August 1940. He joined the Squadron at the same time as Brendan 'Paddy' Finucane, who would go on to become one of the RAF's top scoring aces. *(D.Glaser)*

Top left: WAAFs Joan Bowell née Dudman (left) and Joy Caldwell née York (right) who worked in the Operations Block in Signals at Hornchurch while the bombs dropped during attacks on the airfield in August/Sept 1940.
(Author via J.Caldwell)

Top right: A remarkable photograph showing the bombing of Hornchurch airfield on 31st August 1940 by the Luftwaffe. *(Deere family)*

Middle left: Squadron Leader John Hamar Hill, who led No.222 Natal Squadron through-out the Battle of Britain, seen here wearing the B-type leather flying helmet with canvas D-type oxygen face mask and microphone.
(Author via N. Burgess)

Middle right: A young 'Joe' Crawshaw seated in the cockpit of one of No.222's Spitfires. Joe was a rigger with the Squadron, and it was with his camera that some of the photographs in this book were recorded at Hornchurch

during the height of the Battle of Britain.
(J. Crawshaw)

Above: 222 Natal Squadron ground crew at dispersal, September 1940. Back row (left to right): Webb, unknown, Davis and Dashper; front row: Clarke, Peerless, White, Anderson and Monty. Dave Davis was interviewed during the research for this book. *(J.Crawshaw*

Top left: Two pilots of No.41 Squadron take a break between sorties. Left, P/O Norman McHardy Brown and Sgt Robert Angus.

(Author via F. Mileham)

Top right: Ground crew re-arm and check the machine guns of a No.41 Squadron Spitfire; Sergeant Pilot Terry Healy is pictured on left.

(Author via R. Beardsley)

Middle left: Two Sergeant Pilots of No.222 Squadron find time to have a lark, September 1940. Sgt Iain Hutchinson and Sgt John Ramshaw. Ramshaw was killed in action soon

after this photograph was taken.

(Author via N. Burgess)

Middle right: Sergeant Pilot Jack Stokoe of No.603 'City of Edinburgh' Squadron. He was shot down on September 2nd and managed to bale out safely, but suffered from burns to his face and hands. After spending six weeks in hospital he returned to operations.

(Author via J. Stokoe)

Bottom: A Spitfire of No.41 Squadron prepares to take off on another sortie; in the cockpit is Flying Officer Peter Brown. *(M.P. Brown)*

Top left: South African born Pilot Officer Gerald 'Stapme' Stapleton of No.603. He was to shoot down the German pilot Franz von Werra, who became known by the 1950s film *The One That Got Away*; as a POW he escaped from Canada. Stapleton himself became a POW in 1944 when he was forced to crash-land his aircraft behind enemy lines.
(G. Stapleton)

Top right: An Avro Anson climbs on take-off; below a No.222 Spitfire stands ready. This aircraft was flown by Squadron Leader Johnnie Hill. *(Author via M. Hill)*

Bottom left: A portrait photograph of Pilot Officer Peter Pease. Pease was killed in action on 15th September 1940. Flying with No. 603 Squadron, he courageously dived into a formation of Heinkel bombers, but was followed and shot down by German fighters. He was 22 years old. *(Sir Richard Pease)*

Middle right: In front of his aircraft is Pilot Officer Eric Lock who hailed from Shrewsbury. He would become the top scoring British pilot of the Battle of Britain. *(Mrs J. Statham)*

Bottom right: Pilots of No. 222 Natal Squadron, Hornchurch, September 1940. Left to right: F/O Eric Thomas, Sgt Davis, Sgt Dudley Gibbins, S/Ldr John Hill, Sgt Norman Ramsay, Sgt Rainford Marland and Sgt Leon Patrick.

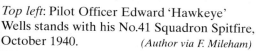

Top left: Pilot Officer Edward 'Hawkeye' Wells stands with his No.41 Squadron Spitfire, October 1940. *(Author via F. Mileham)*

Top right: David Scott-Malden flew with No.603 Squadron. He was one of the few pilots to encounter the only Italian raids against Britain during the battle. This photo was taken later during the war. *(Author via Scott-Malden)*

Middle left: Sergeants Phillip Davis and John Burgess of No.222 take a break between sorties and find time to have this photograph taken at Rochford, Hornchurch's satellite airfield, October 1940. Note the parachute pack resting on the tailplane, ready for the next scramble. *(Author via N. Burgess)*

Bottom left: Sgt McAdam of No.41 Squadron rides his motor-cycle around dispersal, during a lull in the fighting, October 1940.

(Author via F.Mileham)

Bottom right: Pilot Officer Denys Edgar Mileham joined No.41 at Hornchurch on 29th August 1940. He claimed an Me109 destroyed on 5th October. He was killed in action on 15th April 1942, while flying with No.234 Squadron aged 22 years.

(Author via F. Mileham)

Top left: Flying Officer Peter Brown of No.41. He wears the German schwimmveste that he took from Feldwebel Bielmaier whom he shot down over West Malling on 20th October 1940.
(M.P. Brown)

Top right: A group photograph of No.64 Squadron pilots taken outside the Hornchurch Officers' Mess during November 1940. From left to right: P/O A. Donahue, F/Lt J. Thomson, P/O K. Hawkins, F/Lt D. Taylor, P/O A. Towers, P/O A. Tidman, F/O E. Gilbert, P/O Rowden, F/Lt R. Gittens (Engineering Officer), S/Ldr A. MacDonell, P/O E. Watson, P/O R. Jones, S/Ldr J. Rankin, P/O J. Pippett, P/O P. Beare and P/O T. Gray.
(Author via MacDonell)

Middle left: Pilots of No.611 Squadron pose for the camera, on the wing of one of the Squadron's Mk1 Spitfires, during December 1940. Pictured left to right are; Sgt Leigh, Sgt Bye and Sgt Ingram.
(Author via A.C. Leigh)

Middle right: Group Captain Harry 'Broady' Broadhurst was given the command of RAF

Hornchurch on 24th December 1940. He would lead the new 'Hornchurch Wing' onto the offensive against the Germans in 1941.
(Broadhurst collection)

Above: S/Ldr Don Finlay, commanding officer of No.41, strides through a muddy airfield back to the dispersal hut after another sortie in November 1940.
(Author via F. Mileham)

Bouchier, it's been a wonderful day. I've seldom enjoyed a day more. Thank you.' My pilots impulsively rushed out from the Mess to line a short path to the main gates and salute his Majesty as he drove away.

The King departed 1 pm.

Meanwhile across the Channel, Hitler and his High Command were busy detailing plans for the invasion of Great Britain. The part played by RAF Hornchurch during the Dunkirk operations was of great importance, but would be minor, compared to the role that was about to be played out over the skies of southern England within the next couple of months.

CHAPTER 6

THE BATTLE OF BRITAIN
July 1940 – 6th September 1940

During the early part of July, the squadrons from Hornchurch were mainly deployed for the protection of the Merchant Navy convoys that were making their way up and down the Channel routes, bringing supplies to the United Kingdom. The Luftwaffe was now concentrating their daylight operations on trying to sink as much shipping as possible, mostly in the Straits of Dover area.

However, on 3rd July 1940, No.74 Squadron sadly lost another valuable pilot, Sergeant White, who had only been with the squadron nine days. He was killed, while on patrol over Margate, when his Spitfire was struck by lightning, crashing to the ground in flames.

As the squadrons of Fighter Command made ready for the next phase of the war, Hornchurch's No.54 were told to move a flight of aircraft down to the most forward airfield at Manston. They arrived there on 4th July, along with Blenheim aircraft of No.600 (City of London) Auxiliary Squadron.

One of the first squadrons to encounter the Germans over the English Channel was No.74 'Tiger' Squadron. While on convoy patrol over Dover on 6th July, Flight Lieutenant W.G. Measures and Pilot Officer D. Dowding spotted two Heinkel 111s; which they engaged. A burst from Flight Lieutenant Measures' Spitfire badly damaged one of the Heinkels, which changed course and set off home for France, only to crash into the sea near the French coast. Pilot Officer Dowding managed to claim hits on the other enemy aircraft, but he lost sight of it when it went into cloud.

Flying from Manston, one of Hornchurch's forward bases, on 7th July, a section of No.54 Squadron, led by Flying Officer Desmond McMullen, sighted a formation of Messerschmitt 110s crossing the coast near Dungeness. No.54 were about to go into the attack, when they were bounced from above by waiting Me109s, who had attacked with the sun behind them. Two of 54's aircraft were shot down and a third was damaged, but luckily there were no pilot casualties.

On 8th July, another skirmish between Spitfires of No.74 Squadron and Heinkel bombers took place in the morning at 11 am; but only one enemy aircraft was claimed, destroyed by Sergeant Bill Skinner and Pilot Officer Derek Dowding. Later in the afternoon No.74 were up again, and engaged four Me109s of 4/JG 54 over Manston. One of the Me109s was forced down near Elham by Sergeant E.A. Mould, while another was damaged by Pilot Officer Stevenson. The Messerschmitt 109 shot down by Sergeant

Mould was, in fact, the first German fighter aircraft to fall on British soil; another first for a Hornchurch-based squadron. The combat report of Sergeant Mould states that four Me109s had been chasing a single Spitfire, belonging to Squadron Leader Sawyer of No.65 Squadron, who had been on a lone patrol. Arriving on the scene, four Spitfires of No.74 Squadron who, unable to contact or warn Sawyer, had only one course of action, which was to attack. Mould's own combat report gives his version of events:

> I was Red Leader of a section of 'A' Flight of No.74 Squadron with No.2 of Blue Section also in company. The four of us were on an interception patrol over Dover when I sighted four Me109s flying on my starboard beam. I gave the order 'Line Astern' and turned to starboard, climbing up under the tail of the rear Me109. I gave him a short 30 degree deflection shot, and he immediately half-rolled and dived to ground level followed by Red 2.
>
> In trying to follow him, I blacked out and lost sight of him, but I saw another Me109 also flying at low-level, so I dived on him from about 3,000 feet. He immediately dived to ground level, and used evasive tactics by flying along the valleys behind Dover and Folkestone, which only allowed me to fire short deflection bursts at him. After two bursts, smoke and vapour appeared from the radiator beneath his port wing, and other bursts entered his fuselage. He eventually landed with his wheels up, as I fired my last burst at him in a field near Elham. The pilot was apparently uninjured and I circled around him until he was taken prisoner.

The German pilot was Lt Johann Bohm of 4/JG 51 who had been on a free-chasing patrol.

The 9th July found No.54 Squadron flying a number of convoy patrols. 'B' Flight engaged the enemy twice, with losses on both sides. 'A' Flight, on their fourth patrol of the day, was ordered by Hornchurch Control to investigate an unidentified plot five miles east of Deal. After crossing the coast at around 1,500 feet, they spotted a silver painted seaplane and, closely behind and above, a formation of Me109s. One of the 54 Squadron pilots, Johnny Allen, informed his comrade Alan Deere; it was agreed that the seaplane must be German, so they decided to attack.

On seeing the RAF fighters attacking, the German aircraft broke formation, one group turning towards the Spitfires, the other staying to protect the seaplane. No.54 were outnumbered by about six to one. The combat was fierce and deadly, with aircraft twisting and turning about the sky, each trying to outmanoeuvre the other, and gain the advantage. The seaplane was in fact a Heinkel 59, which was being used as air sea rescue for downed German pilots in the Channel; it had Red Cross markings on the fuselage. Flying Officer Johnny Allen led his section to attack the seaplane, and scored hits on the aircraft's engine forcing it to ditch. Flying

Officer Allen also claimed an Me109 probable, while Sergeant Lawrence claimed an Me109 destroyed.

Flight Lieutenant Alan Deere had survived a near head-on collision with an opposing Me109. He recalls:

> I soon found another target. About 3,000 yards directly ahead of me, and at the same level, a Hun was just completing a turn to re-enter the fray. He saw me almost immediately and rolled out of his turn towards me, so that a head-on attack became inevitable. I was using both hands on the control column to steady my aircraft and thus keep my aim steady. We opened fire together and immediately a hail of lead thudded into my Spitfire. One moment the Messerschmitt was a clearly defined shape within the circle of my gun sight, the next it was on top of me; a terrifying blur which blotted out the sky ahead. Then we hit.
>
> The force of the impact pitched me violently forward on to my cockpit harness, the straps of which bit viciously into my shoulders. At the same time, the control column was snatched away abruptly from my fingers by the powerful reversed elevator load. Smoke and flames were pouring from the engine, which began to vibrate. Hastily I closed the throttle and reached forward to flick off the ignition switches, but before I could do so the engine seized, and the airscrew stopped abruptly. I saw in amazement that the propeller blades had been bent back almost double from the collision with the Messerschmitt.

With smoke now pouring into his cockpit, Alan Deere tried to release his cockpit hood, but this would not budge; he tried several times but to no avail. There was no other choice but to try and land the aircraft, by gliding it down on to some open countryside. He finally came down, crash-landing on cornfields some five miles from Manston. He managed to break open the cockpit canopy, by smashing it with his bare hands. He climbed out of the aircraft and took stock of his injuries. Both hands were cut and bleeding, his eyebrows burnt, knees badly bruised, and he had a cut lip. His aircraft was now a burning wreck, and he had to tell interested onlookers who had gathered around, to keep away because of the danger of exploding ammunition. He was picked up by the medical officer from Manston, where he stayed the night, before being flown back to Rochford the next morning in a Tiger Moth. This was to be one of the many lucky escapes that he would have during the war.

10th July 1940: Official start of the Battle of Britain.
Fighter Command engages Me109s and Ju87s in battles over Channel convoys. Changeable weather for the next 32 days enables Fighter Command to build up its strength.

On 10th July, a Channel convoy code-named 'Bread' was sailing off the North Foreland, when it was attacked by German aircraft. No. 74 Squadron who were down at Manston, scrambled both Red and Yellow Sections at 10.40 am to deal with the threat. They encountered only one Dornier 17, escorted by up to 30 Me109s; during the combat they made several claims on the Me109s. Three of 74 Squadron aircraft returned damaged, but repairable; the pilots Pilot Officer Freeborn, Pilot Officer Cobden and Sergeant Mould were all unhurt. The squadron also claimed a Heinkel destroyed on the 12th, when Malan, Stevenson and Mould attacked the enemy aircraft and saw it lose height, crashing into the sea.

Hornchurch played host to a contingent of the East India Trading Company on the 15th July, when eight presentation Spitfires were handed over to No.65 Squadron by Sir Edmund and Lady Benthall, and Sir Alexander Murrey with Mr Rowen Hodge. Sir Alexander Murrey made a speech, and handed over a cheque for £55,000 to the Secretary of State, as the first instalment towards another eight aircraft.

A flypast was undertaken with the new aircraft, led by 65's new CO Squadron Leader Henry Sawyer. The squadron was thereafter known as No.65 'East India' Squadron. The eight new aircraft had been bought by monies raised by the East India Fund. Also in attendance was Air Vice-Marshal Keith Park, AOC No.11 Group, with Captain Harold Balfour, the Under Secretary of State for Air. Later down at Rochford airfield, pilots of 65 Squadron were presented with silver presentation tankards from the East India Company, as was Group Captain Cecil Bouchier.

While on convoy patrol on Sunday 21st July, Pilot Officer J.L. Kemp of No.54 Squadron ran into difficulties 15 miles east of Clacton, when his Spitfire N3184 suffered engine failure. He was forced to bale out at 9.20 am. He was rescued from the sea by a Royal Navy destroyer.

On 24th July, 54 Squadron were scrambled at 8.15 am from Rochford to intercept a raid on a convoy near Dover and North Foreland. At 20,000 feet they were informed about plots of two large enemy formations, which were spotted by Pilot Officer Colin Gray; the enemy formation consisted of about 18 Dorniers, escorted by a large number of fighters. During the fighting Flying Officer Johnny Allen's Spitfire was damaged by Me109s of Stab III/JG 26 over Margate. His engine cut out and he attempted to glide his aircraft to Foreness Point, which was open ground. While making the descent his engine picked up again, and he decided to try for Manston airfield. While he was doing so, his engine stalled again. This time the aircraft's speed was too slow and it fell out of the sky, crashing near the Old Charles Inn, Cliftonville at 12.30 pm. Flying Officer Allen, who 27 days previously had been awarded the DFC by the King at Hornchurch, was killed. He was buried with full military honours at Margate Cemetery, Kent. He was 24 years old.

Five enemy aircraft were claimed by No.54 during the engagement, including an Me109 of 8/JG.52, shot down and destroyed by Pilot Officer Colin Gray at 12.35 pm; it crashed eight miles off-shore from Margate. The pilot Oberleutnant Ehrlich baled out, but was presumed missing. Other aircraft of 54 Squadron were also damaged. Pilot Officer Finnie force-landed at Mayfield, unhurt, and his aircraft P9389 was repairable. Pilot

Officer H.K.F. Matthews had his cockpit canopy shattered during the dogfight; he too was unhurt and returned to base; his aircraft R6710 was also repairable. But Sergeant G.R. Collett was slightly injured when he had to force-land his Spitfire N3192 on the beach at Dunwich, near Sizewell, after running out of fuel pursuing an enemy aircraft.

Later, in the early evening of the 24th, Spitfires of No.74's 'A' Flight patrolling near Dover were told of a raid coming in. They recognised three Dornier 215s flying very low over the water. Once spotted by the Spitfires they immediately altered course and headed back across the Channel, not wishing to mix it with the fighters.

On Thursday, 25th July, the weather forecast announced a fine day with haze in the Straits of Dover, with a northwesterly light wind. Later that afternoon, 54 Squadron was ordered up to protect a convoy which was coming under attack from a force of 60 Ju87 Stuka dive-bombers. The 12 Spitfires of 54 Squadron led by 'B' flight commander Flight Lieutenant Basil 'Wonky' Way, dived into the enemy at about 3 pm. After shooting down one of the Junkers, Way and the rest of his section were jumped by 109s, who had been waiting unseen above. His No.2 was heard to shout over the R/T, 'Break, Wonky, break'. But it was too late and Way was shot down and killed, crashing into the Channel. Pilot Officer D.R. Turley-George, whose aircraft was also damaged during the combat, crash-landed near Dover; he escaped unhurt although his aircraft P9387 was a complete write-off. Later that evening Pilot Officer A. Finnie was killed in combat, again over another convoy off Dover at 6.10 pm, while engaged with Me 109s; his aircraft R6816 crashed at Kingsdown, Kent.

That same evening, with the loss of two of their most senior pilots, No.54 Squadron was ordered to Catterick for rest, while No.41 came down to Hornchurch again.

On 27th July, No.41 Squadron flew seven varied sorties. The first was at 1 pm when they flew down to Manston. Only once that day did they make enemy contact. At 6 pm, 'B' Flight consisting of six aircraft and patrolling over Dover, noticed anti-aircraft fire, and Flight Lieutenant John Webster spotted enemy fighters below. They dived down on the Me109s and a low-level combat followed with the 109s heading back across the Channel. F/Lt Webster claimed an Me109 as a probable after hitting it from 200 yards, and reporting that it went into the sea; but as there was no other confirmation, it could not be written up as destroyed.

Sunday, 28th July, was a fine bright morning, with both No.41 and 74 flying down early to their forward base at Manston. But Operations did not plot any enemy activity until after 12.30 pm, when information began to come in.

At 1.45 pm No.74 were scrambled and vectored to cover Dover, as a raid came in at 18,000 feet. With 'Sailor' Malan out front leading, they continued to gain height to get above the enemy, hopefully above any fighter escort. They soon encountered a formation of about 36 Me109s coming from out of the sun. They first engaged about six of the enemy fighters, getting in amongst them without being seen. Once combat had begun, three of the 109s were destroyed by Malan, Flight Lieutenant Kelly and Flying Officer Freeborn; two were damaged by Flying Officer St.John and Pilot Officer Stevenson. One of the Messerschmitts that had been engaged during the combat and damaged, had been flown that day by the German ace Major Werner Mölders, commander of Jagdgeschwader 51. During the combat, his machine had come under the guns of 'Sailor' Malan. Mölders was wounded, but managed to get his aircraft back across to France, crash-landing at Wissant. This aircraft was also claimed as damaged by Flight Lieutenant John Webster of No.41 Squadron, who during the dog fighting over Dover, fired at Mölders' aircraft which was firing at a Spitfire flown by Flight Lieutenant Lovell. Tony Lovell, in Spitfire P9439, was wounded in the thigh during this action, but he managed to get his damaged aircraft back to Manston. On landing he was transported to Margate Hospital for medical attention.

Pilot Officer G.H. 'Ben' Bennions, also of No. 41 Squadron, claimed an Me109. He had spotted this aircraft creeping up on the tail of his CO Squadron Leader Hood; he chased after it using emergency boost, fired two short bursts, and watched the enemy aircraft turn on to its side and go down vertically.

No.74 lost one pilot killed; it was Pilot Officer J.H.R. Young, who crashed in the Channel near the Goodwin Sands. Sergeant E.A. Mould was shot down off Dover, but baled-out wounded. He was attended to and sent to Dover Military Hospital.

On Monday, 29th July, the weather outlook for the day over the Channel was fair, but hazy. No.41 Squadron were down at Manston for early morning patrol, and were scrambled at 7.15 am. Over Dover at 12,000 feet they were involved in combat with a large force of Ju87s and 109s; there were losses on both sides. Flying Officer D.R. Gamblen was posted as missing in Spitfire N3038, while Flying Officer W. Scott, Pilot Officer G. Bennions, Pilot Officer J. Mackenzie and Flying Officer J. Webster all crash-landed with damaged aircraft, although none of the pilots was injured. They claimed five enemy aircraft destroyed and one damaged.

On July 31st, 'B' Flight of 74 Squadron was the only Hornchurch unit to be in action that day. It wasn't until about 4 pm that they made contact with Me109s of JG/2 'Richthofen', who were 2,000 feet higher than the climbing Spitfires. The Germans, on seeing the Spitfires, split into two formations; one group of six attacked Flying Officer Kelly's section. Sergeant Fred Eley's aircraft was hit immediately and went down in flames off Folkestone pier, killing the pilot. Pilot Officer H.R.Gunn was also killed in the attack. Flight Lieutenant Piers Kelly had to fight his way out of the overwhelming numbers of fighters that they had encountered. He landed back at Manston with a badly damaged aircraft, but was unhurt himself. On landing he was met by some of No.65 Squadron's pilots, who had also moved up to Manston from Hornchurch. Supermarine test-pilot Jeffrey Quill, now flying with No.65, could not believe the amount of damage that Kelly's aircraft had sustained. On looking into the cockpit, it was noticed that the armour plate behind the pilot's seat had taken the impact of the enemy shells, and had indeed saved the pilot.

Meanwhile back at Hornchurch, Flight Lieutenant 'Sailor' Malan and Flying Officer Johnny Freeborn both received notification that they had been awarded the DFC, Freeborn for destroying five enemy aircraft, and Malan for the two enemy bombers at night.

On a lighter note, it was during July that Hornchurch saw the birth of the fictional cartoon figure Pilot Officer Percy Prune. His creator Aircraftman William J. Hooper was a general duties clerk with No.54 Squadron; in his spare time he was very apt at drawing cartoons on the spur of the moment. The late Bill Hooper recalled:

It was during July 1940, after 54 Squadron had engaged the enemy, that one of the sergeant pilots, I think it was the Scot Jock Norwell, landed quite badly shot up. He emerged from his aircraft in a bit of a state, and with his hands shaking began to light up a cigarette. Suddenly one of the other pilots blurted out 'Don't worry, you my son, are privileged to be flying with the gallant Fighting Fifty-Four!' To which he replied, 'Oh aye, I often wonder where the other Fighting Fifty-Three are!'

After witnessing this, I returned later in the afternoon and quietly pinned up a cartoon drawing of the pilot's response in the 'A' Flight hut. It showed an egg-headed, button-nosed Spitfire pilot surrounded by hordes of Me109s. Underneath the caption read, 'Where's the other fifty-three?' So was born the character legend of Percy Prune.

The CO James Leathart thought my drawings were very good, and later when he was posted to Fighter Command Headquarters, he asked me if I would illustrate a slim book of useful tips and ideas for fighter pilots, that he was putting together. The book was called *Forget-Me-Not's for Fighters*. It was from this that I was eventually asked to meet at the Air Ministry with a Flight Lieutenant Anthony Armstrong-Willis, to help illustrate a new training book similar to *Forget-Me-Not's*.

I worked alongside Anthony Armstrong and used the cartoon figure I had created, the book was titled *Tee-Emm* and Pilot Officer Prune was used as the example of what not to do while flying in combat; a complete dim-wit whom no airman would want to copy.

Tee-Emm became a great success throughout the war, and after hostilities had ceased, I received a letter from an intelligence officer who was working with the 'Captured Documents' department in Berlin. With the letter came a German citation, confirming the award to Percy Prune of the Iron Cross, for destroying so many Allied aircraft; this was signed at the bottom with the signature of Herman Göring. This of course was completely faked, but what an honour for Pilot Officer Prune.

On Friday, 2nd August, No.65 Squadron suffered the tragic death of their new commanding officer, Squadron Leader Henry Sawyer. He was killed when undertaking a night take-off from Rochford airfield at 11.35 pm. His aircraft's engine stalled immediately after reaching an altitude of about 1,000 feet, coming down and crashing in flames. He was 25 years old.

Squadron Leader A.L. Holland was posted in as the new CO for No.65. Because of his inexperience in flying duties, it was decided by Holland and his flight commander Gerald Saunders, that Saunders would lead the squadron in the air, while Holland dealt with the administration and paper work, until he had settled in.

On 5th August Sergeant Walker, while in combat with 109s of JG54 just east of Dover, was hit in the petrol tank. He managed to get the No.65 Squadron aircraft back to Manston and carried out a force-landing. Walker suffered only a slight shoulder injury.

Two Polish pilots arrived together on 5th August, to take up their postings to No.74 'Tiger' Squadron. They were Flight Lieutenant Stanislaw Brzezina and Flying Officer Henryk Szczesny. Henryk Szczesny remembers his arrival at Hornchurch:

> My comrade and I arrived at Elm Park station; it was a foggy day and we could not find the airfield, so we asked someone to direct us. When we eventually arrived, I introduced myself. We were shown our rooms in the Officers Mess and given a batman.
>
> I was told I would go to 'B' Flight, commanded by F/Lieutenant Mungo-Park. After a while the members of the squadron named us 'Breezy' and 'Sneezy', as it was far easier for them than to pronounce our Polish names; I was also called Henry the Pole. I was 31 years of age at this time. My English was absolutely nil when I arrived. I was helped very much by the pilots of 74 Squadron to learn English; H.M. Stephen, Malan, and Mungo-Park would help me with phrases like 'Tally-Ho', 'Pancake', and 'Scramble', but I would always follow my leader. Malan would always say we were to stick together; I flew as his No.2 on many occasions.

Pilot Officer E.D. 'Dave' Glaser, had arrived early at Hornchurch on 13th July to join No.65 Squadron, along with Pilot Officer Brendan 'Paddy' Finucane. He remembers some of the incidents and combats during the early part of August 1940:

> Paddy and I joined No.65 together; Paddy went to 'A' Flight, led by Flight Lieutenant Gordon Olive, the Australian, while I went to 'B' Flight, commanded by Flight Lieutenant 'Sam' Saunders. Saunders was a brilliant leader. He had a technique which he used when the big enemy formations started to come in. He'd get right above them, and he would then whistle

down through them, which would cause them to break; the rest of the squadron would then come down and we'd pick out an aircraft to have a go at.

One incident I recall was when we took off from Rochford on a sortie on 7th August. I was flying No.2 to Jeffrey Quill, and as we were climbing up, all of a sudden Gordon Olive's aircraft pulled up and broke away. I didn't hear what had gone on over the R/T, I couldn't quite catch it all at that time, but anyway Gordon had baled out. What had apparently happened was that he had turned the oxygen on in his cockpit, and it had caught fire; they think that there was grease on the tap and that this had ignited. As he came down on his parachute, he was wearing a dark blue uniform with gold braid; the farmers rushed forward, and not recognizing the Australian uniform and the Australian accent, shouted 'What the bloody hell are you doing?' They pitchforked him all the way around the field. [Flight Lieutenant Olive's aircraft R6617 crashed, and burned out at 1.05 pm.]

Down at Rochford we were living in huts; they would bring us jugs of hot water to wash and shave with, and there were showers at the end of the huts. We used to go and pick mushrooms out of the woods, if we had any spare time.

During the afternoon of 5th August, No.41 Squadron sent six aircraft of 'B' Flight up on convoy patrol over Dover. While on patrol they were alerted to an incoming raid. The weather conditions were not ideal as there was a lot of low cloud and haze, but a lone Heinkel 111 was seen by Flight Lieutenant Webster, who went after the lone aircraft, while the rest of the flight stayed above. He caught the bomber and fired several bursts at it, hitting the engines; but he could only claim it as a probable, as he was forced to disengage when enemy fighters were spotted above.

Flight Lieutenant 'Sailor' Malan took over command of No.74 Squadron on 8th August, Squadron Leader Francis White being posted to Fighter Command Headquarters at Bentley Priory. During the day, Green Section of No.41 Squadron was on patrol near Manston, when they were contacted by Operations Control to investigate a plot of six unidentified aircraft.

At 12,000 feet, the aircraft were spotted by Flight Lieutenant J. Webster who confirmed that they were Messerschmitt 109s. The Spitfires dived down to attack; Pilot Officer R.W. 'Wally' Wallens fired on the last aircraft in the formation and shot it down, seeing it crash into the sea. Flight Lieutenant Webster claimed to have destroyed three of the enemy aircraft, and Pilot Officer Wallens two more. After the engagement, RAF Intelligence did not credit the claims because of insufficient confirmation. They were credited with two destroyed and one damaged. Flying Officer Tony Lovell had been flying the third Spitfire, but was unable to take part in the attack, owing to problems with his oxygen supply. Later that afternoon No.41 returned to Catterick, while No.54 returned to Hornchurch.

On 9th August, a large force of about 250 enemy aircraft was picked up by radar, heading for a convoy code-named 'Peewit' sailing near the Isle of Wight. No.65 and 54 Squadrons were scrambled along with other units from No.10 and No.11 Groups. The German formation of Ju87s and Me109s were engaged over the Channel, the RAF claimed 24 German bombers and 36 fighters shot down. No.65 lost two pilots killed: Sergeant David Kirton, shot down in flames over Manston, and Sergeant Norman Phillips. Both were attacked by German fighters at about 11.45 am. Ten minutes later a Blenheim of No.600 Squadron, based at Manston, was also shot down by 109s of lll/JG 26, crashing into the sea off Ramsgate and killing all aboard.

On 11th August, 74 Squadron were kept exceptionally busy; they were involved in four separate engagements from first light till 2 pm. The squadron report for that day reads:

> The first operational order, received at 7.49 am, was to intercept a hostile raid approaching Dover. The squadron with 12 aircraft, led by S/Ldr Malan, climbed to 20,000 feet, and surprised approximately 18 Me109s flying towards Dover. P/O Stevenson's aircraft was hit by enemy fire, and he baled out and came down in the sea. He attracted the attention of a motorboat by firing his revolver.
>
> The second combat took place between 9.50 am and 10.45 am, when 12 aircraft took off to intercept enemy fighters approaching Dover. Several small groups of Me109s were sighted in mid-Channel. Owing to R/T difficulties, part of the squadron did not engage.
>
> The third combat started at 11.45 am when 11 aircraft took off to patrol the convoy 'Booty', about twelve miles east of Clacton. 40 Me110s were sighted approaching the convoy from the east, in close formation, just above cloud-base. The enemy fighters formed a defensive circle on sighting our fighters, but F/O Freeborn led the squadron in a dive into the middle of the circle. The aircraft landed back at Manston at 12.45 pm. The squadron took of for the fourth time at 1.56 pm with 8 aircraft, to patrol Hawkinge at 15,000 feet, and subsequently northeast of Margate where enemy raids were reported. 10 Ju 87s were sighted passing through cloud at 6,000 feet, and twenty Me109s at 10,000 feet; our fighters attacked the 109s which dived for cloud and a dogfight ensued.

During the four sorties No.74 had claimed 23 enemy aircraft destroyed and 14 damaged. The squadron, because of the success of the combats against the Germans, named 11th August 'Sailors' Day. Top scorer that day had been H.M. Stephen who had destroyed five and damaged three. Two pilots were lost, however: Pilot Officer Don Cobden and Pilot Officer Dennis Smith; both had been pursuing Me110s, 30 miles out, east of Harwich.

Hornchurch that evening was buzzing with the news that the famous Windmill Girls would again be performing that night in the station theatre. They were driven down from London, led by Sheila Van Damm, who choreographed the shows. The evening was a great success, and they received several 'encores' from the airmen, who no doubt once more appreciated the scantily clad women.

On 12th August, No.54 Squadron back from their rest at Catterick, flew the early morning patrol. The Luftwaffe launched raids that morning on Dover, at around 7.30 am, in order to divert British fighters from the main targets; these were to be the radar stations along, and just inland, of the coast. No.54 engaged with Me109s at around 8.30 am; three of their aircraft were damaged. Pilot Officer J. Kemp force-landed at Lympne, and Pilot Officer D. Turley-George crash-landed at Denton at 8.40 am; he was admitted to Canterbury Hospital with shrapnel wounds to the head. Pilot Officer Eric Edsall had to force-land his Spitfire near Dartford, Kent.

At 9 am five radar stations were attacked. One of them at Dunkirk in Kent, had lost two buildings, but no vital equipment was destroyed. The radar stations at Rye and Pevensey were also hit, damaging the huts and cutting an electric main.

Portsmouth was also bombed and, nearby on the Isle of Wight, the C.H. radar station at Ventnor was attacked by Junkers Ju88s. At 1.25 pm a formation of low-flying Dornier 17s dropped bombs on Manston airfield, damaging two of the hangars, and leaving bomb craters all over the flightpath. No.54 Squadron were ordered to cover Manston, but could not engage the bombers because of the heavy fighter escort.

Whilst the Germans had been bombing the airfield, they had caught No.65 Squadron Spitfires who were preparing to take off. 'Dave' Glaser recalls the attack:

> The Germans had come in unseen at low-level, and bombs were dropping all over the place. Everybody just opened up their throttles and went hell for leather. A bomb dropped just behind Pilot Officer Wigg's aeroplane, which stopped his propeller. Nobody had ever seen Wigg run for a scramble, but they reported that he ran like blazes for a hedgerow. Dick Kilner, who was a sergeant pilot, had just managed to get out of his Spitfire. He had been waiting for his oxygen bottle to be changed, and his groundcrew suddenly disappeared from view; so he bolted for the nearest shelter where he found his crew. Apart from that everybody managed to get off safely.

The aircraft that had managed to take off, proceeded to join up with the Spitfires of No.54, and then joined combat with Me109s. No.54 landed at

Manston later in the afternoon, and were met by the airmen of No.600 Squadron, who were somewhat shaken by the previous bombing attack on the airfield.

The airfield had taken quite a pasting, with two gutted hangars and burnt-out huts; meanwhile the craters along the flight path were busily being filled in.

13th August 1940: 'Adler Tag' or Eagle Day, heralds the first of the major attacks by the Luftwaffe over England to attain air supremacy and subdue the British people.

Tuesday, 13th August, was the day that the German Luftwaffe conducted its new plans to wipe out the RAF airfields and installations. Both Luftwaffe air fleets would operate; Luftflotte 2 commanded by Generalfeldmarschall Albert Kesselring and Luftflotte 3 by Generalfeldmarschall Hugo Sperrle. The code-name for this operation was 'Adler Tag' (Eagle Day). The weather during the early morning was bad with very low cloud and poor visibility. This caused a postponement at first, but several Luftwaffe bomber units failed to be notified of this in time, and carried out their missions without any fighter escort.

A formation of 74 Dornier 17s of KG2, flying from Cambrai and St Leger, missed their escort of Messerschmitt 110s as they crossed the French coast. They headed for targets at Sheerness and the Coastal Command aerodrome at Eastchurch.

No.74 Squadron were scrambled from Hornchurch, after the Operations Room had received confirmation of the raid coming in. The squadron caught up with the Dorniers over Whitstable at 7 am and engaged the rear section of the enemy formation. Four of the Dornier 17s were destroyed and two claimed as probables. No.74 suffered no pilot losses in the action, although Flight Lieutenant Brzezina was forced to bale out of his Spitfire after his aircraft was hit by return fire, causing an explosion in the cockpit at 7.05 am; he landed unhurt. The other Pole, Pilot Officer Szczesny after shooting down a Dornier 17, which crashed on Whitstable beach, was forced to land at West Malling airfield. He was unable to lower his undercarriage, owing to damage sustained in the attack on the bomber; however the aircraft K9871 was repairable.

On the afternoon of the 13th, larger formations of bombers and fighters crossed the Channel, aiming for targets in the Southampton area, Portland, Andover and Middle Wallop. No further action by squadrons from Hornchurch was conducted that day. But other RAF squadrons continued to destroy and harry the Luftwaffe; the final tally was 34 enemy aircraft destroyed, for the loss of 12 Hurricanes and one Spitfire. RAF casualties were three pilots killed and two wounded.

Unfortunately No.65 did lose one pilot, although not to enemy action. Pilot Officer Felix Gregory was killed, during night-flying practice in Spitfire R6766 at 7.15 pm. With the actual cause unknown, he baled out of his aircraft, but was too low and was killed; the aircraft crashed at Eastry, Kent.

The next day, 14th August, the Germans continued their assault on coastal airfields, attacking Manston yet again. This time they managed to destroy the main power supply and telephone communications line, as well as finish off the destruction of the already damaged hangars. One Messerschmitt 110 was shot down by members of No.600 (City of London) Squadron, who were manning a Lewis Gun on one of the sandbagged dugouts; the German crashed into the middle of the airfield. A second Me110 was hit by ack-ack ground defence fire; this also crashed at Manston at 12.10 pm. All the crews from both aircraft were killed except one, who was wounded and captured. The Me110s were from 2/Erprobungs Gruppe 210.

No.65 Squadron, involved in combat with Me109s over the Channel at 12.45 pm suffered no casualties, but two aircraft were damaged. Spitfire R6602, flown by Pilot Officer L. Pyman had to force-land at Manston, and Sergeant M. Keymer, in Spitfire R6884, returned to Hornchurch with his R/T shot to pieces.

Another squadron arrived to take up its post at Hornchurch on the 14th; this was No.266 'Rhodesia' Squadron. They had come south from Wittering to Eastchurch on the 12th August, led by their CO Squadron Leader Rodney Levett Wilkinson.

An interesting note appeared in the Stop-Press of the *Evening Standard* newspaper. Squadron Leader James Leathart of No.54 Squadron was quoted in his views on the Fighter Boys' determination to resist until victory was won. A full page article in the *Daily Express*, and extracts in other papers were published next day under the title 'The Story of a Spitfire Squadron'.

15th August 1940: On this day 75 Luftwaffe aircraft are destroyed, the highest number recorded in one day during the battle. Luftflotte 5 based in Norway and Denmark, flew major raids against the north of England, but substained 20% casualties on this day. They never flew a major raid again during the battle.

With the weather changing to fine and warm, August 15th was to be a day when all three Luftwaffe fleets, from Brittany to Norway, would mount attacks on Britain. About 11 am No.54 were ordered to patrol over Hawkinge and Lympe. Here they met a first wave of enemy aircraft, consisting of 60 Ju87 Stukas and about the same number of Me109s as escorts. The pilots of No.54 did manage to get in amongst some of the Ju87s; Flight Lieutenant Alan Deere claimed one destroyed before returning to Manston to re-fuel and re-arm. Because of the overwhelming opposition, No.54 suffered two pilots injured. Sergeant N.A. Lawrence was shot down by enemy fighters after destroying a Ju87. He crashed in the sea just off Dover and was rescued by a Royal Navy vessel; he was admitted to Dover Hospital suffering from shock. Sergeant W. Klozinsky crash-landed at Hythe at 11.45 am, also the victim of Me109s; he was sent to Ashford Hospital with injuries.

Later, at about 5 pm, Operations Control plotted a formation of 200 plus, heading towards the Isle of Wight area. No.266 were scrambled along with squadrons from other airfields to intercept. They lost two pilots killed. Sergeant F.B. Hawley was listed as missing after destroying a Heinkel 115 floatplane, and at 6.50 pm Pilot Officer F.W. Cale baled out too low, and was killed following combat with 109s over Kent. His Spitfire crashed at Teston on the banks of the River Medway.

No.54 Squadron were up again early in the evening, against bombers heading for their targets at Biggin Hill and Kenley. They were joined by No.501 Squadron from Gravesend together with aircraft from 266 Squadron.

Led by Squadron Leader James Leathart, the nine Spitfires entered the fray, taking on the escorting fighters; on the first attacking pass two 109s were shot down. Flight Lieutenant Alan Deere latched on to one Messerschmitt 109, who started his turn to go back across the Channel. Alan Deere continues the episode:

> If my recollection serves me, I was chasing a 109 back across the Channel, rather ill-advisedly. I was then engaged over Dunkirk with some 109s and attacked; on the way back one of them made a bit of a mess of me. Returning over on this side I was forced to bale out at 10,000 feet, hitting my wrist against the Spitfire's tailplane as I tumbled out. I landed in a field in Kent, and was picked up by a passing ambulance, and taken to East Grinstead Hospital, where I met Archie McIndoe, the famous plastic surgeon. He came to see me; it was getting late in the evening by then.
>
> I wasn't burnt, but I was in great pain from this injury to my wrist. They gave me an X-ray and found nothing was broken, but it was badly sprained. He said I'd have to have it in a sling, and taped up. He said, 'You could stay here and have a rest for two to three days.' Well the next morning there was an air raid, and everybody evacuated to the shelters; I evacuated myself to the railway station, and got a train back to Hornchurch. He was furious with me; he'd apparently rung the Station Commander at Hornchurch earlier, and said he had got me there at the hospital. The Station Commander's reply to what Archie had said was, 'Keep the little bugger there for a day or two.' When I arrived back at the airfield, much to the surprise of the Station Commander, he didn't say anything, just 'You got back rather quickly.' I was flying again the next day.

Alan Deere's Spitfire R6981 crashed and burned out at Pope Street, Godmersham, near Ashford at 7 pm. The only other aircraft loss to 54 Squadron was Spitfire R7019 piloted by Pilot Officer H.K.F Matthews, who force-landed near Maidstone, after receiving damage during a dog-fight with 109s at 7.05 pm.

The losses for both sides at the end of the hardest day's fighting were, 75

German aircraft destroyed, and 34 RAF aircraft lost, with 17 pilots killed and 16 wounded.

The 16th August saw similar German operations over the south-east; West Malling airfield was attacked again, as were Manston, Tangmere and its satellite Westhampnett, bombed by Ju87s. Ventnor radar station was again attacked and was completely put out of action.

Hornchurch-based No.266 Squadron suffered badly that day in combat with Me109s. Three of their pilots were killed in combat and two wounded, when at 12.30 pm the squadron attacked a Staffel of 109s over the Kent coast; but they in turn were jumped by Me109s at a higher altitude. Among the casualties were Squadon Leader Rodney Wilkinson and Sub-Lieutenant Henry Greenshields who had transferred from the Fleet Air Arm; the other fatality was Pilot Officer N.G. Bowen. Pilot Officer S.F. Soden was slightly wounded in the legs, but managed to force-land near Faversham. Flight Lieutenant S.H. Bazley had to abandon his aircraft over Canterbury, after being set alight during combat; he suffered minor burns.

A large enemy plot was spotted heading for the Thames Estuary, and approaching the Hornchurch sector; No.54 were alerted to the position of the incoming threat. It was in fact a formation of Dornier 17s of 3/KG2. Nine Spitfires of 54 Squadron dived into the Dorniers forcing them to break, some of them jettisoning their bomb loads and heading back to France. Their escort of 109s engaged the Spitfires, but they too soon headed for home due to lack of fuel. Two of the fighters were shot down by Pilot Officer Colin Gray, the New Zealander. Three of the Dorniers were shot down by British fighters on the way back, one crashing east of Canterbury, one listed as missing and another crashing at Calais-Marck. No.65 suffered the loss of one pilot; Pilot Officer L. Pyman failed to return from combat over the Channel in Spitfire K9915.

Unusually, 17th August was a very quite day, although the weather was perfect for flying; no enemy activity was monitored by radar or observation posts. This gave the squadrons a day of well-needed respite.

The Germans resumed their attacks on RAF airfields and radar stations in the south-east of England on the 18th. The first wave of massed bombers and fighters crossed the coast at around midday, coming in over the Dover area, and going for their targets at Biggin Hill, Kenley, Croydon and West Malling airfields.

No.65 Squadron, who were operating from Hornchurch's satellite at Rochford that day, were scrambled to intercept German aircraft near Biggin Hill, where they claimed a Heinkel 111 of 2/KG1 destroyed. The aircraft crashed at Snargate, near Dymchurch at 1.30 pm. During this engagement No.65 lost Polish pilot Flying Officer Franciszek Gruska who was listed as missing. It was not until thirty years later, in 1971, that his aircraft was located by members of the Kent Battle of Britain Museum. After an initial search, they found the aircraft's serial number R6713, confirming the identity of the aircraft and the pilot. In 1976, a team from RAF Bicester re-excavated the crash-site and recovered the remains of Pilot Officer Gruska. After an inquest, he was given a full military burial at Northwood

Cemetery, Middlesex.

No.54 Squadron had gone down to Manston early that morning, after having breakfast at Hornchurch; Colin Gray recalls the day's events:

> Once again we went down to Manston, six of us led by George Gribble. We were scrambled at 10.54 am, against an unidentified aircraft which proved to be a Messerschmitt 110 on a reconnaissance; the poor fellow didn't have much chance. I was the first to fire, using up all of my ammunition from very close range, and knocking off large pieces, which slowed him right up; but four of the others in my squadron managed to have a squirt before he crashed into the sea. This aircraft was subsequently identified as an Me110 of 7(F)LG2 piloted by Oberleutnant Werdin who was killed, as was his radio/gunner. We landed back at Manston and were not ordered up again until 12.40 pm, when Squadron Leader Leathart led the whole squadron against a 300 plus raid over Kent.
>
> We encountered a large formation of Dorniers escorted by Me109s over Dover; during the action I was attacked by another Spitfire, while using all my ammunition on a Dornier at 25,000 feet.
>
> After the combat, we landed back at Hornchurch, which was fortunate for us, because our place at Manston was taken by No.266 Squadron, who were also based at Hornchurch. Sure enough, Manston was once more attacked an hour or so later by Me109s. At 5 pm the squadron was again ordered off from Hornchurch to patrol Manston with 'Prof' again leading. We were vectored north on to a raid of 250 plus, approaching the Essex coast. This included 51 Heinkel 111s bound for North Weald, and 58 bound for Hornchurch airfield. They had a combined escort of about 150 Me109s and 110s. We arrived off Clacton-on-Sea, to find a squadron of Hurricanes already on the scene. I saw 'Prof' Leathart being harassed by several Me110s, so I fired at two, who lost interest in a hurry, and then at another, which I shot down. This fell into the middle of Clacton, fortunately without causing damage or injury to any civilians on the ground. The aircraft buried itself and its crew in the middle of Smith's Sandpit. It was still there, buried, when I paid a visit to England in 1978. The Me110 belonged to 4/ZG26, and was piloted by Hauptmann Ludtke, with gunner Unteroffizier Brillo; it crashed at 5.30 pm.

Back at Manston about 2.30 pm, No.266 Squadron, now led by Flight Lieutenant Denis Armitage, had landed after engaging Dorniers without any success. While refuelling and awaiting new orders, they were caught on the ground by Me109s of JG52.

The enemy fighters strafed the airfield, severely damaging six Spitfires and completely destroying two. Sergeant Pilot Donald Kingaby, who at that time was taxi-ing his aircraft to dispersal, was caught out in the open. He jumped from his Spitfire, and whilst rolling over on the ground, one of his fingers was nicked by one of the bullets and cannon shells that were ploughing up the earth all around him.

The squadron, which had now lost most of its aircraft, was withdrawn from the battle and sent up to Wittering.

19th August 1940: The strain on Fighter Command squadrons caused by the heavy attacks of the previous week is eased by a period of poor weather.

From the 19th up until the 23rd August, the weather deteriorated, with very cloudy skies and rain limiting the amount of German aircraft activity over the Channel and the south-east of England; however small numbers of recon-naissance and 'tip and run' raids by individual enemy aircraft were noted.

Back at Hornchurch, this lull in operations gave the pilots time to unwind and relax, while the ground crews and station personnel could re-equip and repair damaged aircraft, and bring squadrons up to full strength after the losses of the past few days. The replacement of new pilots was much more serious; squadrons were now experiencing the problem of receiving new inexperienced pilots, many with only a few hours on their specific types of fighters. James Leathart remembers the problem at this time:

> I tried to take up my new pilots, at least once or twice, before taking them on ops; otherwise it was like sentencing them to death if I didn't. Most of them did not have the faintest idea about high-speed combat; some had not even fired their guns during training.

Alan Deere recalls two fellow New Zealanders who had just joined No.54 as replacements; he too was shocked at their inexperience when he spoke to the new pilots:

> At that stage of the Battle of Britain, between August and the beginning of September, the aircraft had started to be available again, because Beaverbrook [the Minister of Aircraft Production] had got cracking and we were having them flown in. But we were short of pilots and we were getting pilots who had not even flown Spitfires, because there were no conversion units at that time; they came straight to us from their training establishments. Some of them did have a few hours on Hurricanes, but not on the Spitfire. For example, two young New Zealanders were sent to my flight, and chatting to them I found out that they had been six weeks at sea coming over; they had trained on some outdated aeroplane called a Wapiti back in N.Z. They had then been given two trips in a

Hurricane, and sent here to the squadron. We were pretty busy, so we gave them what is known as a cockpit check. We had by then a Miles Master monoplane; we'd give them one trip in that, and one of the pilots would take them up to see how they handled it. Then we'd brief them on the Spitfire and send them up for one solo flight and circuit; then we'd send them off to battle.

Of course they didn't last long; I think it was two trips before they were shot down, and both ended up in Dover Hospital, strangely enough. One of them was fished out of the Channel, while the other managed to parachute down; they were Mick Shand and Charlie Stewart. All I used to say to the new boys was, 'Don't do anything by yourself, stick with your leader and just watch; unless you are attacked yourself, stay out of trouble until you get a feel of the things.' Well it was pretty hard for a young chap to follow that dictum. In fact what generally happened was that they would follow their leader, and then the next thing they'd be on their parachute, because an Me109 had got up behind them.

Pilot Officer Ken Hart of No.65 Squadron was forced to crash-land his aircraft on 20th August, after his engine was damaged while in combat with an Me109 over the Thames estuary; he put the Spitfire down at Foulness at 3.30 pm.

On 22nd August, Flight Lieutenant George Gribble, leading a section of No.54 Squadron on patrol, ran across a gaggle of 110s and 109s; 54 lost Sergeant Collett, who was hit by a 109 and crashed into the Channel off Deal at 1.15 pm. Later in the day No.65 suffered two aircraft damaged and one lost in combat with Me109s at 7.30 pm; two of the pilots were unhurt, but Sergeant M. Keymer was killed.

Also on this day, Boulton-Paul Defiant aircraft of No.264 'Madras Presidency' Squadron flew down from Kirton-in-Lindsey to Hornchurch, led by Squadron Leader Philip Hunter. They had achieved great success during the Dunkirk operations in May 1940 by shooting down over 50 enemy aircraft destroyed.

Sergeant Fred Barker was the top scoring air-gunner in the squadron, with his pilot Sergeant Edward Thorn. He describes how he operated the Defiant's gun turret and what tactics they used.

As the gunner, I was in control of the MkIID turret with four 0.303 Brownings each with 600 rounds. There was only one main control, which was like a joystick. This moved the guns forward or sideways as you wished, also the firing button; this was no problem at all, it was a smooth working operation. It was better in my opinion than the previous Frasier-Nash turret.

The turret obviously had cut-outs on it, so you did not hit any part of the aircraft when firing. The only problem with it was it didn't carry enough ammunition. The tactics employed by us against the enemy bombers was to find their blind spot, which was usually just below and to the side of the bomber.

Although the squadron began to suffer high casualties during this period, some might suffer from a bit of a twitter before take-off, but once airborne you were too busy and concentrating on your job to worry.

24th August 1940: The Luftwaffe renew and increase their attacks on No.11 Group airfields. Defiant aircraft go into action over the south-east coast.

On Saturday 24th August, the weather was perfect for flying operations, fine and clear. It was about 9 am that the signs of an enemy build up started to emerge on the plotting tables of No.11 Group. The raid of 100 plus showed up over Cap Gris Nez and was heading towards Dover at altitudes from 12,000 to 24,000 feet.

RAF fighter squadrons were scrambled to intercept the raid; the town of Dover was attacked. At about 12.30 pm, the Defiant aircraft of No.264 Squadron landed back at Manston after inconclusive engagements with the enemy. They were ordered up again almost immediately, as a number of Junkers Ju88 bombers were attacking Ramsgate and the edge of the airfield. They took off in twos and threes, as they could not form up as a squadron.

Pilot Officer Eric Barwell had one aircraft with him, and they chased after the bombers heading for France. But before getting within range, the second Defiant flown by Pilot Officer J.T. Jones, with gunner Pilot Officer Bill Ponting, was shot down by one of five Me109s which attacked them. The German fighters then concentrated on Barwell, but by hard dog-fighting, air-gunner Sergeant Martin shot one down. They managed to evade the rest of the enemy fighters, and landed back at Hornchurch without any damage. The rest of No.264 did not fare as well as Eric Barwell.

The Defiant L7021, crewed by Pilot Officer D. Whitley and Sergeant R.C. Turner, was badly damaged in the tailplane by return-fire from a Ju88 they attacked over Manston; but they returned to base unhurt. Squadron Leader Philip Hunter and gunner Fred King were last reported following a Ju88 out across the coast. They were listed as missing, as were Pilot Officer I.G.Shaw and his gunner Sergeant Alan Berry, who failed to return from combat with Me109s off Manston at 12.45 pm.

Eric Barwell remembers flying the Defiant, and the combats that No.264 were engaged in at this time:

> I remember it well. We were caught on the ground at Manston but we managed to get off; my No.2 Pilot Officer Jones was very much a newcomer. We chased out after the 88s, not gaining on them much, when we were then attacked by five

109s; at the time I thought they were Heinkel 113s, but I corrected myself afterwards.

I shouted to Jones, 'Line astern, evasive action'; unfortunately he only did a gentle turn and was shot down immediately. They turned their attentions to me, and they only attacked one at a time; my air-gunner told me when they were coming in and I'd turn very quickly. The 109s couldn't turn quickly enough to allow for deflection in front of our aircraft, which meant they were pointing more or less at our aircraft, giving a dead straight shot for my gunner. I reckoned we hit two or three of them; one of them we definitely downed. They broke off and we set off for home. That one incident confirmed my belief that we could hold our own against enemy fighters. Unfortunately, on that day our CO Philip Hunter was lost, and his place was taken by a squadron leader, who had only been with us a fortnight as a supernumerary squadron leader. He insisted on leading us into action the very next day, although until a fortnight before he had never flown fighters. The net result was that we lost rather more aircraft.

One of 264 Squadron's casualties earlier in the day had been Defiant L7013, crewed by Flight Lieutenant Campbell-Colquhoun and gunner Pilot Officer Gerry Robinson, in combat with a Me109. Their aircraft had been damaged, and bullets from the German aircraft had ignited the Very cartridges in the Defiant's cockpit, causing the coloured flares to shoot all around. Campbell-Colquhoun slammed the Defiant down as quickly as possible on Manston airfield, and vacated the aircraft at great speed with gunner Robinson.

No.54 Squadron had now stopped using Manston as their forward base, because of the amount of enemy activity it was drawing; it was beginning to be quite an unhealthy place to be situated at this time. Colin Gray reflects:

This was the day we stopped using Manston. After one uneventful patrol immediately after breakfast, we were sent off against a raid of about 40 Dorniers and Ju88s, with an escort of 66 109s approaching Dover. Gribble, Robins and McMullen had successes, but Bob Campbell was badly damaged, although he landed safely. I didn't get a shot in, but later found an Me110 at 30,000 feet over the Channel, apparently on reconnaissance. I chased him all the way down to sea level, firing all my ammunition; I watched him crash into the sea, a quarter of a mile from the French coast. I saw one chap bale out at 1,000 feet; the aircraft was of 5/ZG2 and the pilot Leutnant Meyer was killed.

Later in the afternoon, we were scrambled again from Hornchurch against a large build up of enemy aircraft over the

Le Havre area, which developed into two raids. One was to Manston and Ramsgate again, and the second, against targets north of the Thames estuary, including Hornchurch and North Weald. We met up with seven Me109s in the Dover-Manston area, which my section was detailed to deal with. We chased them back to the French coast, threw a fair bit of lead about, but could only claim probables. Whilst we were doing this the rest of the squadron got involved with another formation of 109s and lost Charlie Stewart, who baled out over the sea and finished up in hospital. By the time we got back to Hornchurch, the raid had come and gone, without causing too much damage.

As mentioned, Hornchurch and North Weald were now receiving their share of attention from Luftwaffe raids. No.264 Squadron, who had been withdrawn from Manston after their bad mauling earlier in the day, now found themselves caught on the ground at Hornchurch by an incoming raid. Eric Barwell remembers:

We were about to take off on a patrol, but we were kept on the ground for too long. Then over the Tannoy came a running commentary that the Germans were approaching the area. Somebody contacted Operations over the R/T, and was shouting 'Do you want us to take off, we are here on the ground?' Then over the Tannoy came a cry almost of panic, '264 scramble, 264 Squadron scramble, scramble!' We took off, apart from two of our aircraft that had taxied into one another; the bombs were falling just where we had been before.

We had only managed to put up seven aircraft. I was last man and I told my gunner to keep his eyes skinned, looking up in the sun, when all of a sudden I felt that we had been hit by something. I whipped around quickly to see a 109 going down past us; he had sprayed the lot of us. Squadron Leader Garvin had made us keep right up close together, and he was climbing at full throttle; so it was difficult, after I turned away, to catch up with him. I noticed that one of the other aircraft had petrol streaming from one of his wing tanks, and I could see that I had holes in my wing tanks. I was not flying my usual aircraft that day, so I had no idea whether this aircraft had self-sealing fuel tanks or not. Anyway I called up Control and told them I was here by myself, and they said, 'Oh, patrol Dover at 10,000 feet.' I said, 'You understand that I'm just by myself.' They said 'Yes, understood.' I didn't see anything else and in due course came back.

During the rush to take off, a Defiant, piloted by Flying Officer D.K.

O'Malley with gunner Pilot Officer A. O'Connell, had collided with another aircraft whilst on the ground. Although damaged, the aircraft was repairable; both aircrew were unhurt. Not so lucky was Defiant L6965, flown by Pilot Officer R. Gaskell and shot down by Me109s of JG51 over Hornchurch airfield at 4 pm. Pilot Officer Gaskill survived with slight injuries, but his gunner Sergeant W. Machin died of his wounds.

There was very little activity on 25th August, and there were no German raids sighted until about 5 pm. Only No.54 Squadron lost a pilot; this was Pilot Officer Mick Shand who was wounded in action. Colin Gray was also flying that day:

> We were scrambled against a large raid off Dover and the Thames estuary, and were attacked by Me109s as we were descending through cloud. Mick Shand was shot down, and finished up in bed next to Charlie Stewart in Canterbury Hospital. I was saved by a timely warning from my No.2, Pilot Officer Peter Howes. I managed to get a full deflection shot at an Me109, which burst into flames; the pilot baled out, but his parachute caught fire. The aircraft fell in pieces not far from Manston.

Hornchurch was again on the Luftwaffe target list for 26th August, together with Kenley, Biggin Hill, North Weald and Debden airfields. No.264 Squadron were again in the thick of the action at about midday, when over 150 aircraft were sighted crossing the coast at Deal, in Kent. They engaged a formation of Dornier 17s. Fred Barker remembers that over Thanet they were then attacked by enemy fighters:

> We were basically doing our job, fighting away there, when all of a sudden, out of the blue, appeared this Messerschmitt 109; he came straight at me and started firing. My reaction was that I shouted to Ted Thorn to dive, which he did immediately. As we were going down, the 109 started to come around again; everything appeared to be all right in our aircraft, so I returned fire again. But then all of a sudden we crashed; I thought I saw the Me109 in trouble as well, but everything seemed to happen so fast. The Defiant crashed into a tree on landing, and we had to get away quickly as it was starting to smoke a bit. When we had got out we were then arrested by the Home Guard, so we had a bit of a problem until we convinced them who we were. Then we had to make our way back to Hornchurch.

Again 264 Squadron suffered losses. Defiant L7024 was badly damaged in action against Me109s over Thanet, but somehow managed to get back to base; both Pilot Officer H. Goodall and Sergeant R.B.M. Young were unhurt. Another Defiant L6985 was shot down after the gunner, Sergeant B. Baker, had destroyed a Dornier 17 over Thanet. The pilot, Flight

Lieutenant A.J. Banham managed to bale-out, but Sergeant Baker was listed as missing, after the Defiant crashed two miles off Herne Bay at 12.26 pm. Flying Officer I.R. Stephenson and Sergeant W. Maxwell suffered the same fate; they too were shot down by fighters at about the same time. Stephenson baled out injured, but Sergeant Maxwell was not found.

Eight aircraft of No.54 had also been scrambled, and they ran into 30 109s over Manston. Pilot Officer Desmond McMullen claimed a 109 which crashed near Ramsgate, while Pilot Officer Colin Gray had a good burst at three 109s in formation; the No.2 was seen to break away with damage and was claimed as a probable. The Spitfires landed back at Rochford; while they were there a second enemy raid developed against North Weald, Debden and Hornchurch. By the time they had got back to Hornchurch it was all over, but there was very little damage done.

No.65 Squadron led by Flight Lieutenant Gerald Saunders were also in action that afternoon. They attacked a formation of Dorniers escorted by 109s at 3.20 pm. Gerald Saunders:

> The enemy aircraft had split up and a dogfight had started with the 109s. I was returning to Rochford, and as I broke cloud cover I could see a Dornier 17 in front of me. He was obviously having trouble, but flying quite well. I was overtaking quite quickly, but I opened fire; I saw both of his engines stop, so I pulled to one side. I realised he was going down and he actually crash-landed on Rochford airfield. Later we had the pilot of the Dornier in the Mess and gave him a cup of tea. First of all he would not speak English, but later on he turned out to be a very charming German. All the crew of the aircraft had been wounded, including the Officer Pilot, who had been shot in the backside. The German pilot, who spoke English, said he had been attacked before, but only one shot had hit his aircraft as far as he could tell, and this had hit the compass; that's why he had broken cloud cover.

The Dornier that 'Sam' Saunders had helped bring down, was from 2/KG 2; its crew were Hauptmann Bose, Unteroffizier Schmidt, Unteroffizier Lunghard, and Obergefreiter Roeder. One incident worth recalling, which happened during this period in August, is remembered by Wing Commander Frank Dowling OBE, who was then Pilot Officer Dowling, the Assistant Station Adjutant:

> We had heard that one German aircraft had been shot down near the airfield, and that the surviving crew had been rounded up. They were brought to the station and led into the station adjutant's office; they consisted of a German Major and two NCOs. They were marched into the presence of Flight Lieutenant George Kerr and myself. The Germans clicked

their heels and bowed; they were quite smart looking chaps. I knew that Flying Officer Tubby Markwick, whom I had succeeded as assistant adjutant, spoke German. So he was sent for to look after the Major and take him over to the Officers' Mess. The station warrant officer dealt with the two NCOs, taking them to the Sergeants' Mess.

It was whilst in the Officers' Mess, that one of our chaps reminded the German Major that a German delegation had visited Hornchurch earlier, in 1938. With that the German replied, 'We will all be here soon' or words to that effect. Later that evening Al Deere came in; Al walked over to the German and felt like clocking him one. Al said, 'Why do you buggers always run away, and shout "Spitfire", as soon as you see us?'

We also had a piano in one of the rooms. Tubby Markwick was adept on the keys, so he and the Major were heard singing German songs. As the evening drew on it was time to bed down for the night. I had to take the German over to the guardroom. When we got there, he was told to empty out his personal belongings and lay them on the table for listing; there were all sorts of things, wallet and cards etc. Funnily enough he also had a small packet; the NCO in charge of the guardroom said 'What's this?' I said, 'Put that down in your list as one condom.'

The three of them were put into a large cell together so that they could chit-chat. The next morning I took a photograph of the Major outside the Officers' Mess. Soon after breakfast they were taken away for interrogation. [The Major was in fact the bombing leader of a formation whose target was Hornchurch.]

It was also on the 26th that the No.54 Squadron Diary recorded a change of command:

It was with very mixed feelings that we learned that our Squadron Leader known affectionately as 'Prof' was to hand over his command. Mixed, because on the one hand we had grown accustomed to 'A son of 54 Squadron' leading the Squadron through the most intensive and successful period of its history, whilst on the other, we knew the strain of leading the Squadron both in the air and on the ground would soon begin to take its toll. We say 'Au Revoir' with the knowledge that wherever he may be in the 'Higher Spheres' 54 Squadron will be well and truly cared for.

On 27th August the weather was bad, and there was no significant Luftwaffe activity. At RAF Hornchurch, No.54 Squadron's commanding officer Squadron Leader James Leathart was formally advised that he was to be posted away for a rest period, while his place would be taken over by Squadron Leader Donald Finlay.

The 28th August was the last day that No.264 Squadron would play a role in the Battle of Britain. The German raids started to appear over Cap Gris Nez at about 8.30 am; one formation of 27 bombers was heading for Rochford airfield. Squadrons from No.11 Group were sent up, including aircraft of No.264 Squadron at Rochford. The fighter escort was very strong and the RAF fighters achieved very little success.

The Defiants were again outclassed by the German fighters and paid severely. Two Defiants, N1574 and L7026 were both shot down by Me109s at 8.55 am; their crews, Pilot Officer D. Whitley and Sergeant R.C. Turner, Pilot Officer P.L. Kenner and Pilot Officer C.E. Johnson, were all killed. Defiant N1576 was badly damaged, hit by return fire from a Heinkel 111 over Dover at 9 am; Pilot Officer W.F. Carnaby and Pilot Officer C.C. Ellery returned to base, both unhurt. Defiant L6957 was hit in the petrol tank while in combat over Folkestone at about the same time; the crew, Sergeant A.J.Launder and Sergeant V.R. Chapman, both unhurt, got back to base. Squadron Leader G.D. Garvin and Flight Lieutenant Ash were not so fortunate; their aircraft L7021 was shot down in flames by 109s near Faversham. Squadron Leader Garvin baled out and survived, but Flight Lieutenant Ash was killed when his parachute failed.

At 12.30 pm Hornchurch's satellite Rochford was again the main attention of a second raid. No. 264 were forced to take off when approaching bombers began pounding the airfield; they managed to get off in the nick of time. No. 54 Squadron were scrambled from Hornchurch to engage the raid. Pilot Officer Colin Gray was again in action:

> The first sortie of the day had been uneventful, but on the second we ran into 30 Dorniers and escorting 109s, headed for Rochford. 'Prof' Leathart, who was leading, shot down a Dornier, and George Gribble, an Me109. I fired all my rounds at a Dornier without apparent damage. Al Deere was attacked by another Spitfire and forced to bale out over Detling.

Also in action for the first time, since arriving down at Hornchurch from Turnhouse that morning, was No.603 'City of Edinburgh' Squadron. They engaged Me109s at 22,000 feet, just west of Canterbury. During the fighting, Squadron Leader George Denholm claimed a probable, but their first taste of action down south had cost them three pilots. Flight Lieutenant J.G.L. Cunningham was posted as missing, after last being seen in combat with 109s of JG2, and so was Pilot Officer Donald MacDonald. Flying Officer I.S. Ritchie was wounded, but managed to get his badly damaged aircraft back to Hornchurch. He was then rushed off to Oldchurch Hospital at nearby Romford for treatment.

A third large raid was sighted later in the day, which consisted mainly of fighter-bombers and fighters on sweeps over the Kent area, at a height of 25,000 feet. Colin Gray continues:

We had just re-fuelled and re-armed, when we were scrambled again against a massive fighter sweep of 109s and 110s in mid Channel. As is usual in fighter combat, we became separated as soon as the action had begun. Flight Lieutenant George Gribble put paid to an Me109, and I chased two back to France, firing half of my ammunition without result. On the way back home, I noticed a parachute floating down near Canterbury. This proved to be our new commanding officer, Don Finlay, who had a nasty wound; so 'Prof' had to stay on for some while longer.

'Ricky' Richardson, an engine fitter with No.54 Squadron, looked after Flight Lieutenant Alan Deere's aircraft and they became life long friends. He recalls the events which took place at Rochford, when the airfield received a surprise attack.

One of the things I remember vividly was when we were at our forward base at Rochford. We had just seen our aircraft off, they had gone off on another patrol. We had just decided to have a quick game of football when suddenly 12 machines appeared into the wind and into the sun. We watched them thinking that's funny why are they coming back, and it wasn't until we saw the twinkling of the gunfire along the aircraft's mainplane that we realised that they were Jerries. What happened next was they came down in layers, and I can remember it now as if it was yesterday, one of the German aircraft was flying in really low, unfortunately he ran smack into the gunfire of one of his comrade's aircraft above and they shot the poor young chap down and he was killed.

One of our flight mechanics had come to me before the raid and had asked about the CO's aircraft, as it would not be flying anymore that day, should he cover it up and I had said 'Yes'. Unfortunately they dropped a bomb near the aircraft and it was two days later that they found this poor lad lying dead on top of the hangar. After the attack we ferried the injured off to the local hospital for attention, it was only at the hospital that a doctor noticed that my leg had been hit and sliced open, I hadn't felt a thing at that time.

Also up at 25,000 feet, the pilots of No.603 Squadron were again in dogfights with 109s. Pilot Officer George Gilroy managed to get in behind a 109; he fired all his ammunition from a range of 150 yards, which set the 109 alight, causing the pilot to bale out. Pilot Officer Morton attacked a formation of eight 109s and in doing so managed to make them break. He followed one down to 6,000 feet and fired several short bursts; he claimed it as probable, as he saw it diving straight down, on fire, at 4,000 feet.

Pilot Officer Ronald 'Raz' Berry also claimed a 109 probable and one damaged. This time the Squadron landed without loss of pilots or aircraft.

Squadron Leader Don Finlay was shot down by Me109s over Ramsgate at 5.15pm. He spent nearly a month in hospital before returning to command No.41 Squadron, who by then were also at Hornchurch. Alan Deere was also shot down; this time by 'friendly fire' from another Spitfire. He had been attacking an Me109, when his aircraft R6832 was hit by bullets in the fuselage, port wing, and also cutting his control wires. He had no option but to 'take to the silk'. He landed safely and was back at Hornchurch by 3 pm, having been flown back from Detling airfield in an Anson aircraft.

In fact it was on this day that Hornchurch was visited by no less a person than Marshal of the Royal Air Force Lord Trenchard, who had come down to make an address to the pilots, to praise and give encouragement for all the good work.

The scrambles continued into the early evening, with 603 Squadron airborne again at 6.36 pm. They encountered Me110s and 109s, at 7.36 pm, between Manston and the Isle of Sheppey. Squadron Leader George Denholm's combat report reads:

> In a combat against 10 Me109s, when 10 miles west of Manston at 20,000 feet, I singled out a Messerschmitt and made two stern attacks on it. After my first attack the Me109 started to dive down. I followed it, and after my second attack, it appeared to be in difficulties. I was then able to make two quarter-attacks. The German pilot, who had been heading for France, then turned back towards the English coast and went into a glide. I eventually saw him hit some high-tension wires and crash into a field west of Dover.

No.603's Spitfires returned back at Hornchurch at about 8.15 pm. There was only one casualty from that sortie. This was Pilot Officer Noel 'Broody' Benson, who was listed as missing, until his aircraft was found crashed at Tenterden, Kent; his body was discovered nearby.

During the late evening, Flight Lieutenant Charles Pritchard of No.600 Squadron was sent off in his Blenheim aircraft, 20 minutes before the squadron was due to come to 'readiness'. In his report, he recorded:

> I was told to take off as soon as possible and to patrol base at 'Angels 17'. We took off and started to clamber upwards, for the next hour. We received a good number of vectors and investigated innumerable searchlight concentrations. We were then sent to patrol a line across the route which a lot of enemy aircraft were making their way towards the Midlands.
>
> It was not long before I saw the exhaust flames of an aircraft cross close in front and above, so I turned and went 'Flat Out' after him, only to find that we could hardly climb any higher. All the controls were pretty sloppy, so having

staggered into line astern and positioned at about 400 yards, I let go a good burst of fire. The enemy aircraft turned and dived, moving too fast for us to catch, although we could see him for some time.

Later I saw an exhaust flame below us to starboard, so I dived after it, towards the slipstream. We were getting very close, when we were illuminated from behind, one searchlight coming in from the front, which flicked over the aircraft in front, before fastening onto us. It sufficiently showed us that we were very close to the enemy aircraft. I opened fire before the searchlight blinded us entirely. I exhausted the remainder of the ammunition and again the enemy aircraft dived away, too fast for me to catch. Arriving back at Hornchurch, I had trouble getting in, and after two bad attempts, I finally made it on the third, with brakes hard on.

On the next day, 29th August, after spending six years as one of Hornchurch's home-based squadrons, No.65 'East India' were posted to Turnhouse, in Scotland. They were never to operate from Hornchurch again.

This same day saw the return to RAF Hornchurch of another squadron that had been at the airfield during the Dunkirk period. No.222 'Natal' Squadron arrived from Kirton-in-Lindsey, to replace No.264 who were now withdrawn from the battle.

No. 222's aircraft had been bought and supplied by money raised by the people of Durban and Natal in South Africa. The idea was the brain child of Horace Flather, a South African newspaper editor, who wanted to help the RAF by sponsoring a complete fighter squadron with aircraft and the money to maintain them.

After an article he had published in the Durban *Daily News* titled 'Speed the Planes', the response from the public was phenomenal. One donor sent a cheque for an incredible £25,000. Women gave over their jewellery and wedding rings and some families donated their heirlooms for the fund. Within one month over £200,000 had been raised.

Aircraft Rigger Joe Crawshaw and Engine Fitter 'Dave' Davis of No.222 Squadron, who had travelled down from Kirton-in-Lindsey, recall the squadron's call to go south. Joe Crawshaw:

On the previous day, we had received orders to prepare quickly to go to Hornchurch. Dave and I bundled all our belongings into my car. I had just purchased an Austin Seven motor car, and was told that if I wished to take the car to Hornchurch, it would have to be resprayed in camouflage colours; this I did. We were to travel down by convoy, but it was so long-winded that we decided to part and go down on our own. We didn't go straight to Hornchurch; we went home first. Dave, who had recently married, had his home in the East End of London. I went and stayed with some friends in

Welling, Kent. We eventually arrived at Hornchurch the next evening at about 5 pm.

'Dave' Davis, Engine Fitter No.222 Squadron:

> The first thing they gave us when we arrived were tin helmets, 'Battle Bowlers'; I thought, well it looks like things are going to get interesting down here. The squadron was pretty quiet the first day, doing circuits and bumps, and we settled into the scheme of things. Then in one foul swoop it really started; we were called to 15 minutes readiness. I sat in the cockpit ready to start up the aircraft, while Joe stood ready to press the electric trolley button as soon as the scramble was ordered. When this happened, Joe would help the pilot on with his parachute, and strap him in; by then I would already be out of the cockpit.

No.222 Squadron had flown down with 19 Spitfires, led by their Commanding Officer, Squadron Leader Johnnie Hill. Their first sortie from Hornchurch was at 4.25 pm on the 29th, when Squadron Leader Hill led four Spitfires of 'A' Flight on a defensive patrol over the Hornchurch area; no enemy contact was made during this flight.

There was little activity that day until about 3 pm, when units of Luftflotte 2 were picked up on radar over Cap Gris Nez near Boulogne. This consisted of over 500 Me109s and 150 Me110s, with a small number of bombers to draw up the RAF fighters. Back at Hornchurch, 603 Squadron were scrambled off at 3.15 pm and engaged the enemy formation. In the following combat Flying Officer J.C. Boulter destroyed one Me109, while Pilot Officer Gerald 'Stapme' Stapleton, Pilot Officer Richard Hillary and Pilot Officer Bill Read all claimed probables. Only the 'A' Flight Commander, Flight Lieutenant William Rushmer, was hit by 109s and had to force-land at Bossingham, slightly wounded.

Another massive German fighter sweep was plotted 40 minutes after No.603 Squadron had landed back at Hornchurch, for refuelling and fresh ammunition. They were back in the air again at 6.10 pm to meet the new threat coming in at 25,000 feet. They engaged the 109s over Manston at 6.50 pm. Pilot Officer Colin Pinkney claimed a 109 before being attacked from astern by at least four Me109s. His aircraft was hit badly and he baled out, slightly burned, and on landing was admitted to hospital.

In the meantime Flying Officer Brian Carbury, from New Zealand, attacked an Me109 with a head-on pass; the 109 completely disintegrated. Pilot Officer Richard Hillary also claimed a 109, but soon afterwards his own machine was hit by 20 mm cannon shells, when he became separated from the rest of the squadron. He had latched on to a flight of Hurricanes from No.85 Squadron, and was acting as their 'weaver' at the tail end, when he was hit by a 109. Fortunately he was able to control his damaged Spitfire, and force-land near Lympne, Kent. He returned to Hornchurch unhurt.

It was while at Hornchurch on 30th August 1940, that No.222 Squadron received a signal from HQ Fighter Command which read:

By an Order dated August 30th 1940 from HQ Fighter Command:
That the Province of Natal has made a gift of money sufficient to buy a complete Squadron of fighters, therefore in future No.222 Squadron will be known as 222 (Natal) Fighter Squadron

The Germans continued their assault on the airfields on the 30th; the weather forecast was for fine clear skies. They sent over three large waves of over 100 aircraft consisting of Heinkels, Dorniers, Me110s and Me109s.

At 10.35 am, 603 Squadron were scrambled; over Dover they met a formation of about 80 Me110s at 17,000 feet. 603 dived down into the attack and the 110s split up and formed four defensive circles. Only Pilot Officer 'Black' Morton made a claim, a probable, while the CO Squadron Leader George Denholm was shot down by a 110 at 11.15 am; he baled out unhurt. Flying Officer R. 'Bubble' Waterston was also hit during the combat, his aircraft's oil tank being punctured. He managed to return to Hornchurch, as did Sergeant A.R. Sarre whose Spitfire had been severely damaged, with most of his tail rudder shot away.

No. 222 Squadron, sent up on their first scramble since arriving at Hornchurch, were ordered to patrol Gravesend. Sergeant Pilot Iain Hutchinson was only minutes into his flight when he was bounced. Iain Hutchinson remembers the incident:

It was due to stupidity on my part first of all, because I was up at about 20,000 feet looking out for enemy aircraft in the wrong place, when all of a sudden four Me109s passed underneath me. It took me about 20 seconds to realise what I should be doing, and in that time somebody attacked me from behind, and got the engine, so I couldn't carry on. I had to come down to try to make the airfield. I was unable to do this so I had to crash-land in a field. I remember seeing a farmer with his horses pulling a plough in the field about 50 yards to my left; I am sure I could see a look of surprise on his face. We then hit the deck, not damaging the aircraft too badly. After a short while I was picked up by a truck from Hornchurch, as I had landed just down the road at Damyns Hall Farm in Rainham.

In the afternoon No.222 were told to move down to Rochford to operate there for the next 24 hours. At 2.30 pm 14 Spitfires of 222 (Natal) Squadron left for Rochford, but during the flight were told by Ops to patrol over Lympne at 16,000 feet. While over the Canterbury area, they spotted an enemy formation of over 50 aircraft. They went in to attack the enemy bombers, but were then attacked in turn by Me109s. Pilot Officer William Assheton was shot down, but managed to crash-land his Spitfire on

Bekesbourne aerodrome, Kent. Also shot down during this engagement were Sergeant Sidney Baxter, who landed his badly damaged aircraft at Eastchurch, and Pilot Officer John 'Chips' Carpenter, who was forced to bale out of his burning Spitfire. He landed without injury, and his aircraft crashed at Cherry Orchard Lane, Rochford at 4.30 pm. Pilot Officer Tim Vigors claimed an Me109 probable.

A young 20-year-old old Sergeant Pilot, John Burgess, remembers his first day's action against the Luftwaffe:

> I was the most junior pilot in the squadron, and I didn't fly in the morning. But in the afternoon we were sent to a satellite aerodrome at Rochford, and we took off at about 2 pm; by that time we were down to 14 aircraft. We weren't intended to go into action, and the distance between Hornchurch and Rochford was no more than ten minutes, straight flying time. When we were about halfway there, we were told to start climbing because an enemy raid was coming in; we were told to patrol the line between Maidstone and Ashford. I'd never seen any enemy aircraft in the air, and as I say, I was the most junior pilot. We climbed up to 17 to 20,000 feet, and suddenly, they said over the R/T that the enemy raids were approaching us. Then the CO of the squadron said, 'There they are down below, down below.' I looked down, and couldn't see a thing, just beautiful countryside. We went into line astern, which was the standard attack formation at that time. When you are fourteenth aircraft in a line, it is very difficult to keep up with the string of aircraft in front of you, weaving about the sky. All I could do was to go full throttle, and try and keep up with the others. I kept the pilot in front in view, but the rest of the squadron had disappeared into the distance. Then suddenly I saw him roll over and go straight down, so I proceeded to do the same. As I levelled up there were the enemy, I suppose a formation of about 40 110s.
>
> I dived down towards them, and to be honest, I was not fearful or worried, just excited and intrigued; this is what it was really all about. I dived towards the 110s and as I came towards them, they broke formation and formed a great big circle. I fired my guns as they moved across in front of me, and I could see flashes of gunfire coming from the back of their aircraft. I turned on my back and dived away. As I dived I could see that I'd got a bullet hole in the tip of my wing; I thought, there you go, an 'ace' at last.
>
> I looked around and could see some aircraft spinning down in the distance, nothing to do with the formation of 110s. But there were engagements everywhere; you'd just see a flickering silver flash as an aircraft was going down out of control.

I was pretty low on ammunition at that time and so went back to base; whether I'd shot down any 110s I don't know. I landed at Rochford with the souvenir of a single bullet hole.

Anyway in the evening we took off, and were told to patrol Dover. We were flying along in a vic formation at the time, when suddenly there was a loud crack. I looked down, and there seemed to be some smoke between my legs, but only a little puff. I was formating on the man on my right, and I looked away from him to my engine to see white spots appear all the way down the cowling. I looked back again to my friend on my right, and he was in flames. Overhead there suddenly appeared a shadow that went over the top of us, and a duck-egg blue wing with black crosses on it. We'd been bounced by some 109s, and we didn't even see them coming; the white spots had been bullets. I broke away, and then I realised that I'd been hit; the engine was running normally, but I noticed that the radiator temperature was rising quickly. So I headed back for Rochford, and landed just in time before the engine overheated. We lost two or three pilots that day, principally because we were so inexperienced.

In fact 222 Squadron had six aircraft written off that day due to combat, with two further aircraft damaged, but repairable. They lost one pilot killed, Sergeant Pilot Joseph Johnson, while two pilots were wounded; Pilot Officer Hillary Edridge suffered burns to the face, and Flight Lieutenant Geoffrey Matheson was badly injured after crash-landing his Spitfire near Sittingbourne. Squadron Leader Arthur 'Dagger' Spears was then a Sergeant Pilot with 222 Squadron; on their third scramble of the day, he describes the following events that befell him:

We had been in engagement with the enemy, but without any success from my point of view. When we landed back at Rochford, our advanced landing ground, we went and grabbed a cup of tea. Suddenly the gong went again; I dropped my tea and ran to take off. The result of that was we met up with German aircraft in quantity, and not being very practised I was shot down, having to bale out.

After landing without injury, I was taken to Eastchurch airfield, where I met up with Billy Baxter, another pal of mine from No.222. We spent the night at Eastchurch, but the following morning before we'd had time to have breakfast, the Jerrys came over and bombed the airfield. We made for the open countryside in company with a chap from a Fairey Battle squadron. We got clear of the airfield but were actually bombed that time. I remember that the ditch we had jumped in was heaving like a boat at sea, like a cork on water. Afterwards we picked up our railway warrants and headed for the railway station at Sheerness. After a long trip into London, we transferred to the District Line on the Underground; I was carrying my parachute pack. I remember on the train the old cockney saying 'Good for you mate' and patting us on the back; they'd had it pretty bad at that time.

When I got back to Hornchurch the airfield had been bombed, including my car, a small Ford 8, which had suffered rather badly, but was still workable. It had a rather large dent in the bonnet and the back windscreen was blown in. Fortunately Flight Sergeant Roberts, our ground crew chief, who had been looking after the car for me, said it was repairable. There was a stock of old cars situated around the fields near to the airfield. These had been placed there to deter and obstruct the landing of any German aircraft. From these wrecks I managed to scrounge bits to make good the repairs.

Sergeant Spear's Spitfire P9323 crashed at South Lees Farm, Minster, on the Isle of Sheppey at 6.29 pm.

No.603 Squadron were scrambled for the last time that day at 3.55 pm. They were vectored on to a raid that had already attacked Kenley, Tangmere and other airfields. At 25,000 feet they met 109s. Flying Officer Brian Carbury engaged with three of them, firing at one from a range of 50 yards; this aircraft went down streaming glycol. A 109 was also claimed by Pilot Officer Waterston, which crashed into the River Medway. Sergeant Sarre was obliged to bale out of his aircraft however, when the entire tail section was blown off by enemy cannon fire; he landed safely by parachute.

31st August 1940: Very heavy fighting by Hornchurch squadrons. Hornchurch airfield bombed. Fighter Command severely stretched at this time.

On 31st August, the Hornchurch squadrons were to be involved in some of the heaviest fighting so far, and the airfield would also take punishment. At 8 am, radar stations first reported a build-up of four large waves of German aircraft; one of the raids was headed for Dover while the other three were headed for targets up the Thames estuary.

No.222 Squadron had flown down to Rochford at dawn, and at 8.20 am was given orders to put up a standing patrol over the airfield. Because of the heavy losses of the previous day's fighting, they could only muster seven aircraft. No.603 was scrambled from Hornchurch at 8.55 am; they encountered a formation of 109s and claimed three of the enemy fighters without loss to themselves. No.222 were scrambled again at 12.45 pm and, between Gravesend and Biggin Hill airfields, made contact with over 60 Heinkel and Dornier bombers, with the usual escort of Me109s. This raid was making its way to attack RAF Hornchurch. Pilot Officer Tim Vigors destroyed a 109 and claimed another as a probable. Flying Officer Robinson also claimed a 109 destroyed, and Sergeant Iain Hutchinson a

109 damaged. They suffered no casualties.

No.603's second scramble of the day was also at 12.45 pm. They were given instructions to intercept two waves of Dorniers and Heinkels, with Me110s and 109s, heading for Croydon and Biggin Hill. Almost immediately after take-off, Flying Officer Brian Carbury was involved in a combat with an Me109 of 1/JG26. He shot the aircraft down, and it crashed in flames at Bridge Road, Rainham. The pilot, Oberleutnant Hafer, baled out, but his 'chute failed to open; his body was found two days later in the Ingrebourne Creek. Flight Lieutenant MacDonald also claimed an Me109 destroyed, which crashed at Hunton. In all the squadron claimed seven enemy aircraft destroyed.

At about 1 pm German raiders approaching Dungeness turned and headed for their target, Hornchurch. The Station Diary recorded the raid:

> A large formation of enemy bombers, a most impressive sight in Vic formation at around 15,000 feet, reached the aerodrome and dropped their bombs (probably sixty in all); the bombs landed in a line from the other side of our dispersal pens to the petrol dump, and beyond into Elm Park. Perimeter track, dispersals and barrack-block windows suffered, but no other damage to buildings was caused and the aerodrome, in spite of its ploughed up condition, remained serviceable. The Squadron (No.54) was ordered off just as the first bombs were beginning to fall, and eight machines safely left the ground. The remaining Section, however, had just become airborne as the bombs exploded. All of these machines were wholly wrecked in the air. The survival of the pilots is a complete miracle. Sergeant Davis, taking off across the airfield towards the hangars, was thrown back to the other side of the River Ingrebourne, two fields away; he scrambled out of his machine unharmed.

The following pilots, ground crew and WAAFs now retell their memories of the bombing of the airfield. Squadron Leader James Leathart, who was leading No.54 Squadron that day, remembers the hectic scramble to get airborne:

> We were all at standby at our dispersal point, expecting to be scrambled at any moment, when suddenly I saw German bombers appearing over the horizon, coming closer and closer; and still we weren't scrambled. I did the most unspeakable thing; I decided to take off without permission, alas ten seconds too late. I got away with it, but Eric Edsall, Al Deere and Sergeant Davis were caught as the bombs began to drop.

Flight Lieutenant Alan Deere:

I was caught taking off by a German raid on the airfield. We were ordered to take off and then ordered to cancel the order. You must remember that the radar, which was the reporting chain, only worked effectively up to the coast; then inland it was up to the Observer Corps, and there was a bit of an overlap. If they couldn't visually see the enemy aircraft, there was a bit of indecision and they'd get raids mixed up. This was no criticism, it was just the system ironing itself out; one minute there would be an X Raid, then the next minute it would have disappeared from the plotting board.

However, we were told to get to readiness, which we did, then to standby, which meant in your cockpits, all ready and strapped in; we were then told to go back to readiness. As we got out and were walking back to dispersal, the phone rang and dispersal said 'Scramble as quickly as possible.' So we had to run back to the aircraft, and that's when we were caught taking off; the Germans were already overhead and dropping their bombs.

I was leading the section on the right, and I was held up from taking off by a new pilot who'd got himself stuck in the take-off lane, and didn't know where to go. He delayed me and, by the time I'd got him sorted out, I was the last one off and caught the bombs. I was blown sky high, the three of us were; we all got away with it. I was pretty badly concussed and my Spitfire was blown up. I finished up on the airfield in a heap, and my No.2 had his wing blown off. No.3 was not seen for two hours, until he re-appeared at dispersal with his parachute. He had been blown in his aircraft about a mile away, into what we called 'Shit Creek'. He landed the right way up and got out, and had to walk all the way around the airfield to get back in.

I was pretty well shaken, and I'd had the top of my scalp badly torn from my head scraping the ground, when the aircraft had careered upside down along the ground. The doctor plastered and bandaged me up and said, 'Forty-eight hours' rest, then report back.'

Well, 24-hours and I felt all right, so I just went back. We were under tremendous stress at the time, so I took just the night off, and went back flying the next day all bandaged up.

Jack Shenfield was a 'B' Flight mechanic with No.54 Squadron. He too remembers the raid:

At the time, we had just got the aircraft away when the bombs started falling, and I ran towards the air-raid shelter. What I also remember well, was that there was an ack-ack unit or gun emplacement near to Sutton's, where our dispersal point was.

There was so much dust from the bombs and the guns going off, it made me wonder how these people could see what they were shooting at with these ack-ack guns. Once I got into the shelter, we were all packed in there, and the sergeant had closed the door. We had been only in there a minute or so when there was a banging at the door. He opened the door and it was the driver of the Bowser; this was the vehicle that carried all the high-octane petrol for the aircraft. He'd parked the thing outside the shelter with all the bombs falling all around. The sergeant said, 'Sod off, and take that bloody thing with you, and park it somewhere else before you blow us all to pieces.' The driver had to go back and park it before they'd let him into the shelter.

After the raid was over and we came out, some of the lads got on top of the shelter and started shouting, 'Oh look they've shot a German down, I can see the crosses on the back.' What they didn't realize was, that it was the three kites from our squadron, Al Deere and the others, the crosses were the victory scores on the side of the aircraft. Poor old Sergeant Davis appeared hours later, asking for a cup of tea after being blown up. The whole fuselage went, the wings were left on the aerodrome, and the fuselage blown into the river, which was quite a distance. How they all survived was a miracle.

Joy Caldwell was 18 years of age when, as a WAAF, she worked in the Operations Room in Signals at RAF Hornchurch. She can vividly remember the raids:

The worst day was my father's birthday, that's how I remember it. My friend Joan and I were on duty in or around Ops; anyway we knew there were plots of hundred pluses coming in. Ronnie Adam the Ops Controller, used to say 'Tin hats on', which some of us had already done. The Ops Room was sand-bagged all around, so you felt perfectly secure; but then it would start to rattle and bang a bit once the bombs started falling and get a bit unpleasant. But I don't think we were ever frightened because we were too ignorant; we didn't realize what could happen.

When they came over again at lunchtime, they really did paste us then. I think they dropped something like 60 on us, and I think three airmen were killed; that wasn't very pleasant because they were too near. We walked back from our billets and they came over again at teatime and hammered us again. But Ronnie Adam, with that lovely calming voice, he was great; you felt that he never altered despite whatever was going on. He was completely calm, and the pilots loved him because of his calm actor's voice.

Ronald Adam, Hornchurch's Controller was an ex Royal Flying Corps pilot. He served on the Western Front in France with No.73 Squadron, before being shot down by one of Manfred von Richthofen's pilots on 7th April 1918. Adam survived the crash, but was badly injured and spent the rest of the war in hospital as a prisoner of war. After the war, he entered into the theatre and became an actor. With war imminent in 1939, he joined the RAF, and after training was sent to Hornchurch. His calm controlled voice coming over the aircraft's radio was very much appreciated in times of anxiety by many of the young pilots at that time. He would write two fictional novels based on his time while serving at Hornchurch, *Readiness at Dawn* which was published in 1941 and later *We Rendezvous at Ten*. Post-war, he returned to acting and appeared in many films including classics like *Reach for the Sky* and *Angel's One-Five*.

A second raid by German Squadrons II/KG3, 4/KG3 and 5/KG3, pounded the airfield again at about 6 pm, but much of the damage was to the flight path and a few aircraft. No real damage was done to the main airfield buildings, except the newly built Airmen's Mess which was about to be opened. This was hit, much to the anger of the men who were looking forward to the new facility. Some of the bombs had unfortunately hit residential housing at Elm Park.

All the Hornchurch squadrons had been airborne by the time this raid had reached the airfield, and they harried the German bombers and fighters over Hornchurch, and all the way back over Kent and the Channel.

Flying Officer Brian Carbury of No.603 Squadron claimed two Me109s destroyed over Southend, but in return was attacked from behind by a 109. He was wounded by shell splinters from a 20mm cannon shell, which also knocked out the pneumatic system of his aircraft, and he was forced to make for home. Meanwhile Pilot Officer 'Raz' Berry, also of No.603, had managed to latch on to a 109 just off Shoeburyness, flying at 1,000 feet. In his combat report he states:

> As I had no oxygen left, I had to leave the squadron at 22,000 feet, and waited below in the sun for any straggling enemy aircraft. After patrolling for 30 minutes, I saw an Me109 proceeding very fast. To overhaul him I had to press my emergency boost, which produced an indicated airspeed of 345 mph; I caught the enemy off Shoeburyness. I opened fire at close range and fired all my ammunition, until the enemy aircraft streamed with smoke and pancaked on the mudflats at Shoeburyness.

The Me109 that Pilot Officer Berry had shot down belonged to 3/JG3 and was flown by Oberleutnant Rau who was captured.

No.54 Squadron, who had been caught earlier in the day by the first raid, claimed several enemy successes during this engagement. Pilot Officer Colin Gray encountered enemy fighters over Maidstone, Kent at 6.40 pm:

I was on patrol over Maidstone at 28,000 feet when I sighted some fighters behind and below me. I then saw approximately 30 enemy bombers, in Vic formations of three, going west at 15,000 feet. I followed Red Section and attacked the bombers from the front and above, firing a good burst at the leading enemy section. I then pulled up to 20,000 feet and engaged an Me109, giving it short bursts with deflection at close range. I observed a stream of glycol and followed the aircraft down, firing as I went. The enemy aircraft force-landed two miles north of Headcorn, which is ten to twelve miles south-east of Maidstone.

Colin Gray's victim had been Oberleutnant Fronhoefer of JG26, who landed his stricken aircraft at Jubilee Hall Farm, Ulcombe, and was captured by the local Home Guard.

The courage and dedication of the RAF fighter pilots during the Battle of Britain goes without saying, but down on the airfield there was also the bravery and hard work of the unsung ground crews, who kept the aircraft re-fuelled and re-armed, sometimes under enemy attack.

Iain Hutchinson, a Sergeant pilot with No.222 (Natal) Squadron while at Hornchurch, had this to say of their ground crews:

The airfield was under attack and chunks of shrapnel were raining down on the airfield. When I taxied towards the dispersal no one was to be seen; they were all in the air-raid shelters taking cover. Before I rolled to a halt and cut the engine, 'B' Flight ground crew, under their flight sergeant, were swarming around my Spitfire; the bowser was racing out to refuel the aircraft, while the armament men, laden with ammunition, were reloading the guns. The noise from the explosions going on around us was terrifying, but not one of those magnificent men faltered for a moment in their tasks. I was frankly relieved to be taking off again.

Joe Crawshaw was an airframe rigger with No.222 Squadron. He recalls his fellow ground crew servicing the Spitfires coming in after combat on 31st August.

I certainly recall that before the air-raid all-clear had sounded, some of our aircraft had come back on to the airfield, managing to avoid the bomb craters; but one or two of them had stopped suddenly in the middle of the runway, having run out of fuel. A corporal and myself jumped into a van; one of us grabbed some rope, and went out on to the airfield to tow these aircraft away, which hopefully left more space for others to land. There were some casualties that day, just near our dispersal; there was a truck standing near the perimeter track, which appeared to be abandoned, but when we looked, the men inside were dead.

In fact, I managed unofficially to take a few photographs on the next day, September 1st, with a 35 mm Agfa Karat camera that I possessed at that time. The photographs showed some of the damage to our squadron's aircraft caused by the previous day's raid.

In between the raids and the squadron sorties, the Station Commander, Group Captain Cecil Bouchier, had been busy organising ground staff to help keep the airfield operational. Every person who was not already busy with important work was mustered onto the flight path, given a shovel and told to help fill in the craters caused by the bombing; this was also done with the help of a traction steam engine roller which flattened any large uneven surfaces. There was no real time for anybody to have a proper meal, so the NAAFI wagon was very busy supplying tea and sandwiches etc, the station personnel taking it in turns to get food and refreshment throughout the day.

By the late evening of the 31st, the squadrons were stood down after one of the most hectic days in the history of RAF Hornchurch. The aircraft and pilot casualties for the day for No.54 Squadron was: four aircraft destroyed during an air raid on the airfield, and only one Spitfire shot down during combat; this was flown by Sergeant D.G. Gibbins. He baled out unhurt from Spitfire X4054 which crashed at Hildenborough at 7.28 pm. No pilots were lost.

No.222 Squadron had two aircraft destroyed during this raid, including one Spitfire P9337 shot down by Me109s over Ashford, Kent. Pilot Officer G.G.A. Davies baled out, burned, but survived. A Spitfire N3233, piloted by Flight Lieutenant A. Robinson, was damaged in combat with 109s but he landed at Eastchurch slightly wounded; the aircraft was repairable. One of No.222 ground crew was killed during the second raid. No pilots were lost.

No.603 Squadron had two aircraft destroyed while in combat. Spitfire X4273 was shot down over Ilford at 6.30 pm; Flying Officer R.M. Waterston was killed when the aircraft crashed at Repository Road, Woolwich. Spitfire X4271 was also shot down in flames, its pilot Pilot Officer George Gilroy baling out, wounded from shell splinters. He landed and was attacked by civilians who mistook him for a German parachutist; fortunately a woman bus conductress intervened, recognising his RAF uniform. Afterwards he was taken to the King George V Hospital at Ilford for treatment. His aircraft crashed onto a house, No 14 Hereford Road, Wanstead, but the only casualty was a dog. The Mayor of Dagenham was so appalled after hearing of the incident, that he visited Gilroy in hospital and handed him a cheque for ten pounds. Thereafter, when Gilroy shot down an enemy aeroplane, he would buy a round of drinks for his fellow pilots, telling them that they were 'On the Mayor of Dagenham'.

Spitfire R6835 flown by Flying Officer Brian Carbury was damaged in combat, and he was slightly wounded, but he successfully returned back to base. The total 603 Squadron casualties, were one pilot lost.

The 1st September was very quiet compared with the previous few days' excitement at Hornchurch. But nevertheless the Luftwaffe put up a strong force of aircraft to attack the airfields at Biggin Hill, Detling, and Eastchurch, and the docks at Tilbury. These raids started at 10.15 am and continued throughout the day.

Back at Hornchurch later, at 10.23 am, Squadron Leader Johnnie Hill led eleven aircraft of No.222 Squadron on a patrol over Canterbury and the Manston area, after which they were to fly to Rochford. But at 11 am they encountered Me109s who were seen making their way back across the Channel. Squadron Leader Hill recalls:

> I was flying at about 17,000 feet, when I spotted two Me109s in company, making for France. I dived down behind the right hand one and put a long burst of fire into him from about one hundred yards range. It burst into flames and I saw it diving towards the ground.

Also in action this day was Pilot Officer John 'Chips' Carpenter; he was flying with 'B' Flight during the encounter and the account from his combat report reads:

> On September 1st 1940, 222 Squadron were patrolling over Manston Aerodrome when we ran into Me109 fighters. I failed to engage one but, while returning to base, I came out of cloud in the middle of enemy fighters. Using cloud as cover I attacked one 109 fighter at a hundred yards range. Immediately I opened fire the 109 burst into flames; I continued firing until my guns stopped due to a separated case. I then dived away to a lower height, from where I noticed a plume of white smoke descending to the ground; I took this to be the 109. I had a camera gun in my machine which will confirm my report.

A third wave of bombers was plotted on radar in mid afternoon, and No.603 Squadron was sent up from Hornchurch to deal with the threat, along with other squadrons in No.11 Group. Sergeant Pilot Jack Stokoe, a 20-year-old from West Cornforth, County Durham, was the only member of the squadron to claim an aircraft destroyed that day. While over Manston at 12,000 feet, No.603 was told that Canterbury was being bombed. Jack Stokoe recalls:

> We were about three miles south of the town, when at 3,000 feet a Messerschmitt 109E painted silver with large black crosses, went past my nose, flattened out at about fifty feet above me and headed south. I executed a steep turn, pushed

my boost into override and sat on his tail. At about fifty yards from him, I gave him a one second burst with little effect, and then closed to thirty yards to give him a slightly longer burst of fire. Black smoke poured from him as I overshot. The aircraft crashed in a field, turned over two or three times, and then burst into flames against a clump of trees.

The only casualty for No.603 that day was a Spitfire L1020 flown by Pilot Officer Philip 'Pip' Cardell, who during a routine flight, suffered mechanical problems and was forced to crash-land the aircraft. This was written off in the process, though fortunately the pilot was unhurt.

The weather was very good; it continued to be fine and very warm, which was ideal for the Luftwaffe. On 2nd September, the Germans would launch over 900 aircraft sorties; they hoped that these would finally stretch the RAF fighters of No.11 Group to breaking point.

Pilot Officer Gerald 'Stapme' Stapleton of No.603 Squadron hailed from South Africa, and had joined the RAF on a short service commission in January 1939. He recalls that summer of 1940 while at Hornchurch:

It became a routine. We'd get up about 4 am; this was one of the best summers Britain had ever known. Out we'd go and have breakfast in the Officers' Mess, and then afterwards sit around down at dispersal. Then we would go on an early morning patrol, if there was any activity over the Channel and over France. We would patrol over Maidstone at 15,000 feet; we found that patrolling over Maidstone was not really economical, because we would run out of petrol if the enemy came over later. So the radar plots of aircraft over France or the Channel had to be fairly positive, before they would put us up on to a patrol. In between sorties we would entertain ourselves in all sorts of ways; some chaps would play chess, others would do crosswords or read magazines. When you were on five minutes readiness to take off, you would always have butterflies in your stomach until you got into your aeroplane. We use to sit around in a Nissen hut, and you could get into your aircraft from there in about a minute; that's how close we were to the aircraft. Our CO 'Uncle' George Denholm would always get his aircraft going long before us, but we found out his secret; he never strapped himself in before taking off. He just jumped in, started up, and moved into position for taking off; then he'd strap on his parachute and Sutton harness while we were catching him up on the ground.

The feeling once you were in the air, for me, was one of excitement; I suppose these days you would call it a rush of adrenalin.

The German formations were picked up on radar over Cap Gris Nez, stacked up to 20,000 feet; the raids were headed for Rochford, North Weald, Biggin Hill and Eastchurch. At 7.30 am No. 603 Squadron was scrambled from Hornchurch, and became involved in combats against fierce opposition from the German fighter escorts.

Sergeant Pilot Jack Stokoe has cause to remember this engagement in, what for him, was going to be a day full of unforeseen circumstances. He had encountered a formation of Dornier 17s and Me110s over Hawkinge at 8.15 am:

> I was attacking an Me110 and saw some of my bullets striking it. Then, either from that aircraft or some other, (there were a lot of aircraft around at the time) a bullet hit the hood of my cockpit and shattered it. This sent Perspex splinters into one of my hands slightly damaging it, but it was nothing too serious. I landed back at Hornchurch on that occasion without a hood.

Pilot Officers Berry, Hillary, and Haig all claimed successes against Me109s, as did Flying Officer Carbury.

At first light Squadron Leader James Leathart led No.54 Squadron down to operate from Rochford. They were scrambled and told to patrol over Kent. At about 8 am they were engaged in combat with Me109s of 1/JG51; the squadron claimed two of the enemy fighters destroyed for no loss to themselves.

Squadron Leader 'Prof' Leathart shot down an Me109 which crashed in flames near Leeds Castle, Maidstone, its pilot Leutnant Thoerl baled out and was captured. Another was shot down by Pilot Officer George Gribble, and crashed at Womanswold near Barnham; the pilot Leutnant Ruettowski was killed.

Nine Spitfires of No.222 Squadron were airborne at 8.38 am, to patrol over Chatham, Hawkinge and Manston, but did not encounter any aircraft. They then flew down to Rochford airfield. At midday, a German formation of 250-plus was picked up heading for the Isle of Sheppey and the Thames Estuary.

No.603 Squadron were scrambled again at 12.08 pm, and were involved in various skirmishes with bombers and their escorts. Flight Lieutenant William 'Rusty' Rushmer claimed a Dornier 17 destroyed. Two Me109s were shot down by Pilot Officer Richard Hillary and Pilot Officer 'Black' Morton, but Pilot Officer J. Haig was forced to break off combat due to damage sustained to his aircraft; he landed wheels-up back at Hornchurch and was unhurt.

The squadron were scrambled again for a third time at 4.04 pm; they were vectored to intercept a raid which was near Dungeness. Again Pilot Officer Hillary claimed another victory, shooting down a 109; Pilot Officer Stewart-Clarke also claimed a 109. Sergeant Pilot Jack Stokoe was again in action during this raid, flying his Spitfire N3056; he remembers the action and what happened next:

On that occasion I was attacking an enemy aircraft. I remember either bullets or cannon shells hitting my Spitfire, followed by flames in the cockpit, where my petrol tank in front of me had been hit. I thought, 'I've got to get out of here,' because you don't hang around when there's fire around. I undid my straps and opened the canopy, which unfortunately made things worse, causing a forced draft of air and pushing flames into the cockpit; it felt like being in front of a builder's blow-torch. Because we had a hurried scramble from Hornchurch, I was not wearing my gloves at the time, but I had to put my hands back into the flames to the control column to be able to turn the aircraft on to its side, so that I could just drop out. I remember as I put my hand back, I could see sheets of skin just peeling off of my hand like tissue paper. The side of my face and hair were also burnt, but not severely. I was a bit concerned after getting out of the aircraft, that my parachute might not function, as it too had been in the cockpit which was aflame. I pulled the ripcord and it opened, and I landed in a field. Almost immediately the Home Guard, strangely enough, appeared on the scene; they started to query my identity and consider whether I might be an enemy spy. But a few choice words in English soon convinced them I was genuine. Thereafter I was rushed to Leeds Castle, which was being used as an emergency hospital, and treated for burns to my hands, face etc. For four days I was actually listed as 'missing in action'. I spent the next six weeks in hospital before returning to operational duties.

While returning from their last patrol of the day, No.222 Squadron ran into German bombers that had just bombed the edge of Hornchurch airfield. They had dropped their bombs, but only six had actually hit the airfield, causing slight damage and fortunately no casualties. The squadron attacked the homeward-bound formation and Flight Lieutenant Andrew Robinson claimed an Me109 destroyed, as well as damaging a Heinkel 111. He was himself attacked and forced to crash-land at Hornchurch airfield, after his aircraft was hit in the petrol tank. Robinson was wounded in the leg.

An Me110 was destroyed and a Dornier 17 damaged by Sergeant Sidney 'Clot' Baxter; a Dornier was damaged by Sergeant Ernie Scott and another Me110 by Sergeant Douglas Chipping. Two other Spitfires of No.222 were damaged in combat, but were repairable.

Throughout this intensive three-week period, when the Luftwaffe tried to destroy No.11 Group's Fighter airfields and squadrons day after day, the strain on the pilots was enormous, and daily they grew more tired and weary. Cecil 'Boy' Bouchier remembers the strain on his men, but also the part played in keeping up their spirit by the station chef.

The long summer days provided very short hours of sleep

available to them, and they had to spend long hours of daylight on the airfield at dispersal. The constant flying at high altitudes, squadrons being called upon daily to do five or six sorties, with the constant strain of combat plus the loss of close friends. All these things took their toll, and were of heartfelt concern to me.

The strain could be seen on many of the faces, a weariness so complete that on occasion I found a young pilot too tired even to eat. Fortunately throughout the Battle of Britain we had at Hornchurch a splendid Officers' Mess, good food, and 'Freddie' our magnificent Mess chef.

From mid-day onwards each day, Freddie, dressed in immaculate white coat, trousers, apron and a tall starched chef's hat almost two feet high on his head, would preside at a long side table, on which large dishes of roast sirloin of beef, vegetables etc would be laid out. On more than one occasion I would be behind a weary young pilot at Freddie's table, and I would see the young pilot hesitate, and slowly shake his head as if he had no appetite for food. Seeing this Freddie with deep concern, would bend down towards the youngster and say, 'Come on, young Sir, you must keep your pecker up, you know. Let me cut you a nice slice of this lovely roast beef with a little bit of crisp brown fat.' The pilot would smile up at him, and reach out for a hot plate to take to him. Freddie's obvious admiration and affection for 'his pilots' as he called them, was always very touching, and we loved him for it.

Tuesday, 3rd September started hazy, but soon developed into fine and warm weather, although further north there was some cloud and drizzle. The Luftwaffe targets arranged for this day were again to be airfields in the south-east; also Liverpool and small raids over South Wales.

The first raid, consisting of around 50 Dorniers and 80 Me110s, headed up the Thames estuary at 20,000 feet. The Operations Rooms at Hornchurch, North Weald and HQ No.11 Group waited to see where this formation might break off its course, and what its target would be. At 9.45 am the Germans had already made their move and headed towards North Weald; because of the last minute change of direction, some of the operations controllers were caught out, and British fighters were sent off too late. North Weald was severely damaged, the Germans dropping over 200 bombs, some with time-delayed fuses. The operations block was hit and there was damage to two of the hangars and main stores; two ground personnel were killed and several were injured.

The three squadrons from Hornchurch were ordered up to intercept the raiders. No.54 Squadron engaged the raid returning from North Weald, a few miles east of Hornchurch at 13,000 feet. They attacked the tail end of the German fighter escort, which consisted of about a dozen Me110s and some 109s, who were busy trying to avoid the heavy ack-ack barrage that was being thrown up from batteries near the Thames.

The Spitfires of No.54 went into attack, but only Pilot Officer Colin Gray claimed an Me109 destroyed, while Pilot Officer Baker claimed a half share of an Me110; Pilot Officer McMullen claimed an Me110 damaged, and Squadron Leader Leathart a 109 damaged.

No.222 was ordered to patrol over Hornchurch at 20,000 feet. They also met the enemy, a formation of Dorniers with their escort of 30 Me110s flying at 5,000 feet below 222 Squadron. Squadron Leader Hill led the squadron down to attack the formation which had formed itself into a defensive circle, but he managed to hit one of the Me110s; this turned out of formation and dived out of control. Pilot Officer Tim Vigors also destroyed a Me110 and damaged another; his combat report for this action states:

> I dived with the squadron on twenty Me110s, opening fire at two hundred and fifty yards. I gave one of the enemy a four second burst. Both engines caught fire issuing black smoke and flames; the aircraft dived away from the formation. I then found myself in the middle of the 110 formation; I gave four further bursts at fifty yards range to separate the 110s. I noticed that the engine of one of these caught fire.

Sergeants Baxter and Scott also claimed an Me110 and Dornier 17 destroyed. In 'B' Flight Pilot Officer 'Chips' Carpenter and Flying Officer Brian Van Metz each claimed an Me110 destroyed, and Sergeant Iain Hutchinson an Me110 damaged.

No.603 Squadron, which had been scrambled at 9.15 am, was bounced by a Staffel of Me109s at 20,000 feet, while they were about to attack a formation of Dorniers over Manston. Pilot Officer 'Stapme' Stapleton managed to claim a Dornier 17 bomber and Pilot Officer J.R. Caister and Pilot Officer Peter Pease an Me109 each.

Pilot Officer Richard Hillary in Spitfire X4277 was also to claim an Me109, but he was shot down in flames almost immediately at 10.04 am, just off Margate, by a German fighter coming in on his tail. His combat report of this action was written after he had spent many months in hospital, recovering from severe burns to his face and hands:

> I took off with the rest of the Squadron in a Spitfire that was suffering from a damaged hood; there was difficulty in opening and closing it. Twenty miles east of Margate, we sighted thirty Me109s 1,000 feet above our level, and coming straight for us. They came down and we split up. I climbed and from slightly below and to starboard, opened fire with a three-second burst on a 109 at three hundred yards range, closing to one hundred and fifty yards. Bits came off, but he did not go down. I continued to fire in line astern, giving him a burst of four seconds as I did so. He took no evasive action, burst into flames and spun into the sea. I was then hit from astern by an

incendiary bullet. The cockpit caught fire but I could not open the hood and passed out with the heat. When I came to, I was free of the aircraft, and pulled my chute to come down in the sea.

Hillary was now very badly burned and drifting in the water off Margate; he was rescued by the Margate lifeboat, the *J.B. Proudfoot*. He was to spend many months in the East Grinstead Hospital, in the Burns Unit, under the care of the pioneering plastic surgeon Archibald McIndoe. Later, while recovering from his injuries, he would write the book *The Last Enemy*, which would become a classic, describing his memories of that time at Hornchurch during the Battle of Britain.

Pilot Officer Dudley Stewart-Clark, in Spitfire X4185, was also shot down by a Messerschmitt 109 of II/JG26 piloted by Hauptmann Erich Bode, at 10.08 am, just four minutes after Hillary had been shot down. Stewart-Clark baled out wounded, landed, and was admitted to Chelmsford Hospital for treatment.

The only other Hornchurch aircraft loss that day had been during early morning, and this was not due to enemy action. Sergeant Pilot Reginald Johnson, flying Spitfire L1010, was on a routine patrol, when his aircraft developed a glycol leak; he had to abandon the aircraft at about 7.30 am. The Spitfire crashed at Lower Raypits, Canewdon, Essex and Sergeant Johnson was slightly injured.

By the end of the day, No.54 Squadron had received orders to go back up to Catterick for a rest period, while in return No.41 Squadron came down to take their place. The Station Diary records the departure of No.54 Squadron.

In the late afternoon, 54 Squadron left us for a period of rest and recuperation at Catterick. During the previous fortnight, they had been bearing the brunt of the work in the Sector, for they had to hold the fort, while various new squadrons arrived and settled down into the Sector routine. With the exception of two very short breaks, they had been with us continuously during the first year of the war, and in this period had destroyed ninety-two enemy aircraft.

Also that day, Flight Lieutenant George Gribble of No.54 Squadron was presented to His Majesty King George VI at Buckingham Palace to receive his Distinguished Flying Cross.

On 4th September, No.222 Squadron started their first patrol of the day over the Canterbury area at 9 am, but there was no enemy activity to be found, and they returned to Rochford. They were scrambled again at 12.35 pm to intercept a hostile raid approaching from the south. While at 27,000 feet they sighted a formation of 15 Me109s at 7,000 feet below and dived to attack. In the ensuing combat two Me109s were destroyed and three probably destroyed; but 222 Squadron had also paid dearly. Flying Officer John 'Comic' Cutts had been shot down and killed, crashing at Amerfield

Farm, Chart Sutton. So was Sergeant John Ramshaw, who crashed at Mockbeggar, near Yalding. He was carried from the wreckage of his aircraft, but died on the way to hospital. Aged 24 years, he had lasted only five days in front line service with the squadron.

The other casualty was Pilot Officer John 'Chips' Carpenter, who believes he was a victim of friendly fire from the ground defences whilst attacking an Me109. He remembers:

> There were dots all over the sky and getting nearer these turned out to be Me109s. I chased after two or three of them in the distance, when all of a sudden my machine disintegrated around me; one second I was in the cockpit, the next I was feeling around to see if I still had a parachute. Luckily, although I couldn't see anything because my eyes were blinded by the slipstream, the parachute opened and I landed in a tree. I was then carted off to hospital; it was just a lucky escape I suppose.

Finally, No.222 Squadron received a signal from H.Q No.11 Group. This read:

> 4th September: Telex to Hornchurch. Pass to 222 Squadron, Repeat 11 Group, Repeat Fighter Command:
> Following from Chief of Air Staff – Well done in your hard fighting yesterday. Keep it up

No.222 Squadron were put up on patrol at 9.45 am on 5th September, and later in the day at 2.20 pm; but at neither time did they see or engage any enemy aircraft. They were operating from the satellite airfield at Rochford when, at 3 pm, they were caught on the ground, as an enemy raid started to attack the airfield. They managed to get all their aircraft airborne without loss, and proceeded to go after the enemy formation. Catching up with them Sergeant Ernest Scott attacked, and claimed to have probably destroyed one Me109 and one Me110; Sergeant Pilot Douglas Chipping destroyed an Me110, before he himself was shot down by fire from our own ground defences. He was wounded, but was able to bale out; his Spitfire X4057 crashed to the ground at Pineham.

No.41 Squadron had flown down to Manston during the early morning. At 9.40 am they engaged two formations of Dornier 17s at 16,000 feet, escorted by at least 50 Me109s at various heights up to 22,000 feet. Squadron Leader Hilary 'Robin' Hood led Green and Blue Sections down to attack the bombers, while Flight Lieutenant Norman Ryder was ordered to keep 'A' Flight up above, to protect the attacking Spitfires from the 109s. Squadron Leader Hood, who had attacked a Dornier 17, was forced to break off his attack after his engine began to suffer from mechanical problems; he managed to return to Hornchurch. During this action the squadron suffered their first aircraft loss at 10.20 am; Sergeant Pilot Robert Carr-Lewty in Spitfire N3098 was hit by enemy fire, and had to force-land his aircraft at Stanford-le-Hope in Essex. He remembers:

I had dropped the idea of gliding to my home airfield at Hornchurch, because I might overload the R/T channels which other less experienced pilots, also in need of help, might need; I decided to go it alone. I did not want to risk baling out over Essex, because of the dangers of an abandoned aircraft swooping down out of control on to a village; so I decided to look for a suitable field. I spotted a small triangular field that sloped upwards from its base, the base being a hedge with a haystack in the left hand corner and a five-barred gate.

I had enough height in hand to make a descending turn around the field for a final inspection, and managed to lower the wheels. I came into land at 75 mph, missed the haystack as planned by about a wingspan, and passed about three feet over the gate; I touched down about 20 to 30 yards into the field, pointing up the slope. Unfortunately, on touching down the undercarriage collapsed, the Spitfire skidded straight on for a further 70 to 80 yards, but luckily did not catch fire. I hopped out as soon as I came to my ignominious halt, and was quickly surrounded by the friendly people of Corringham, who refreshed and resuscitated me with their treasured bottles of drink. I then put the aircraft into the custody of the local police, and I was driven off by a Dr Pat Daly to his surgery in Stanford. Later an RAF corporal and three men were sent to guard the plane. They too were supplied with cups of tea and cigarettes by the local residents.

After the fighting, No.41 claimed the following enemy aircraft; Flying Officer Boyle one Me109 destroyed, Flight Lieutenant Webster one Me109 destroyed, Flight Lieutenant Ryder, Pilot Officer Bennions and Sergeant Carr-Lewty, one Me109 probable each.

No.603 Squadron were also involved in combat that morning over Kent. Taking off from Hornchurch at 9.43 am, and led by Squadron Leader 'Uncle' George Denholm, they engaged a raid over Biggin Hill at about 10 am; they were involved in dogfights at 20,000 feet with escorting Me109s, who were covering a formation of Dornier 17s. After the fighting, two enemy aircraft were claimed to have been destroyed, an Me109 by Pilot Officer Morton and another by Pilot Officer Gerald Stapleton.

Gerald Stapleton's Me109 has an interesting story related to it, as its pilot was Oberleutnant Franz von Werra. He was to gain fame later as the only German prisoner of war to escape from captivity, albeit from Canada, where he was sent to spend his time until the war ended. A book and film of his escape were made in the 1950s, titled *The One That Got Away*. Gerald Stapleton now retells the shooting down of von Werra:

I had just broken away from combat and was at about 6,000

feet, when I noticed a pilot coming down by parachute; he was being circled by an Me109. I didn't know who he was at the time, but later found out it was Pilot Officer William 'Robin' Rafter who had baled out. I don't know if it was von Werra flying around Rafter, because as soon as I made an appearance he flew off. A few seconds later I came across another 109; he dived straight down for the ground, and started a low-level trip heading back to France. I caught up with him, and I got a fright when he flew low over a village when I was firing at him; I don't know where all my bullets finished up, but they must have been very close to that village. He eventually crash-landed; the pilot got out and he was waving at me, so I waggled my wings at him. I felt a darned fool when I realised that he had dipped his Schwimmweste (German lifejacket) into a petrol tank, and was waving this thing about trying to set his aircraft alight. I later found out that this was Franz von Werra.

Franz von Werra, who was flying with Stab II/JG3, had force-landed at Winchet Hill, Loves Farm, Marden, Kent. Pilot Officer Rafter, who had been descending by parachute at the time, landed and was taken to the local first aid post. He was then sent to the West Kent Hospital at Maidstone, where he was treated for shrapnel wounds to the right leg. He did not return to the squadron at Hornchurch until 7th November.

The only other casualty from this engagement was the sad death of Flight Lieutenant William Frederick Rushmer, who failed to return from combat. His Spitfire X4261 crashed at Buckman's Green Farm, Smarden at 10.00 am. His body was laid to rest at All Saints Churchyard, Staplehurst, but his gravestone read only 'unknown airman'. This was due to the absence of formal identification and identity discs on the body; also there was a mix-up in RAF records of two Spitfires crashing in the same area that day.

He had been a very good and popular flight commander with 603 Squadron, and had been nicknamed 'Rusty' because of his darkish red hair. At 30, he was a lot older than the average pilots in the Squadron, but he would help out the younger pilots with any difficulties if he could. On 6th September 1998, 58 years later, a new headstone was re-dedicated to William Rushmer. This was achieved, after many years of campaigning, by local resident Mrs Jean Liddicoat, who had tended Rusty's grave for many years. She finally persuaded the MOD and others to recognise that this was indeed the last resting place of Rusty Rushmer.

A service was held at All Saints Church, Staplehurst, and was attended by relatives of the pilot, along with veterans of No.603 Squadron and represen-tatives of the RAF. It concluded with a flypast by aircraft of the Battle of Britain Memorial Flight. A final fitting tribute to one of the Hornchurch Few!

At 3 pm No.41 Squadron were again heavily involved with a large formation of Heinkel and Junker Ju88 bombers over the Thames estuary at a height of 15,000 feet.

As the squadron went into line astern, turning the aircraft into a head-on attack, they were bounced on from above by the Me109 escort. Tragedy struck, as 'B' Flight broke to avoid the enemy fighters. Squadron Leader 'Robin' Hood and Flight Lieutenant John Webster collided with each other. Squadron Leader Hood's Spitfire P9428 disintegrated over Wickford; his body was never recovered. Flight Lieutenant Webster managed to bale out, but he was killed, as his parachute failed to open; his aircraft R6635 crashed in flames opposite Markham Chase School, Laindon, Essex.

Pilot Officer 'Wally' Wallens baled out badly wounded, after he was hit in the thigh by a cannon shell; his damaged aircraft, Spitfire X4021, crashed near Nevendon Hall, and he landed at Rawreth, Essex. He did not return to operational duties until April 1941.

Flying Officer Tony 'Lulu' Lovell was also shot down; he baled out unhurt, his aircraft crashing at South Benfleet. The only other casualty from this disastrous engagement was Pilot Officer Eric Lock, who after shooting down a Heinkel 111 into the sea, and while attacking another, failed to see an Me109 closing into attack. The Me109 gave a burst of fire, which damaged Lock's Spitfire, and slightly wounded Lock in the leg. When the German aircraft turned to break away it presented Lock with a perfect target; his machine gun fire caused the 109 to explode. Pilot Officer Lock returned to Hornchurch and landed his damaged aircraft N3162. In his combat report for that action, Eric Lock states:

> I was Red 2 flying in formation with the rest of the squadron, when we intercepted a formation of enemy aircraft; we attacked the bombers first. After we engaged we broke away to port, and then I saw Red 1 shoot down an Me109 which exploded in mid-air. It then developed into a dogfight. I then attacked an enemy Heinkel 111 which crashed into the river and I followed it down.
>
> I climbed back to 8,000 feet and saw another Heinkel, which had left the main formation. I attacked and set his starboard engine on fire. I closed in to about 75 yards and after two long bursts, smoke began to emerge from the fuselage.
>
> The enemy aircraft then put his wheels down and started to glide; I stopped firing and followed him down. I was then attacked by an Me109 who fired at me from below, wounding me in the leg. As he banked away he stalled turned; I fired at him and he exploded in mid-air.
>
> I then followed the bomber down; it landed on the sea about ten miles from the first one in the mouth of the river. I circled around a boat which was at hand. I also flashed my downward light, and saw the boat go to the enemy aircraft. I was then joined by Red 3; on our return up river we saw the first bomber still floating, and a small rubber dinghy.

The squadron's tally was increased by Pilot Officer Wallens, Pilot Officer Morrough-Ryan and Flight Lieutenant Ryder who each claimed one Me109 destroyed; Pilot Officer Bennions claimed one Ju88 destroyed and one damaged, and Sergeant Ford an Me109 probable.

Friday 6th September: No.11 Group under the command of Air Vice-Marshal Keith Park, had received orders to maintain patrols over all aircraft factories which might come under attack. German orders that day had target listings for raids on the Hawker Aircraft works at Brooklands, Surrey, amongst others.

During the morning No.41 Squadron sent twelve Spitfires up on patrol. While on this patrol Pilot Officer Eric Lock suffered from lack of oxygen and passed out while at an altitude of 20,000 feet. Luckily he regained consciousness at 8,000 feet and pulled the Spitfire out of its fall. While continuing on his own, he encountered a Junkers Ju88 over the Channel and proceeded to shoot it down.

No.222 Squadron were ordered up to patrol twice that day, without any engagements. Not until their last patrol at 5.30 pm did they encounter enemy aircraft, a large formation of Me109s near Hawkinge, Kent, at around 15,000 feet. Two of the enemy fighters were claimed as destroyed; one by Pilot Officer Tim Vigors, which forced-landed at Vincents Farm near Manston airfield. The other shot down by Sergeant Iain Hutchinson, which crashed at Plumtree Farm, Headcorn. Both enemy pilots baled out and were captured.

During an engagement with fighters of I/JG54 over the Channel at 1.30 pm, Pilot Officer J.R. Caister, flying his Spitfire X4260, was attacked by an Me109 flown by Hauptmann von Bonin, who damaged Caister's aircraft. He was forced to land his aircraft in France, on the wrong side of the Channel, and was captured.

After their morning patrol, eight aircraft of No.41 Squadron were sent down to Rochford, led by Flight Lieutenant Norman Ryder. They were put up on patrol at 5.35 pm and encountered large groups of Me109s over the Thames Estuary. During this combat Flight Lieutenant Ryder shot down an Me109 which crashed into the sea just off Southend pier.

Flying Officers MacKenzie and Lovell claimed an Me109 destroyed each, while Flying Officer Scott and Sergeant Darling claimed an Me109 probable each. Pilot Officer 'Ben' Bennions was successful again; he claimed two enemy fighters destroyed.

During the evening an ENSA party was held in the workshops at 8 pm. This ended a little hurriedly when flares were dropped over the aerodrome, and the 4.5 ack-ack battery opened fire. Shrapnel pattered down on the top of the glass roof, and although the lights went out, the show went on to the end.

No.600 Squadron were sent up that evening, as their Squadron Operations Diary records:

> Three patrols took off, but no interception of enemy aircraft was made. Enemy dropped parachute flares above aerodrome which were extinguished with gunfire. Bombs dropped and one house bordering the Station was set on fire. F/Lt Clackson had a blip on the A.I. radar, but failed to catch enemy aircraft.

CHAPTER 7

THE TURNING OF THE TIDE
7th September – 31st October

7th September 1940: First Luftwaffe massed bombing raids on London by day and night, the City of London is set on fire, acting as a beacon for the enemy night bombers.

Commander of the Luftwaffe, Reichsmarschall Hermann Göring, had arrived at Pas de Calais on 7th September, in order to witness the change of operations, which Hitler had ordered. He was outraged at the bombing by the RAF on Berlin, a few nights earlier. Hitler's order directed Göring to switch from bombing the RAF airfields, to attacking London. When this happened, it was to catch out many of the RAF fighter squadrons, which were in the wrong position to intercept the incoming raids.

At 3.50 pm a Blenheim of No.600 (City of London) Squadron was destroyed, when it crashed during its landing approach to the airfield; its port engine failed and the aircraft turned over onto its back at 200 feet, crashing at East Close, Rainham. The two crewmen, Sergeants A.F. Saunders and J.W. Davies, were killed.

Squadrons from Hornchurch were not scrambled until the afternoon, when Operations received confirmation of the biggest raid yet, then developing over Calais. Consisting of over 300 bombers and 600 fighters, it covered an airspace more than 20 miles long; the first wave flew straight up towards the Thames estuary, heading for London.

Both No.222 and No.603 Squadrons were scrambled at 4.50 pm, and No.41 at 4.55 pm. During the following enemy engagements, all three squadrons had successes against the bombers and fighters; the following combat reports by the pilots on this day, show the courage of these men, in face of such large enemy numbers.

Sergeant Ernest Scott, 'A' Flight 222 Squadron, 17.45 hrs:

> I was flying behind the S/Ldr in line astern, when we dived to attack a formation of thirty bombers. I picked a bomber, which looked like an Me110 and commenced firing with a beam to astern attack. I opened fire at three hundred yards and closed until I had difficulty in avoiding the bomber's tail. My ammunition was completely exhausted and before breaking away, I saw the machine dive with its port engine in flames; I

did not see the machine crash. On returning to base to refuel and re-arm, a group of airmen said they had seen a bomber dive towards the ground, until it disappeared from their view, in the district where I had attacked it. This engagement took place over the southeast of London. I observed no fire from the Me110, and believe the rear-gunner had been put out of action.

Sergeant Rainford Marland, 'A' Flight 222 Squadron, 18.00 hrs:

On the afternoon of the 7th September at approx 18.00 hrs, I was on patrol with 222 Squadron, when we sighted and attacked a formation of enemy bombers. 222 Squadron were patrolling at 29,000 feet and the bombers were approx 5,000 feet below us. I was at the tail end of the line astern formation and as I went down, I saw Me109s coming into attack me. I therefore turned off and regained height. When I saw one Me109 below me, I dived to attack him and closed to approx 400 yards at 17,000 feet. We were then southeast of Thameshaven, and flying due east towards the sea. I opened fire at 400 yards and closed to about 150 yards, firing bursts all the time. I followed the enemy machine down to approx 9,000 feet, when I had to break away as I was attacked by Me109s. As I broke away, the enemy machine was going straight down in the sea, and volumes of black smoke were trailing behind him. The Me109 which I attacked, had a yellow nose and wing tips. After my first burst of fire, no evasive action was taken by the enemy.

During the action, 222 Squadron claimed six enemy aircraft destroyed and five probables; the squadron suffered no casualties. Two aircraft were damaged, including that of Flying Officer Brian van Mentz, whose aircraft was hit in the glycol system; he returned to base. Sergeant Pilot John Burgess force-landed at Sutton Valence, near Maidstone, following combat; he too was unhurt, and his aircraft repairable.

No.603 suffered no pilot casualties, but three aircraft were damaged and one destroyed. Pilot Officer Peter Pease belly-landed his aircraft, Spitfire L1057 back at Hornchurch. Squadron Leader George Denholm also had to force-land back at base, after his aircraft X4250 had been hit in the main plane by a cannon shell. Sergeant Pilot A.R. Sarre in Spitfire P9467 was slightly wounded, being shot down over the Thames at 5.30 pm; his aircraft was written-off. Pilot Officer Gerald 'Stapme' Stapleton, had to make a forced landing at Sutton Valence. He now recalls the event.

I remember it very well. We'd been in action and were reforming just north of London; we didn't have our rearguard aircraft weaving behind us. It was also the day Peter Pease was hit. A cannon shell hit between my number two and three guns, on my starboard wing, and laid them flat; the ammunition was trailing over the wing. I had no aileron control and as soon as I opened up the throttle, the glycol fumes came into my cockpit. The first thing I did was to open the cockpit hood. I then tried to fly as straight as I could, until I saw a stubble field, which I aimed for. I did a flat turn on the rudder, overshot the stubble field and landed in a hop field; I landed with my wheels up of course. I 'torpedoed' across the hop field, and I was about two feet off the ground. Once I landed, I got out and there was a country lane close by. There was a family there having a picnic, and they offered me a cup of tea, which I gratefully accepted. They then offered me a lift in their Austin Ruby saloon.

No.41 Squadron claimed several enemy aircraft. Flying Officer W.J. Scott attacked an Me109, his bullets setting the aircraft on fire. Flying alongside the enemy aircraft, the German pilot signalled his surrender as if going to force-land; he was last seen flying at 200 feet near Dover. Sergeant John McAdam destroyed a Dornier 17, and he claimed another as probably destroyed. His aircraft had developed engine trouble, and he just managed to get the aircraft back to Hornchurch, making a forced-landing; the aircraft caught fire and was partly burnt out.

Another two No.41 Squadron pilots had to make forced-landings that day, due to damage sustained in combat. Sergeant Roy Ford landed his aircraft N3266 at West Hanningfield, Essex, and Pilot Officer Morrough-Ryan, his undercarriage wrecked, landed his aircraft X4318 at Great Wakering, Essex.

Despite the desperate fight put up by the British fighters, who had been caught out by the change of target, the German bombers succeeded in getting through to the East End of London, and dropped their bombs on targets from Thameshaven and Purfleet, to Millwall, Limehouse, and Silvertown until the whole of the docks area was alight. At 8 pm, the code word 'Cromwell' had been ordered; this for the services, meant that invasion was imminent. The church bells were rung, and roadblocks, manned by regular and Home Guard troops, were set up.

At Hornchurch, the local Home Guard patrolled the outskirts of the airfield, along with the detachment of Glasgow Highlanders, while the 33rd Canadian 'Rough Riders' Regiment operated the four Bofors guns around the airfield. Fortunately, they were not needed to act that night, and the order that the German invasion was imminent was rescinded. The bombing continued into the night, the glow of London set alight being seen for miles around; this also helped the German raiders to their target. By the morning, over 300 civilians were dead and nearly 1,500 were seriously injured.

The 8th September brought the prospect of the same level of attack by the Luftwaffe, but owing to a change in the weather and through fatigue, the Luftwaffe raids were very much reduced on this day. At Hornchurch at 12.20 pm, No.222 Squadron carried out their only patrol of the day, with no enemy sightings. No.41 Squadron were also sent up on patrol to cover the Dover area. It was during this sortie that one of the Spitfires, R6756 flown by Flying Officer W.J.Scott, was shot down in flames; sadly Scott was killed, presumably a victim of a surprise Me109 attack.

No.41 also received a new commanding officer, Squadron Leader Robert Lister, to replace 'Robin' Hood. Unfortunately the new CO lacked experience on fighter operations, and it was felt unfair to put him in the position of leading from the front; Flying Officer Tony Lovell was therefore promoted to stand in for about a month, until the new CO had settled in. That night, bombers of Luftflotte III again attacked London, with over 200 aircraft from 7.30 pm until dawn.

On 9th September, the Luftwaffe raids did not start until the afternoon. No.41 Squadron were scrambled at 4.44 pm when 12 Spitfires were told to patrol Maidstone. They engaged a large formation and combat was met. After the fighting No.41 claimed seven Me109s and one Heinkel 111 destroyed, and one Me109 and one Heinkel 111 damaged. No.222 were in action by 5 pm, between Maidstone and Ashford, at around 20,000 feet. After the engagement the squadron had claimed two Me109s, one each by Pilot Officer Tim Vigors and Laurence Whitbread; Sergeant Ernest Scott claimed a probable Me109 and Pilot Officer John Broadhurst damaged an Me110.

Although Pilot Officer Vigors had destroyed an Me109, his own aircraft was attacked in turn by 109s and was hit by three cannon-shells in the engine. He was forced to crash-land his aircraft X4058 at Southfleet at 5.45 pm; he climbed out unhurt.

Pilot Officer John Broadhurst returned back to Hornchurch; his Spitfire P9469 was badly damaged, with a large section of his tail plane shot away. His combat report confirms this:

> I was returning to base after my aircraft had been damaged by a cannon shell, when I saw an Me110 travelling very fast in a southeasterly direction. I chased it, and fired a number of short bursts at it. The port engine was emitting clouds of brownish smoke, and the speed of the enemy aircraft had dropped considerably, and then my ammunition ran out. When I landed, I found that only four guns had been firing.

On 10th September, Hornchurch was not involved in any air activity. There were very few enemy sorties during the day, except for single raiders attacking targets such as Tangmere, West Malling and Biggin Hill airfields. It was not till the late evening that nearly 150 aircraft attacked London; others attacked targets in South Wales and Merseyside.

The 11th September was another big day for operational sorties by the Luftwaffe. There were to be three very large raids on Portsmouth and Southampton, as well as London. The German invasion, 'Operation Sealion', had now been postponed until the 14th September, provided air superiority had been secured.

Luftflotte II put up three raids, while Luftflotte III sent a raid against

Southampton; at 3.45 pm a third wave came in near Folkestone. Targets that day included London, Biggin Hill, Kenley, Brooklands, and Hornchurch. No.222 Squadron were ordered to patrol over the Hornchurch area at 3.30 pm. During this patrol they encountered several German types of aircraft, Heinkels, Junkers Ju88s, Me109s and 110s. After the action, the squadron claimed eight enemy aircraft damaged or destroyed, without loss to any of the 13 Spitfires that had been on patrol. However Pilot Officer William Assheton was forced to crash-land his Spitfire R6638 at Parsonage Farm, Fletching, owing to an engine problem.

Sergeant Ernest Scott destroyed a Heinkel 111 during the raid; his combat report states:

> I was flying in line astern, when I saw what appeared to be a broken formation of twelve to fifteen Heinkel 111s going south. I dived on one, and commenced a beam attack, opening fire at three hundred yards and closing into about ten yards. The enemy aircraft began to dive steeply, but I was unable to follow it down because my hood was hit. This was either by a piece of metal from the bomber, or by fire from another enemy aircraft, which I assume was an Me109. The hood was completely smashed, and I was blinded for a few seconds by what appeared to be a flash. I commenced a steep dive with evasive action, to rid myself of any following enemy aircraft. On reaching five hundred feet, I began to check my aircraft to see if the damage was any greater than the hood.
>
> My aircraft seemed to be in perfect condition, so I began to climb, and then noticed burning enemy wreckage. I circled it, to try and confirm it as the Heinkel that I had attacked, but the wreckage was spread over such a wide area, that I could not be certain as to what type it was. I had circled the wreckage for a minute or so, when I saw two parachutists descending. They were immediately pounced upon by farmers or L.D.V.

No.41 Squadron had been sent off to patrol over Maidstone at 3.15 pm. The formation of eleven Spitfires cruised up and down the patrol line; one of the Spitfires, flown by Sergeant Pilot I. Howitt, was detached from the rest, and sent to carry out a spotter patrol over the coast. It wasn't until nearly an hour later, after using quite a lot of fuel, that the remaining ten Spitfires made contact with an enemy formation of 70 plus, consisting of Junkers Ju88s and Me110s. It was Flight Lieutenant Norman Ryder who led No.41 into the attack, by diving his aircraft into the middle of the enemy formation, which he hoped would cause them to break. Once this had been done, the pilots picked out their targets. Pilot Officer Eric Lock attacked a Ju88, and after several bursts of fire, the aircraft fell from the sky and crashed south of Maidstone; he then latched on to an Me110, and sent this spinning to the ground. Pilot Officer 'Ben' Bennions engaged one of the Me110 escorts, but was in turn hit by enemy fire; his aircraft was damaged and he was wounded when a shell splinter hit his left heel. His aircraft's pneumatic system had been knocked out; this operated all the aileron controls, brakes and guns. He was forced to break away, and landed at Hornchurch safely, despite the damage to the aircraft. Pilot Officer Gerald Langley had just fired on a Ju88, when he too lost control of his aircraft, after being hit from behind; he was forced to bale out over Sevenoaks at 4.35 pm, and landed safely.

Sergeant Pilot Howitt, who had been sent off as a spotter aircraft, had done an excellent job of work, detailing the incoming enemy raids to operations control from a height of 32,000 feet. However after his last radio communication, he was attacked by a Messerschmitt 109, and had to take evasive action; after a few minutes he managed to lose his attacker. He finally decided to return to base, but on the way back his aircraft's oil cooler system developed a problem, probably caused by enemy fire from the Me109 he was trying to lose. He managed to get the aircraft, Spitfire N3059, nearly all the way back to Hornchurch when the engine seized, and he had to carry out a forced-landing on the airfield; he was fortunately unhurt. The squadron claimed two enemy aircraft destroyed and two damaged.

At 4.25 pm, 'B' Flight of No.603 Squadron was engaged over South London at 20,000 feet with other RAF squadrons, against a force of 100 Me109s, 110s and Heinkel 111s. Pilot Officer Gerald Stapleton's combat report states:

> When patrolling with the Squadron, I saw a large 'Balbo' of enemy aircraft approaching from the east. At that moment my oxygen gave out and I dived to 18,000 feet. Then I sighted an Me110 at 20,000 feet heading southwest. I did two beam attacks and damaged both engines; by this time I was over the coast at 15,000 feet. Glycol was streaming from both engines of the enemy aircraft, but he was not losing much speed.
>
> After that engagement, I came down to 4,000 feet over Dungeness. I sighted an Me109 at 2,000 feet heading for France. When the pilot saw me he dived to approximately 100 feet and continued on a steady course. I caught it up after five minutes and gave it two long bursts from dead astern at 250 yards; glycol issued from his radiator. By this time I could see the coast of France quite plainly, so I turned back.

Pilot Officer Stapleton claimed the Me110 as a probable and the Me109 as damaged.

There was very little enemy activity over the two days of the 12th and 13th September, owing to the unsettled weather over the Channel, with lots of cloud and rain. Although on the 12th, the day's inactivity was broken towards the end of the afternoon, when a solitary German bomber dropped a stick of six 100lb bombs close to the emergency Operations Room at Rainham. Two of the bombs fell by the side of the V.H.F. Signal Tender, turning it over. Two other bombs landed in adjacent gardens but there were no casualties.

It was no doubt a blessing to the pilots and ground crews of Fighter Command, who needed the break from the long days they had had to endure. The German Luftwaffe were beginning to feel the strain as well; after all their bombing of the airfields, and in spite of all their exaggerated claims of RAF fighters shot down, they were still encountering strong opposition from the British squadrons.

On 14th September, Hitler met with his High Command in Berlin, and again postponed Operation Sealion, stating that if the Luftwaffe could not get five good days of weather between the 14th and the 17th, to achieve results, then they could not start the invasion.

London was again the main target; other targets were Cardiff, Ipswich, Farnham and Gloucester. But the raids did not start to develop until about 3 pm, when three raids, one after the other, crossed the English coastline at Deal and Dungeness. Hornchurch was notified of the threat, and squadrons were put at readiness; meanwhile two squadrons from No.12 Group were ordered to protect Hornchurch and North Weald airfields, while the base squadrons dealt with the raids.

Earlier in the afternoon at 1.30 pm, No.222 Squadron were ordered to operate from Rochford airfield. It was from here at 3.25 pm that they were scrambled, and told to meet up with No.603 Squadron at 14,000 feet. This was to intercept an incoming raid over the Canterbury area, which consisted mainly of Me109s who were at an altitude of 21,000 feet. When combat was met, it was fast and fierce, the sky a swirling mass of twisting and turning aircraft. Sergeant Iain Hutchinson downed one of the German fighters, which crashed at Boxley Hill, Detling. He in turn was attacked, and had to make a forced-landing at Detling airfield in Spitfire X4265. Another Sergeant Pilot, Reginald Johnson, had to bale out of his Spitfire X4249 after damage received in combat. He landed safely by parachute at Aveley, his aircraft crashing at Cockhide Farm, Aveley at 4.20 pm.

It was while returning to Rochford with his aircraft badly shot up, that Sergeant Sidney 'Clot' Baxter was killed. Dave Davis was an engine mechanic with No.222 Squadron, and he recalls what happened next:

> We were watching our aircraft returning, waiting for our own particular Spitfire. Suddenly Sergeant Baxter's Spitfire appeared, and you could see straight away that he was in trouble. His tailplane was very badly shot up, and he was valiantly trying to land. He had just crossed over the airfield boundary hedge at a height of 50 feet, when the whole of the tailplane structure dropped off. His aircraft just turned over, straight into the ground. There was nothing anyone could do; it was a great shame as he was a very nice gentleman. He had earned the nickname of 'Clot' after forever questioning his ground crew about his Spitfire; when they asked him why he was always checking up, he replied that he was the clot who had to fly the aircraft, after they had serviced it.

Earlier that afternoon, Pilot Officer Eric Lock had been detailed to fly his Spitfire on a spotter patrol. While at 32,000 feet just over the coast near Dover, he observed a formation of about 12 Me109s; these were flying below his position at 25,000 feet. Always the hunter, Eric Lock dived his aircraft on to the last couple of 109s in the formation; the following account from his report states:

> I attacked the last section of the formation, which were flying in a diamond shape. I was just about to close in, when I was attacked from above by some Me109s. They peeled off from about 3,000 feet above and carried out a head-on attack on me. I waited till one of them was in range, and gave him a long burst of fire. He passed a few feet above me. I carried out a sharp turn to the right and saw him in flames. Just then I was attacked again from head on. I waited till he was at point blank range. I saw my bullets go into the enemy aircraft, and as he was about to go underneath me I gave him another burst.
>
> I then saw more enemy aircraft coming down on me, so I half rolled and dived through the clouds. I had just passed through the clouds when I saw someone who had baled-out; I followed him down to the ground. I am pretty certain it was an Me109 pilot, as I saw he was wearing a tin hat. I saw some of our troops rush up to him, and he appeared to be holding up his arms. I flew low over the field and he waved back. This was afterwards confirmed by the police.

No.41 Squadron were scrambled again that afternoon against the enemy, but no further enemy aircraft were claimed. The only casualty sustained was the new CO Squadron Leader Robert Lister who was shot down by an enemy fighter. Although wounded he managed to bale out of his Spitfire R6605 and spent several weeks in hospital. Squadron Leader Lister's replacement was to be Squadron Leader Don Finlay, who had recovered from his injuries after being shot down in August, when flying with 54 Squadron.

No.222 Squadron were airborne again early evening at 6.15 pm. Eight of the squadron's aircraft were ordered to patrol with aircraft of No.603 Squadron, over the Dungeness area, where enemy bombers and fighters were coming in across the coast. During the encounter Flying Officer Desmond McMullen claimed an Me109 destroyed. The squadron's tally for 14th September was two Me109s destroyed and one probable.

15th September 1940: Two successive massed raids on London intended to destroy what the Luftwaffe believed were the last remnants of Fighter Command. The raid was repulsed with high casualties to the Luftwaffe; on this day the Germans realised that Fighter Command was still intact and that invasion in 1940 was impossible.

On 15th September, the day started at Hornchurch with the early morning preparations by the ground crews. This consisted of wheeling the aircraft into position, checking them over, and warming the engines ready for the first patrols of the day; this was at about 4.30 am. The pilots were awakened later; they would then get something to eat, and then make their way down to dispersal, ready to prepare for the dawn patrols. The Germans were up early too, sending up reconnaissance aircraft over the east and south coasts at dawn. At 11 am the radar stations' began to pick up enemy formations building up over Calais, and as the plots began to increase it was becoming obvious that a massive German attack was developing.

All the RAF sector stations were contacted and told of the situation. At 11.20 am Kenley, Hendon, Middle Wallop and Hornchurch squadrons were ordered to scramble. The first German raid to cross the Kent coast consisted of 100 Dornier bombers of KG.3 and III/KG76, covered by a large fighter escort; this was at 11.30 am. They were first intercepted by squadrons from Biggin Hill. No.41 Squadron sent off ten of their aircraft from Hornchurch at 11.40 am and met the incoming raid over Kent; but before being able to deal with the bombers, they were forced to battle it out with the Me109 escort fighters. Pilot Officer George 'Ben' Bennions managed to deal with one Me109, which he shot down west of Ashford, as did Flying Officer Tony Lovell, who saw the pilot bale out of his machine. Sergeant Pilot E. Darling engaged a Dornier 17 trying to make its way back to France; he fired at the aircraft and damaged its port engine, but was forced to break off the attack, when an Me109 appeared on the scene. During this engagement No.41 lost Pilot Officer Gerald Langley, who was killed when, after being shot down in combat with Me109s, his aircraft crashed and burnt out at Wick House, Bulphan near Thurrock at 12.30 pm.

It was not until 2.05 pm that No.222 Squadron which was down at Rochford, were sent off on their first scramble of the day; they were ordered to patrol over Sheerness at 20,000 feet along with No.603 Squadron. No.222 Squadron could only muster seven aircraft that afternoon. Both squadrons sighted large formations of enemy aircraft covering many miles of airspace, and stepped up at various altitudes.

Both Squadrons dived in to attack the bombers and had several successes. P/O Eric Thomas claimed a half share with a pilot from 603 Squadron on a Dornier 17, which crashed at Maidstone. Flying Officer Brian van Mentz destroyed a Junkers Ju88 while Flying Officer Desmond McMullen destroyed an Me109 and damaged an Me110. Both Pilot Officer John Broadhurst and Sergeant Arthur Spears claimed probables with an Me109 and an Me110.

In the meantime, some of No.603 Squadron's Spitfires, with Hurricanes from other squadrons, were trying to get to grips with a bomber formation over Maidstone. The Heinkel bombers of Geschwader 26 were on their return trip after hitting the East End of London, and were heavily defended by a large fighter escort. The RAF fighters were finding it very difficult to attack or get near the bombers, because of overwhelming enemy fighters. One of 603's pilots, Pilot Officer Peter Pease, tried to penetrate the fighter screen; he dived steeply from above and managed to break through to the bombers. He fired several bursts, attacking from a head-on position, and hit one of the bombers, but he was pounced on from behind by an Me109. His Spitfire was hit, and it pulled up and then rolled on to its back out of control, and dived earthwards trailing black smoke. The Spitfire, X4324, crashed at Kingswood, near Chartway Street, Kent at 3.05 pm; sadly Peter Pease was killed.

Squadron Leader George Denholm, who led 603, was forced to bale out of his aircraft, when his Spitfire was hit by fire from a Dornier 17; his aircraft R7019 crashed near Hastings at 3.10 pm. Pilot Officer Gerald Stapleton, flying with 603 Squadron at 20,000 feet south of Chatham, at 2.50 pm, describes his experiences in his combat report:

> When patrolling with my Squadron, I sighted 25 He 111s and 50 Me109s. While diving to attack, I found myself going too fast to be able to line up on the enemy, so I continued my dive.
>
> About ten minutes later, I sighted two Me109s in tight formation. I fired two deflection bursts at one and glycol streamed from his radiator. They dived into cloud. Later I saw one Dornier 17 over the Thames Estuary, heading for the clouds. I did several beam attacks and he dived to one hundred feet. He flew very low indeed and pancaked on the sea, five miles northwest of Ramsgate. I experienced no return fire.

At 2.10 pm, No.41 Squadron had been ordered up on their second patrol of the day, and told to patrol over Hornchurch at 25,000 feet. A few minutes later they sighted an enemy formation below them at 19,000 feet, consisting of 30 Dornier 17s and their fighter escort. No.41, led by Flight Lieutenant Norman Ryder, formed into line astern formation, and broke up the German raid by diving through the centre of it. No.41 were joined by Hurricane aircraft from other squadrons, after the enemy formation had been split, and they shared in the claiming of several enemy aircraft.

Pilot Officer Lock claimed an Me109 destroyed, Pilot Officer Henry Baker shared with two Hurricane pilots the shooting down of a Heinkel bomber, as did Sergeant Darling who claimed a probable. Flying Officer Boyle and Flying Officer Mackenzie each claimed an Me109 destroyed, and Flying Officer Lovell a 109 probable.

The Germans had suffered heavy losses; they had not expected such stiff fighter opposition from the RAF, and by so many aircraft. This was due partially to the fact that squadrons from No.12 Group, who wanted to try out the 'Big Wing' theory of attack, which involved the use of large formations of Spitfire and Hurricane aircraft, had been brought into the fight from their airfields, such as RAF Duxford in Cambridgeshire. This did have an effect on the Germans' morale, since they had been told by their commanders that the RAF were struggling to survive; suddenly they were confronted with the sight of 60 British fighters from No.12 Group, along with the squadrons of No.11 Group who had held the line since July. At the end of the day the losses for both sides were counted. The BBC Radio announced that evening that the Germans had lost 185 aircraft; in fact the true figure was 56. The RAF aircraft losses were 20 Hurricanes and seven Spitfires; the pilot casualties were 12 killed, four wounded, and one prisoner of war. The 15th September is today celebrated as Battle of Britain Day, the day the RAF turned the tide against the Luftwaffe.

Perhaps at this time it is worth mentioning the anxiety and stress that the wives and families had to endure every day, while their loved ones fought high in the skies above them. Frances Norah Hill, wife of Squadron Leader Johnnie Hill, who was leading No.222 Natal Squadron at Hornchurch, wrote in a letter, dated 15th September, to a friend while living in Upminster.

My dear Jane,

Tomorrow is supposed to be invasion day, and I'm watching the weather anxiously. So far it doesn't look as if it's going to be on our side, as usual it's in favour of Jerry.

We have had three very large battles over our heads today, the noise has been terrific. Johnnie usually rings on the blower every night to tell me the day's score, and I just sit and sit and sit for what seems like years instead of hours.

Johnnie says they are all expecting this blasted invasion any day now, I simply can't bear the idea. The Squadron have a bag of nearly 40 so far, and it will probably be a good many after today.

Johnnie had a very bad day yesterday, he took up 14 aircraft and came back with only 5. One of the boys was killed, a couple wounded and the rest had to bale out.

The boys are so tired Jane, its wicked to keep them at it as they are doing. I could kill the Station C.O. Johnnie looks an absolute wreck, he doesn't even have time to have his hair cut, his nerves are bad and he looks so tired.

We have had raids all night and all day here, shrapnel and bombs falling all around, the noise is absolutely terrific. One battle just finished overhead about half an hour ago, and damn me if the sirens haven't just started again.

I would love to meet you up in town some day. At the moment from this end it's impossible, because the railway has been bombed in several places and it is not very comfortable being out these days.

Johnnie, poor lamb only gets out for a couple of hours once every three days. This war is absolute hell for some people. What I'd give to have one really good night's rest. All the Jerries on their way to London get attacked over here.

You joke about Johnnie having a little leave, it's about as far away as the moon. While at Lincoln we were promised seven days at the end of September, but that was before we were posted to Hornchurch.

I hope you are all well, please give my love to all,

With love, God Bless.
Norah

P.S. I've just heard from Johnnie that 102 Germans were brought down today.

At Hornchurch on 16th September there was no action required by the three squadrons. The weather conditions that day restricted flying, owing to rain and low cloud, with only enemy reconnaissance aircraft making an appearance.

While Göring discussed his next move with his Luftwaffe commanders, No.11 Group Commander Keith Park issued orders to the Hornchurch and Biggin Hill squadrons that they should operate in pairs in clear weather, to attack the German high fighter cover during enemy raids. The Germans however were not deterred from coming over to bomb London by night.

17th September 1940: Hitler cancels the invasion for 1940.
Two days later, invasion barges and personnel start to disperse,
returning to their home bases.

On 17th September, Hitler decided to postpone the invasion of Britain indefinitely. The weather was still variable that day; the only enemy activity was a large fighter sweep with small bomber formations over the south-east coast, during the afternoon. No.41 Squadron were scrambled and engaged Me109s over Manston at 3.30 pm. During the skirmish with the enemy fighters, Pilot Officer Bennions shot down one of the Germans and watched him crash near Canterbury. Sergeant Jock Norwell, who had been posted from No.54 Squadron to No.41, managed to claim a damaged Me109 after diving on to a formation of three, who were making back for France. However No.41 did not get away unscathed; Pilot Officer John Mackenzie's Spitfire R6887 was badly damaged by enemy fire, but he managed to get it back to Hornchurch. Others who were badly shot up included Pilot Officer Harold Chalder in Spitfire N3266, Flying Officer Boyle in Spitfire X4178, and Pilot Officer Henry Baker in Spitfire X4409 who had to make a forced-landing at Stelling Minnis. Fortunately all the pilots were unhurt, and returned to operations immediately.

No.222 Squadron had been scrambled to patrol over Hornchurch at 3.25 pm, but they were recalled at 4.40 pm without sighting the enemy. That evening, the squadron were celebrating in the Officers' Mess at Hornchurch, after receiving the news that Flying Officer Desmond McMullen and Pilot Officer Tim Vigors had both been awarded the Distinguished Flying Cross.

The weather had brightened again on 18th September, and the first German raids of the morning appeared at 9 am over Calais; these were mainly fighter formations coming in between North Foreland and Folkestone at 20,000 feet.

Both No.222 and No.603 Squadrons were scrambled, and ordered to patrol over Maidstone at 20,000 feet. At 10.10 am No.41, led by Pilot Officer Bennions, noticed large numbers of Messerschmitt 109s flying at 7,000 feet above their position.

The enemy fighters in turn saw the Spitfires and dived down to attack. During the ensuing dogfight, Pilot Officer Bennions claimed an Me109 destroyed, as did Pilot Officer Lock. Sergeant Frank Usmar claimed an Me109 as a probable, after hitting the aircraft and watching it turn over and spin down. They returned to Hornchurch without loss. Another raid was intercepted at about 1 pm near Gravesend, Kent. Down at Rochford No.222 Squadron were sent up, and No.41 and No.603 were scrambled from Hornchurch.

After the combat had finished, No.41 claimed three enemy aircraft destroyed and two probables. Pilot Officer Bennions returned to base with his Spitfire damaged from combat with 109s. The pilots of No.222 Squadron were also heavily engaged. Sergeant Pilot Iain Hutchinson, in combat with an Me109, was forced to bale out of his Spitfire when bullets from his opponent hit his aircraft's fuel tank which caught fire. He remembers:

> The fuel caught fire and I opened the hood and attempted to bale out. However, the aircraft was diving steeply at the time, and the slipstream pinned me to the opened hood, while the parachute snagged on it.
>
> The flames were fanned by the airflow and reached my face. I had given up hope of escaping when I found myself floating free, having been ejected and knocked out temporarily. I could see out of the corner of my eye shreds of something, which I took to be remains of my parachute, but I pulled the ripcord and to my great relief, the chute opened. The shreds I'd seen turned out to be bits of skin burned off my face.
>
> After landing heavily with Mother Earth, I was succoured by a delightful group of ladies; unfortunately I could not see properly, so I could not identify them, but they received my grateful thanks.

He had landed at Molash, while his Spitfire R6772 crashed at Clock House Farm, Challock and burnt out at 1.53 pm.

No.41 Squadron were sent up on patrol late afternoon at 5.15 pm; they sighted an enemy formation of Junker Ju88s with escort. Sergeant E. Darling claimed a Ju88 damaged during the attack. Once the enemy fighters had entered the fray, Pilot Officer E.Aldous claimed a 109 damaged and Sergeant Bob Beardsley claimed two damaged.

No raids were intercepted by the squadrons from RAF Hornchurch on 19th September. The weather that day was showery, and the only intrusion by the Germans was a series of lone raiders, who carried out hit and run raids over London and Liverpool.

On 20th September, the Germans sent over only one large fighter sweep, coming in over Dungeness and Dover. 'B' Flight of No.222 Squadron were scrambled, along with No.603, at 10.55 am. Unfortunately No.222 were caught in the climb up to height by Me109s; they suffered three casualties from the enemy attack.

Pilot Officer William Assheton was shot down over the Thames estuary at 11.35 pm; he baled out with slight burns, landing at Latchingdon. He was then taken for treatment at St Peter's Hospital, Maldon. His aircraft K9993 crashed at Linkhouse Farm, West Haningfield. Pilot Officer Eric Edsall, in Spitfire R6840, was hit by enemy fire and his controls were badly damaged. He managed to get back to Hornchurch, where he landed without flaps, and although he overshot the grass flight path and crashed through the perimeter fence, he stepped from his aircraft only slightly injured.

The only pilot loss was Pilot Officer Laurie Whitbread, who was shot down by German fighter ace Oberleutnant Hans 'Assi' Hahn of II/JG2 'Richthofen'. Pilot Officer Whitbread's Spitfire crashed into the garden of Pond Cottage, Hermitage Road, Higham, near Rochester in Kent. His body was thrown from the aircraft when it crashed, and he was killed instantly. Mr Perry, who lived in the cottage, covered his body, until the ambulance arrived.

Flying Officer Eric Thomas, however, managed to claim one of the Me109s. His combat report gives an insight into the surprise attack over Sittingbourne:

> I was climbing to patrol with five other aircraft, when at 25,000 feet, a squadron of yellow nosed Me109s attacked us from the sun in a quarter attack. I saw tracer shells going past P/O Edsall, and I broke away and got on to the tail of an Me109. I opened fire from astern at approximately two hundred yards, and gave two long bursts of five seconds. I then saw trails of white vapour come from the enemy aircraft. I broke away and carried out a deflection attack on two more 109s circling round in tight formation; but I saw no results, as I had to break away, as I was then being attacked myself.

Pilot Officer George Bennions of No.41, whose aircraft was damaged in combat with 109s, had to make a forced-landing at Lympne, Kent. His was the only other aircraft damaged that day, from Hornchurch. The next two days were fairly quiet for the Hornchurch-based squadrons.

At 10.30 am on 21st September, a bomb disposal team arrived at the airfield to deal with a German parachute mine that had been dropped on the flight-path the night before. After safely defusing the mine, Lieutenant Commander Ryan was given lunch at the Officers' Mess, before moving on to his next assignment at Dagenham, where another two mines had landed. At 4.40 pm, a loud explosion was heard at the airfield; both Ryan and his petty officer had been killed dealing with one of the mines.

No.222 were sent up on a patrol at 6 pm on the 21st, but no enemy contact was made. Pilot Officer Edridge and Sergeant Patrick had to divert to Shoreham airfield and land, because of extremely bad weather. During the night of the 21st/22nd, a 1,000lb bomb was dropped on the airfield, which exploded near one of the hangars; fortunately there were no casualties and very little damage apart from shattered windows. The weather was so bad on 22nd September that two of the squadrons were stood down from duty.

The next day, on 23rd September, No.41 Squadron were scrambled, when a formation of 200 enemy aircraft was detected at 9 am, consisting mainly of Me109s. They met the formation at 33,000 feet over Dover and attacked. Pilot Officer Bennions hit one of the 109s, forcing its pilot to ditch into the sea, while other pilots claimed another four of the enemy as probable or damaged.

No.222 sent off two Spitfires at 11.35 am, Flying Officer Brian van Mentz and Pilot Officer Eric Edsall, who were ordered to patrol over the Hornchurch area, after a report of a lone enemy aircraft in the vicinity had been received. While searching, they came across a single Me110; Flying Officer van Mentz engaged the aircraft and proceeded to shoot it down.

Later in the day, No.41 Squadron received orders to send three of their aircraft to escort an Avro Anson on a reconnaissance sortie across the Channel. During the mission they encountered some Me109s, of which they destroyed one and damaged another; none of the RAF aircraft was lost.

On 24th September at 2.45 pm, No.222 Squadron were sent down to operate from Rochford airfield, but the weather was so overcast that they were not ordered to carry out any patrols. They stayed there overnight instead of returning to base. No.41 lost two aircraft in combat over Dover to enemy fighters at 1.45 pm. Sergeant John McAdam baled out of his stricken aircraft, wounded, and parachuted into the sea. He was rescued by a ship, and then admitted to Dover Hospital. Sergeant E.Darling crash-landed just outside Dover at 1.50 pm; he was unhurt.

Only a couple of patrols were carried out by Hornchurch squadrons on 25th September, but again because of deteriorating weather, little enemy activity was seen.

On 26th September, most of the Luftwaffe raids were targeted on the Bristol and Portsmouth areas; so again Hornchurch was not involved that day.

27th and 30th September 1940: The last two massed bomber raids on London. They are of no strategic value.

Heavy raids on London and one on Bristol, were the Luftwaffe orders for 27th September. At 11.40 am, both No.41 and No.222 Squadron's aircraft scrambled to intercept a large formation of bombers over the Maidstone area, but as usual they were interrupted before dealing with the bombers, by their Me109 escorts. During the battle, Sergeant Scott of No.222 destroyed a 109, which crashed into what appeared to be a school playground; luckily there was nobody around at that time. Pilot Officer

John Broadhurst also claimed a 109 destroyed, having watched it dive into the sea off Dungeness. Sergeant Norwell claimed an Me109 for No.41 Squadron.

Both squadrons suffered casualties during this action. Sergeant Frank Usmar was shot down over West Malling at 12.15 pm, and wounded in the leg. He managed to bale out, and after landing was admitted to Preston Hall Hospital. Also shot down was Sergeant E. Darling who was wounded in the shoulder; he also baled out and met up with Sergeant Frank Usmar in the same hospital.

Sergeant Reginald Gretton of No.222 was bounced by 109s over Maidstone and crash-landed at Wennington, near Rainham in Essex at 12 pm. He remembers that landing:

> It was another one of those occasions when the sky had cleared of aircraft. I had looked all around and hadn't spotted anything, when suddenly I was hit; whoever it was had got my glycol tank. Once the glycol started streaming out, I just switched off the engine and dived down. I undid my straps, and pulled back my cockpit canopy ready to bale out. When I had got down to about 5,000 feet, I realised that the engine was not going to catch fire. The aircraft was not flying very well and by the time I got down to 100 feet, ready for a crash landing, I realised that I still had my Sutton harness straps loose; there was now no time to tighten them. The aircraft stalled at about ten feet and smacked onto the ground. I'd turned off the switches and the petrol, and so there was no fire. I hit my head on the gunsight and passed out. I had also badly damaged my back and pelvis, and I remember being lifted on to the wing by my rescuers. I was then rushed off to Oldchurch Hospital in Romford, and spent the next five months recovering from a fractured pelvis and spine. After I had recovered in February '41, it wasn't until June that I was posted to the Aircraft Delivery Flight at Hendon.

No.222 Squadron lost Sergeant Ernest Scott on their second patrol of the day; he was reported missing in action at 4 pm. It was not until the 1970s that the crash site, of what was thought to be Sergeant Scott's aircraft, was located at Greenway Court, Hollingbourne, Kent. Unfortunately the landowner was not agreeable to having his land dug up to recover the aircraft. After many attempts by various groups to have the aircraft recovered, Sergeant Scott's sister Irene and his brother Albert, sent a letter to Prince Charles asking for his help and support in the matter. Finally the landowner gave his permission. The RAF Salvage and Transportation Flight at Abingdon was sent down to recover the aircraft.

When they located the aircraft, they found Sergeant Scott's remains inside the wreckage, along with some personal belongings and maps. He was finally laid to rest on 1st February 1991. He was given a full military funeral at St John's Cemetery in Margate, which was attended by members of his family, with pilot and ground crew members of the No.222 Squadron Association.

No.603 Squadron's only casualty that day was Pilot Officer Philip 'Pip' Cardell, who was tragically killed after baling out too low, after his aircraft had been hit by Me109s. Flying with Pilot Officer Cardell during that sortie was Flying Officer Peter Dexter; they had attacked a pair of Me109s flying at low-level over the Channel at around mid-day. Peter Dexter wrote the following report on what happened next:

> We were returning to base, when I saw an Me109 heading back towards France. I chased him, and when within range, fired a burst which caused him to throw out white smoke from the starboard wing root. The Me109 pulled up to about 500 feet and the pilot baled out. At this time P/O Cardell was in combat with another Me109, which he destroyed. I saw it dive vertically into the sea. Five more Messerschmitts joined in, diving at us from out of the sun. After a short engagement, I saw P/O Cardell break off and head home. While following, I saw he was having difficulties in flying his aircraft. He then jumped and opened his chute at five hundred feet. The parachute failed to deploy properly, and he went into the sea about a quarter of a mile off Folkestone beach. I circled over the pilot for about ten minutes. No attempt whatsoever was made by the people on the beach to reach P/O Cardell. I then force-landed my aircraft on the beach, commandeered a rowing boat, and picked him up. By that time however, he had drowned.

On 28th September, No.222 Squadron carried out two patrols from their forward base at Rochford airfield, the first at 10.05 am, and later at 1.20 pm; neither time did they sight the enemy. But both No.41 and No.603 Squadrons were involved in fighter combats at about 10.15 am, when they engaged Me109s over Charing in Kent. No.41 suffered two pilot casualties. At 10.37 am Flying Officer J.G. Boyle was shot down and killed, his Spitfire crashing at Lynstead. Pilot Officer Harold Chalder was badly wounded during combat; he baled out of his aircraft, which then exploded over Chilham. Pilot Officer Chalder landed at Garlinge Green, and was immediately taken to Chartham Hospital. He finally succumbed to his wounds, and died on 10th November 1940. No.603 suffered the loss of Flight Lieutenant Harold K. MacDonald, who was bounced by 109s over Gillingham at 10.20 am; his aircraft crashed on to Brompton Barracks.

In the afternoon at 12.30 pm, No.41 Squadron were ordered up to patrol over Hornchurch; this they did with only seven serviceable aircraft. Once up, they were vectored by Hornchurch Control to intercept a raid coming in over Kent. In doing this they were attacked by escort fighters who damaged two of the Spitfires, although the pilots were unhurt. Pilot Officer

Bennions claimed two 109s probably destroyed, but in return, he had his aircraft badly shot up by 20mm cannon shells from a Me109 while over Hornchurch at 1.45 pm; however he landed safely back at base.

The Hornchurch squadrons carried out a few patrols on 29th September. There was very little Luftwaffe activity, except for attacks on shipping in the Channel during the morning.

Two German raids on 30th September started at 9 am. The first raid consisted of 30 bombers with over a 100 fighters, and the second raid numbered about 60 aircraft. They were met by RAF fighters, who managed to break up the raids before they reached London.

Another enemy raid was plotted around noon, and the Hornchurch squadrons were scrambled. No.41 took off from Rochford at 1.06 pm, after No.222 had already left from Hornchurch at 1 pm. No. 41 were ordered to patrol with their 12 Spitfires at 30,000 feet over the Thames Estuary, while No.222 were vectored over south-east London. Here they met with 20 enemy bombers and their fighter escort at 20,000 feet. No.222, who were flying at 28,000 feet, went into line astern formation, and dived into the attack. They broke up the enemy formation, but were soon having to fight it out with the Me109 escort fighters. Sergeant Rainford Marland claimed two Me109s as probably destroyed, and Pilot Officer Eric Edsall one Me109 destroyed, and another probable. Sergeant Iain Hutchinson, however, was forced to bale out of his Spitfire, when his fuel tank was hit by machine gun fire, but from where it came he had no idea. He landed safely but was badly burnt on his face and hands, as well as heavily bruised after hitting the tail of the aircraft whilst baling out. He played no further part in the Battle of Britain.

No.41 which had been in the action over Dungeness against a formation of approximately 30 Dornier 17s, were able to claim some success before being forced to fight it out with the enemy fighters. Flying Officer Tony Lovell had fired bursts at a Dornier, when his own aircraft was hit from behind by an Me109. His aircraft was hit in the starboard wing by 20mm cannon shells, which had damaged his undercarriage. On returning to Hornchurch, he discovered his wheels were jammed and he had to carry out a crash landing; he was lucky and stepped from his aircraft unscathed.

Sergeant Bob Beardsley attacked a Dornier 17 and claimed it as a probable. He then attacked an Me109, which he also claimed as probably destroyed. After this he was forced to take evasive action when he was set upon by six enemy fighters. His aircraft was eventually hit and his aircraft's engine began to catch fire with smoke billowing into the cockpit. He managed to steer his aircraft down over the Folkestone area and then force-land at the airfield of RAF Hawkinge. He was back flying with the squadron the next day. Other claims were made that day by Pilot Officer Henry Baker who shot down an Me109, and a Dornier 17 damaged by Flying Officer Peter Brown, who had just been posted from No.611 Squadron on 28th September.

Flying Officer Maurice Peter Brown had been stationed at No.12 Group, flying with the 'Big Wing' squadrons led by Squadron Leader Douglas Bader; he recalls the difference between the two operational groups, No.11

and No.12, and the change in tempo he experienced now operating from Hornchurch:

> On my first sortie from Hornchurch with 41 Squadron, my logbook records that I damaged a Dornier 215; that wasn't special, because I had already been in action against bombers before, with 12 Group. But during the next few sorties, when we were intercepting 109s very high up, I wasn't fully aware of what was going on. I was so busy staying in formation, that I didn't see the 109s early enough; this happened to almost every replacement pilot. It took time to acclimatise to the speed of events down in 11 Group, and the first few early sorties were especially dangerous. Fortunately I quickly acclimatised.
>
> The intensity of operations in No.11 Group at Hornchurch, was quite different from that in 12 Group, where you could sit around all day waiting for action. But once I moved to Hornchurch, I found myself in the real battle; squadrons were being scrambled all the time, and on my third day I did five sorties; so it was an altogether different tempo. 11 Group squadrons had been fighting desperately against the German raids with high casualties. Most of the time in October we were meeting 109s; apart from the first sortie, I don't remember getting in amongst the bombers.

1st October 1940: The Luftwaffe change offensive tactics using high flying Me109s and Me109 bombers. It is difficult to intercept the high and fast enemy aircraft, but the Luftwaffe incurs heavy casualties. The poor weather conditions did not permit mass formations to operate.

So another month began, Tuesday, 1st October, 1940. London, Southampton and Portsmouth were the designated targets for that day. The first raid came at 10.45 am when 100 enemy aircraft headed for Southampton and Portsmouth. They were met by British fighters with a fierce resistance; no aircraft from Hornchurch were involved in combat that morning.

It was not until around 2 pm that No.41 Squadron led by Squadron Leader Don Finlay sighted a formation of Me109s below them and decided to attack. Only one of the enemy aircraft was claimed as damaged during the combat; the claim was shared by Squadron Leader Finlay and Pilot Officer Dennis Adams.

No.222 Squadron had been sent up on three patrols that day, but no enemy contact was made. Nine Spitfires of No.41 were vectored over Maidstone at 3.50 pm. Flying at 30,000 feet, they spotted an enemy formation of 25 Me109s. No.41 dived in to the attack, but could claim only one Me109 damaged, before the enemy fighters headed for cloud cover. The claim was made by Flying Officer Tony Lovell.

On their return trip back to Hornchurch, the pilots of No.41 saw some Hurricane aircraft in trouble with Me109s. One of the pilots, Pilot Officer George Bennions, broke away from his comrades and decided to try and help out the Hurricanes. He latched on to the rear of an Me109, and fired two short bursts of gunfire into it, causing it to catch fire; the German pilot quickly took to his parachute. Seconds later Pilot Officer Bennions was attacked by an enemy fighter. In his own words, he tells what happened next:

> I was engaged with a few 109s just north of Brighton, at about 20,000 feet, when a cannon shell exploded in the cockpit, blinding me in the left eye, and damaging my right arm and right leg. I could not use my right hand; the median nerve had been severed. My face and right leg were bleeding profusely, so I decided to bale out. I disconnected the oxygen tube with my left hand, and pulled out the R/T plug. I then opened the canopy, lowered the side door, and then rolled the aircraft to the left and dropped out. I experienced great difficulty trying to pull the parachute ripcord with my left hand, but I eventually succeeded. The parachute opened with a terrific jerk causing me to pass out completely. When I regained consciousness, I had already landed and was being attended to by a farmer, Mr C.J. Shepherd; I asked him would he please inform my Squadron. After emergency treatment at Horsham Base Hospital, I was transferred to the Queen Victoria Hospital, East Grinstead, for plastic surgery by Sir Archie McIndoe, and thus became a member of the 'Guinea Pig Club'.

George Bennions had been very badly wounded. A cannon shell had pierced his skull, and had destroyed his left eye; it was a miracle that he had survived. After many months of treatment, he returned to duty as an operations controller based at Catterick. His aircraft crashed on Heatenthorn Farm, near Aldborne, Sussex.

On 2nd October, both No.41 and No.603 Squadrons carried out standing patrols; No.603 made contact with the enemy at 10.15 am. Pilot Officer Peter Dexter, who had just shot down an Me109 over Croydon, was in turn shot down himself and was wounded in one leg. He was trapped by his leg as he tried to abandon his aircraft, and fell 15,000 feet before wrenching his foot free of his flying boot. He just managed to open his parachute with enough height to spare. He landed safely and was treated for his wounds, spending the next six months in hospital.

The only other Hornchurch aircraft casualties were two Spitfires of No.41 Squadron, which collided while taxi-ing to take off at 1.30 pm. One of the pilots Sergeant Jock Norwell was slightly hurt and his aircraft was written off.

During the night of the 2nd/3rd, the Germans mounted a raid of 180 aircraft. These attacked London, and dropped bombs on airfields at

Northolt, Kenley, Hendon and Hornchurch, although very little damage was caused.

There was very little flying on 3rd October. The weather with mist, rain and poor visibility, made it impossible for the Germans to launch any significant attack. The weather on the 4th October was again much the same.

The weather lifted slightly on the 5th October, the Germans carrying out fighter-bomber sweeps over Kent, with formations of 30 to 40 aircraft. These consisted of Me109s, with bomb racks fitted beneath the fuselage carrying a 250lb bomb. On their first sortie of the day, No.41 engaged a small formation of Me109s at 25,000 feet. During the action, at 12.10 pm, they were able to claim two of the enemy destroyed, and another three damaged, although one of No.41's Spitfires was hit in the wing by enemy fire. Flight Lieutenant Lovell returned back to base with his damaged aircraft, landing safely.

No.603 Squadron, which had also been involved in combat over Dover, suffered one casualty; it was Pilot Officer J.S. Morton. He was shot down at 11.55 am and baled out, having received burns; his aircraft, Spitfire K9807, crashed at Chilham. No.41 claimed two more enemy aircraft destroyed on their second patrol, shot down by Pilot Officer Eric Lock and Flying Officer John Mackenzie. On their final patrol of the day, Pilot Officer Lock was again able to claim another Me109 as a probable.

At Rochford, No.222 Squadron had carried out three patrols that day, but had not encountered any enemy aircraft; they returned back to Hornchurch in the evening. During the evening of 5th October, at 10 pm Hornchurch was bombed by a single enemy bomber which dropped incendiaries on to the airfield. One bomb went through the roof of the Operations block, and another into the Officers' Mess, but the incidents were quickly dealt with and the fires put out. At 10.45 pm another bomber dropped its load of delayed-action bombs, but these were also dealt with and no damage was caused.

The following day, 6th October, two Spitfires from No.222 Squadron were sent on a weather reconnaissance patrol over Kent at 11 am. The pilots, Pilot Officer Tim Vigors and Pilot Officer Graham Davis, did not sight any enemy aircraft, nor did any other members of the squadron, who went up on another four patrols that day. Most of the day was dull with continuous rain.

During the morning of 7th October, the Germans sent over 120 aircraft on raids over Sussex and Kent. No.222 and No. 603 were scrambled and encountered the enemy. Flying Officer Henry Matthews of No.603 was shot down, and killed during a dogfight with Me109s of II/JG26. His aircraft N3109 crashed at Hurst Farm, Godmersham Park at 10.45 am. During the afternoon, while engaging a bomber formation, Pilot Officer John Broadhurst was shot down in his Spitfire P9469; he baled out, but was killed. His body was found at Longhurst, Kent, after his aircraft crashed at Baileys Reed Farm, Salehurst. He was buried in the military plot of the cemetery at St Andrew's Church, at Hornchurch. A major recovery of Pilot

Officer Broadhurst's Spitfire was undertaken by the Robertsbridge Aviation Museum in the 1970s; the Merlin engine and other items can be now seen on show at the museum.

It was on this day that Flying Officer David Scott-Malden had flown his first sortie with No.603 Squadron having been posted down from No.12 Group. He remembers:

> My first sortie from Hornchurch was on 7th October 1940. I had been posted to 603 Squadron as a replacement pilot as they had suffered quite a lot of casualties. I had started flying with No.611 Squadron, which was a 12 Group squadron. They flew from Duxford in the 'Wing' led by Douglas Bader, so I came into 603 at Hornchurch with some experience under my belt.
>
> The first sortie I did, I managed to get a few bursts at some Messerschmitt 109s. It was always a tense moment if you were climbing up to height and you were heading to where Control had sent you, then suddenly you saw a lot of black silhouettes heading your way. You would be trying to decide whether the leader you were following was going to position you right to carry out a good attack or whether you were likely to be set on and have to fight for your life. Once the fighting had started, as a new boy hanging onto and covering your leader, it was considered bonus points if you emerged after the action still with the pilot you were covering. But the extraordinary thing was, all this could be going on for a few moments of absolute mayhem, then the sky appeared to be empty of aircraft, I think most pilots had that experience.
>
> I didn't know many of the pilots of 603 Squadron when I first arrived there, Richard Hillary had been shot down shortly before I arrived. I remember clearly George Denholm who was the CO of the squadron who was a very remarkable man, because he managed to keep the Scottish spirit of 603 Squadron going in the most extraordinary fashion even though we lived a very chaotic life. He always insisted on the squadron dining together in the Hornchurch Mess, at the same table, as it were 'after dark' not on duty, and always considered we should finish dinner with a round of Drambuie drink to keep the spirit of the Edinburgh squadron going. I also remember him being up at first light and immaculately dressed for virtually every dawn sortie I can think of, he was the most inspiring commanding officer.
>
> It was a fairly chaotic and very charged atmosphere at Hornchurch because we were operational a great deal of the time, flying about four or five sorties a day, unless there was bad weather. In the evenings we would visit the local pubs and I can remember the civilians would come up to you in a very

touching way, shake you by the hand and offer to buy you a pint of beer. Although we knew food was rationed, there always appeared to be eggs and bacon available in the pub, I think they felt that rather like the gladiators of old, we were the chaps who were going to fight the enemy, while they had to put up with all the bombing, rationing and whatever else.

London again received the Luftwaffe's attention on the morning of 8th October, when two enemy raids of over 100 plus dropped their bombs on Charing Cross, Horse Guards Parade, and other buildings around central London. Just after mid-day, another enemy formation arrived to continue the battering. Pilot Officer Tim Vigors of No.222 claimed a Junkers Ju88 bomber destroyed at 11 am, shared with a Hurricane pilot of No.605 Squadron.

A heavy German raid was met by the two combined Squadrons, No.41 and No.222, on the 9th October at 2.45 pm. No.41 had just sighted a group of four Me109s over Maidstone; they dived down to attack, but were themselves attacked by a formation of twenty Me109s who had been watching at a higher altitude. Luckily No.222 were able to give support, and dived in to break up the German fighters; this then turned into a large dogfight between individual pilots. Pilot Officer Lock of No.41 was able to claim one Me109 destroyed, while Flight Lieutenant Eric Thomas of No.222, shot down an Me109, which crash-landed near Hawkinge; the pilot Feldwebel Schweser of 7/JG54 was captured. During the fighting No.41's CO Don Finlay, flying in his Spitfire X4558, was hit by enemy fire and his aircraft damaged. He returned to Hornchurch and carried out a forced landing at 4.15 pm. The squadron claimed two enemy aircraft destroyed and two as probables.

On Thursday, 10th October, Hornchurch received a signal from No.11 Group Commander, Air Vice-Marshal Keith Park, to pass on to both No.41 and No.222 Squadrons.

Congratulations to 41 and 222 Squadrons on their very successful combined operation in combat on Wednesday October 9th, resulting in the destruction of three Me109s plus four others driven down without loss to our pilots or aircraft.

On October 11th, Hornchurch was covered in thick fog during the early part of the morning, and it did not really start to clear until 11 am. It was at this time that aircraft of No.222 Squadron were ordered aloft to patrol over base. At 2.10 pm they were sent to the airfield at Rochford to operate from there. During the day at Hornchurch, a bomb disposal team arrived to attend to three German delayed action bombs, which had been dropped on the airfield a couple of days earlier; they were dug up and taken to the Gerpins Lane sandpits, near Rainham, and safely detonated while an air raid warning was sounding.

At 4 pm No.41 and No.222 Squadrons were scrambled to an incoming raid, but only No.41 made enemy contact. Flying at 30,000 feet they sighted a formation of 50 Me109s who were above them. It was during the squadron's climb to get at the enemy that two of No.41's Spitfires collided in mid-air. Spitfire X4554 flown by Sergeant L.R.Carter hit Spitfire X4042 flown by Flying Officer D.H. O'Neill. Both pilots baled out, but Flying Officer O'Neill's parachute failed and he was killed; Sergeant Carter landed safely, unhurt.

Once battle was joined, only Pilot Officer Eric Lock was able to claim an Me109 destroyed, while another No.41 Squadron pilot was lost. Pilot Officer John Lecky, aged 19, who had only been with the squadron for two days, were shot down and killed: his aircraft P9447 crashing at Preston Hall, Maidstone at 4.30 pm. He was buried at Tilford Churchyard, Surrey.

On 12th October, No.222 flew down to Rochford at dawn, and at 9.15 am were ordered up on their first patrol of the day, to cover the Gravesend area. While doing so they were contacted by Operations and told to head for Maidstone. While at 30,000 feet over Deal, they sighted a formation of Me110s. They were about to attack, when they spotted a large formation of Me109 fighters, waiting at a higher altitude above. The wise decision to break off, rather than to face the overwhelming odds, was made. Flying Officer Brian van Mentz of 'B' Flight did however manage to attack a lone Me110 at 25,000 feet. He fired his guns from 800 yards, and watched as smoke began to pour from the enemy aircraft's starboard engine; he eventually lost the Me110 in cloud, and could only claim it as damaged. Pilot Officer Eric Edsall had also engaged the enemy; he had sighted 15 Me109s in line abreast formation over Chatham at 25,000 feet. He was about to try his luck, when two of the 109s broke off to attack him; he managed to let off two bursts of fire, but his guns failed due to freezing. He was forced to withdraw and returned to Hornchurch safely.

No.41 lost one aircraft that day, but not through enemy action. Sergeant J. McAdam suffered engine failure in his Spitfire while taking off at 4.40 pm, his aircraft crash-landing in Globe Road, Hornchurch. Thankfully Sergeant McAdam was unhurt, although his aircraft was a write-off.

Flying Officer Brian van Mentz of No.222 received the telegram signal that evening that he had been awarded the DFC, for shooting down six enemy aircraft confirmed and two probably destroyed.

On the 13th October, the Luftwaffe sent out small raids against convoys off the east coast, and, later in the day, fighter sweeps over Kent. No enemy contact was made by squadrons from Hornchurch this day. The weather on 14th October was very overcast and it rained almost all of the day. No operational sorties were flown from Hornchurch, although two aircraft from No.222 Squadron were sent up on weather tests.

Early morning of 15th October saw the Luftwaffe build up over the Cap Gris Nez area, and at 9 am 30 enemy aircraft were sighted heading for Hornchurch and London. It was at this time that 23-year-old Sergeant Pilot Philip Lloyd of No.65 Squadron was shot down and killed in Spitfire X4178, during a surprise attack by an Me109 flown by Hauptmann Fozo of 4/JG51. His aircraft crashed into the Channel, but his body was not recovered from the sea until 27th October; he was buried in the grounds of the Church of the Holy Innocents, High Beech, Essex.

No.222, already on their third patrol of the day, made enemy contact for the first time at 2.30 pm, when Flying Officer Desmond McMullen and Sergeant Jack Dunmore sighted two Me109s between Maidstone and Sheerness. They managed to destroy one of the Me109s between them, while Sergeants Burgess and Gibbins also claimed another shared Me109 destroyed. Sergeant Burgess's combat report states:

> With the rest of the Squadron, I sighted two aircraft coming from the south and travelling towards London. We followed and intercepted these aircraft, which upon seeing us went into a steep dive. I delivered about six bursts at one of them, some dead astern and some with a slight deflection. With the exception of seven rounds and one gun which had a stoppage, I used all my ammunition on this aircraft. This aircraft crashed near Whitstable, and I understand that it was also fired on by Sergeant Gibbins. I think my firing was at least partly responsible for the destruction of this aircraft. I fired at ranges varying from 100-300 yards.

Because of the long flight time and consequent shortage of fuel, pilots Flying Officer Hallam, Sergeant Burgess and Sergeant Dunmore had to make forced landings. Pilot Officer Edridge force-landed his aircraft K9795 at 4.20 pm at Tillingham Hall, near Hornden on Hill, Essex. Earlier that day, the emergency Operations Room at Rainham was finally abandoned, and full operations began at the Masonic Temple Hall in Romford. On 16th October, weather prevented any real German activity, with widespread fog over France; a very quiet day in the Hornchurch sector.

On 17th October, German raids began just after 8 am when 90 Me109s and Me110s strafed and bombed Margate, Stanmore and Broadstairs. But it was not until mid-afternoon that Hornchurch squadrons were scrambled to cope with the Luftwaffe. At 3 pm No.222 were ordered to patrol Maidstone, and sighted 20 Me109s; once combat was joined fierce dog fighting was the order of the day. Flight Lieutenant Ian Hallam attacked one of the enemy fighters from astern, and claimed it as damaged. Flying Officer Desmond McMullen claimed an Me109 destroyed, after it had crashed into the sea off Sheerness. Pilot Officer Charles Stewart claimed another damaged and Sergeant John Burgess an Me109 probable. The squadron suffered no loss. No.41 Squadron were also over Maidstone, when they attacked and broke up an Me109 formation at 3.40 pm. Pilot Officer Edward 'Hawkeye' Wells and Pilot Officer F.J. Aldridge each destroyed an Me109.

For the next two days the weather was very overcast, and heavy fog and poor visibility kept the Hornchurch squadrons grounded; the Luftwaffe sent over a few patrols, but it remained fairly quite.

On 20th October, the weather had cleared for flying, though it was still mainly cloudy. The Germans again continued their fighter-bomber raids over the south-east and the capital. The first enemy sweeps were detected on radar at 9.35 am.

At Hornchurch the scramble bell was sounded, and at 11.15 am, No.222 Squadron were sent off to patrol over Maidstone at 30,000 feet. At 11.45 am they received instructions from Operation Control to descend to 15,000 feet; it was while doing so that Flying Officer McMullen sighted a single Me110 fighter-bomber. He led Red Section down to attack the aircraft, while the rest of the formation stayed on patrol. Both Flying Officer McMullen and Pilot Officer Edridge fired bursts at the enemy aircraft, and saw their bullets striking home; Spitfires from No.92 Squadron also attacked the Me110. Shortly afterwards, at 12.50 pm, the enemy aircraft crash-landed at Horsmonden; the pilot, Oberleutnant Lemmerich was captured, but his gunner Unteroffizier Ebeling was killed.

Both No.41 and No.603 Squadrons flew together during the afternoon, and at about 2 pm intercepted a formation of approximately 60 Me109s at 25,000 feet. Together both squadrons between them claimed several kills; No.41 claimed three destroyed, one probable and one damaged. One of the Me109s destroyed was claimed by Flying Officer Peter Brown. He remembers:

> We were flying at 25,000 feet in the Biggin Hill area, when we intercepted a formation of 50 to 60 Me109s. They appeared not to have seen us, and we were able to attack from the rear. Flying as Red 2, I singled out an Me109 at the rear of the formation.
>
> I opened fire with a short burst at 150 yards and could see tracer bullets hitting the aircraft. Glycol coolant streamed out of his engine and I closed to 100 yards and fired another short burst. The 109 dived down apparently out of control. I followed him down for several thousand feet when he suddenly climbed up again. I gave him two more bursts at 100 yards – he half rolled and I followed him down again.
>
> He baled out, landing near Wrotham unhurt, and his aircraft crashed in woods near West Malling airfield. I decided to land at the airfield, and the Intelligence Officer took me to the Bull Inn at Wrotham, where the German pilot was being held prisoner in the cellar. After a chat with him – more as fighter pilots than as enemies – I managed to acquire his Schwimmweste as a souvenir and as evidence to my claim; also his pilot's badge which he had great difficulty in removing from his tunic. He asked for a knife to prize the badge off, whereupon the soldier who was on guard loaned the German his bayonet, still fixed to his rifle, and the badge was handed over.
>
> I returned to Hornchurch, and found that two of my guns

had not fired due to the cold. This often happened at 25,000
feet and above, which not only reduced the gun power, but if
the failure occurred on one side only, then the aircraft slewed
round, making accurate shooting very difficult.

Again, over 21st, 22nd and 23rd October, bad weather prevented most
flying operations over Britain. On 24th October, No.41 Squadron replaced
their trusty old Mk1 Spitfires in return for 14 MkIIs, belonging to No.611
Squadron, who were stationed up at Digby in Lincolnshire.

Messerschmitt 109 fighter-bomber sweeps were the order of the day for
25th October, starting at about 8 am. Kent received most of the bombing
during the day, but some enemy aircraft got through as far as London. Two
aircraft from No.222 Squadron were sent on convoy patrol at 7.40 am that
morning but nothing was reported. No.41 and No.603 were sent off to
patrol between Hornchurch and Rochford at 9 am and told to fly at 23,000
feet. They were then vectored over Kent and told to climb to a higher
altitude, which they did; a few minutes later they sighted an enemy
formation of about 30 Me109s.

Moving into a position to attack, with the sun directly behind them, the
Spitfires dived into the enemy, who broke in all directions. Sergeant
McAdam was able to claim one of the 109s destroyed, while other pilots
reported four probables and three damaged Me109s.

It was not all one way however: No.603 suffered two aircraft written off
and one damaged, and Pilot Officer John Soden in Spitfire P7325 was shot
down and forced to bale out. He landed, injured in the right leg, at
Perryfields and was admitted to the East Sussex Hospital; his aircraft
crashed at Stonelink Farm, Brede.

Pilot Officer Peter Olver was also wounded and had to 'hit the silk'; his
Spitfire P7309 crashed at Pickdick Farm, Brede at 10.20 am. Polish Pilot
Officer Ludwick Martel was forced to crash-land his Spitfire P7350 after
being damaged in combat; he was unhurt, and the aircraft was repairable.
The Spitfire of No.41 Squadron Pilot Officer Aldridge was also slightly
damaged, but thankfully no pilots were lost.

At 1 pm No.222 were scrambled and given instructions to join up with
No.74 Squadron which was now flying from Biggin Hill. The orders were
changed after No.74 had already sighted enemy aircraft. No.222 were
ordered to climb up to 30,000 feet; while doing this they noticed RAF
fighters just below them at 28,000 feet, and Me109s further below.

Flight Lieutenant Eric Thomas, who was leading No.222, gave his
instructions to his pilots over the R/T to dive down in line astern formation
on to the enemy fighters below. Flight Lieutenant Thomas positioned
himself on to the tail of one Me109 and opened fire from a range of 200
yards; as he closed to 75 yards, the Me109 manoeuvred three downward
flick rolls and then pulled straight up. He followed the 109 and fired
another burst into it; at that moment glycol from both radiators streamed
out. The aircraft was then attacked by Pilot Officer Hilary Edridge; the
Me109 rolled over and went straight down. The German pilot baled out,

and almost collided with Flight Lieutenant Thomas's aircraft. The pilot Feldwebel Joseph Gartner, landed safely although slightly wounded, and was then captured.

Flying Officer Desmond McMullen attacked two 109s, and shot one down into the sea. Pilot Officer Eric Edsall claimed another as a probable, as did Sergeant Rainford Marland. Pilot Officer Graham Davies claimed a 109 damaged, after seeing his victim's aircraft falling to pieces, bit by bit, before disappearing into cloud. The squadron carried out one more patrol that day at 3.30 pm, but no further enemy contact was made.

No.41 Squadron were involved in combat once again that day; this was over Dungeness at 4.00 pm again against Me109s. During the encounter Sergeant Bob Beardsley had just destroyed a 109 and damaged another, when his Spitfire came under attack, and a 20 mm cannon shell went through the starboard camshaft casing of his engine. He broke away from the combat zone and force-landed his aircraft at Hawkinge; he was unhurt himself. Flying Officer John Mackenzie also claimed one enemy aircraft destroyed, but he too was obliged to force-land when his aircraft ran out of fuel. He landed uninjured at Tandridge at 4.30 pm. Flying Officer Peter Brown, also in combat that day remembers:

> At about 25,000 feet over Ashford we intercepted a formation of 30 Me109s. The squadron dived into the attack and I followed Red Leader. I attacked an Me109 with no apparent result. As often happened the sky appeared to be empty and I climbed up to 25,000 feet again. I then saw about nine Me109s on my starboard beam and slightly lower. I attacked one of the 109s, and after two short bursts, glycol streamed out of his engine. I gave it two more bursts with slight deflection – the aircraft rolled over on its side and dived straight down into cloud. I estimated that the aircraft had crashed in the vicinity of Rye.
>
> I then attacked another 109 and followed it down over the sea, but after one burst my ammunition ran out. Once again two guns failed due to the cold, and two other guns failed after a few seconds. As I hadn't seen the 109 crash I could only claim a probable. In fact the pilot baled out and was taken prisoner. He later reported that my first burst hit the engine and the second had destroyed his instrument panel.

It was on 26th October, that RAF Hornchurch received following information from No.11 Group Headquarters and Air Vice-Marshal Keith Park, regarding the arrangements for the Duxford Wing to operate in No.11 Group.

> As soon as the Group Controller gets a clear indication of raids building up over the French coast, he is to request No. 12 Group Controller to despatch the Duxford Wing to patrol east of London on

approximate line north and south of Hornchurch.

The arrival of the wing patrol will be communicated to No.11 Group Controller who will indicate to No.12 Group Controller the best position in the estuary or northern Kent to which the Wing should be directed to effect an interception.

The No.12 Group Controller will inform No.11 Group immediately the Duxford Wing has left the ground.

No.11 Group Controller is then to inform Senior Controller at Hornchurch who is to fix the position of the Duxford Wing. This will be possible as two aircraft of the VHF Squadron in the Duxford Wing are fitted with Hornchurch fixer crystals (one working, one in reserve).

On arrival on the patrol line Hornchurch will give zero to the Duxford Wing on its operational frequency.

Hornchurch will hold a crystal of the leading squadrons frequency in the Duxford Wing and set up a channel on air frequency with R/T facilities as indicated. Hornchurch Controller will be able to fix the Duxford Wing and inform the Observer Corps liaison officer, flank sector and group operations of the position of the Duxford Wing at frequent intervals.

It would appear in retrospect, that Leigh-Mallory's Big Wing had on a few days made an appearance, and had helped the Germans realise that the RAF was far from being beaten. However, by the time these new orders were being put into effect, Operation Sealion had already been cancelled indefinitely, and the daylight bomber raids were being reduced, owing to the Luftwaffe losses, and the difficulties imposed by bad weather, and the approach of winter.

During the 26th, Hornchurch squadrons carried out patrols, but no enemy aircraft were engaged, except for one Me110, which was fired on by Flying Officer Brian van Mentz of No.222, at 10.15 am. The Me110 headed for cloud cover and was not sighted again.

Sergeant Phillip Davis was on his last patrol of the day, when his Spitfire's engine caught fire. He managed to crash-land the aircraft, with no injury to himself at Purleigh Barns Farm, Latchingdon, at 5.45 pm.

Both No.41 and No.222 were sent off to patrol over London at 7.45 am on Sunday, 27th October. They sighted an enemy formation way into the distance, but because of the distance and lack of oxygen, were forced to turn back. No.603 Squadron were heavily involved in combat with 109s over the Maidstone area, when they were victims of a surprise attack by aircraft of III/JG27. It was during this action that they lost two pilots killed. Pilot Officer Claude Goldsmith, from South Africa, was shot down in Spitfire P7439 crashing near Waltham at 2.05 pm. He was rescued from the wreckage of his aircraft and quickly taken to a hospital, but died of his injuries the following day.

Also lost was Pilot Officer Robert Dewey, when his aircraft was badly damaged and crashed into a tree at Apple Tree Corner, Chartham Hatch;

Robert Dewey was killed instantly. Both of the pilots were returned to Hornchurch for burial in the military churchyard plot at St. Andrews Church. Fortunately, although Pilot Officer D.A. Maxwell's Spitfire was severely damaged, and he had to force-land at Throwley, he escaped unhurt.

All three squadrons were involved in a combined patrol over the south coast at 4.40 pm. Me109s were sighted during this sortie and engaged; No.41 claimed two enemy aircraft destroyed. Pilot Officer Eric Edsall of No.222 ran out of fuel while in combat with Me109s. In trying to force-land his aircraft at Hailsham, he ploughed through high-tension cables and crashed heavily. He was badly injured and admitted to Hellingly Hospital. He recovered, and in July 1941 was posted to No.602 Squadron.

Heavy mist on the morning of 28th October restricted German raids; it was not until the afternoon that the Luftwaffe tried any large formations. No.222 and No.603 joined forces over Maidstone at 30,000 feet at 1.20 pm; after an hour patrolling the line and running short of oxygen, they descended to 17,000 feet. Towards the end of the patrol, Flying Officer Desmond McMullen sighted aircraft in the distance; his combat report states:

> Towards the end of a patrol over Maidstone on 28/10/40, at approximately 14.30 hours, when at 17,000 feet, I sighted five unidentified aircraft which I investigated. After a stern chase I found that they were Me109s, with another four enemy aircraft some way off over Dungeness, in line astern at 15,000 feet.
>
> I attacked from astern and saw glycol streaming out, but had to break off immediately on being attacked myself. The enemy aircraft was in a dive, with glycol damage, when last seen.

Flying Officer McMullen could only claim the Me109 as damaged. Pilot Officer George 'Sheep' Gilroy of No.603 Squadron also claimed an Me109 destroyed; this crashed near Pinewood Garage, London Road, near Maidstone, at 2 pm. The pilot, Unteroffizier Gonschorrek, baled out wounded, and was captured.

At 4.12 pm both No.222 and No.603 were given vectors to intercept an enemy raid. Flying Officer McMullen, leading Red Section of No.222, sighted 12 Me109s flying in a line abreast formation, but on seeing the Spitfires they formed into a four line astern formation and went into the attack. Combat was met, but only one enemy aircraft was claimed destroyed by McMullen and this crashed into the sea off Dungeness.

On Tuesday, 29th October, the weather was hazy over the Channel and overcast inland. German targets were Southampton and London, the first attack coming at 11 am, when 30 enemy aircraft were engaged by RAF fighters over Kent. No.222 Squadron were scrambled at 12.45 pm; they sighted an enemy formation of up to 80 aircraft at 15,000 feet. Led by

Flight Lieutenant Eric Thomas they attacked the formation from astern, joined by eight RAF fighters from another squadron. Sergeant John Burgess managed to position himself into a firing position behind an Me109; his report of the action states:

> 'B' Flight. Ashford area at 13.35 hours at 8,000 to 9,000 feet. Whilst on patrol with the squadron, I sighted an aircraft diving, and leaving a white smoke trail, being pursued closely by another aircraft. After a little while, the second aircraft flattened out and the emission of white smoke ceased. I pursued this aircraft, which was flying just above the clouds, and after two to three minutes, I caught up and saw it was an Me109. I gave it a seven second burst from slight deflection round to dead astern, closing from three hundred to fifty yards. As I broke away to the side, I saw his hood go up, and the pilot baled out. The machine crashed, just to the south of Pluckley Station, West of Ashford. I force landed, wheels down, at Lenham, as I had been shot at myself, and was hit in the glycol system.

Sergeant John Burgess landed safely in his Spitfire P9318 at a dummy aerodrome at Lenham. His victim was pilot Oberleutnant Otto Hintze of 3/Epro 210, who damaged his shoulder whilst baling out; he landed and was taken prisoner. Both pilots were to meet again after the war, when the remains of Otto Hintze's aircraft were recovered in April 1976.

No.222 were instructed to patrol over Hornchurch, when an unidentified formation was plotted heading towards the airfield at 4.21 pm. But the formation did not arrive, and however, it was presumed to be a false alarm.

On 30th October, No.41 and No.222 flew together on patrol over base at 30,000 feet, No.222 acting as rearguard for No.41. They were told of a raid coming in over the Dover area at 25,000 feet and when this was sighted No.41 went into the attack. The German formation of 30 Me109s was broken up. Flight Lieutenant Norman Ryder, Flying Officer John Mackenzie, and Pilot Officer Aldridge destroyed one Me109 each, while another three enemy machines were claimed as damaged by other pilots of No.41 Squadron.

A smaller formation of six Me109s was spotted by Flying Officer Brian van Mentz of No.222; the 109s were flying above the Spitfires of No.41 Squadron, waiting to bounce them. Flying Officer van Mentz chose the fifth enemy machine to attack, which he did, and after firing a few bursts it began to pour brown smoke. Pilot Officer John Carpenter also attacked one of the enemy aircraft; his report states:

> While flying as the Section protecting a number of 222 Squadron on the Maidstone patrol line, height 27,000 feet, a section of six Me109s were observed about 2,000 feet above us, and circling around as if to attack the squadron.

I immediately climbed up to their height and engaged one
Me109. I got in a burst of five seconds from a range of one
hundred yards, and I noticed my tracer hitting him and bits
falling off. While attacking this Me109, I was myself attacked
by two Me109s, which dived out of the sun and opened fire,
and damaged my airscrew and engine. I managed to get back
to Hornchurch aerodrome O.K.

Unfortunately No.222 did not return from this action unscathed; two of
their pilots had been killed during this action. Pilot Officer Alfred Davies
was killed when his Spitfire's wing was shot off during combat, his aircraft
crashing at Upper Wilting Farm, Crowhurst at 12.11 pm. The other casualty
was Pilot Officer Hilary Edridge, whose Spitfire was badly damaged by
enemy fire. He attempted to crash-land, but his aircraft burst into flames on
Longwood Farm, Ewhurst at 12.15 pm. Rescuers managed to pull him from
the wreckage, and he was rushed to an emergency hospital at Brickwell
House at Northiam, but he died of his injuries later that day.

They carried out their second sortie of the day at 3.30 pm, in company
with aircraft of No.41 Squadron, to patrol over Ashford at 30,000 feet.
Flight Lieutenant Andrew Robinson who was leading 'B' Flight of No.222,
sighted what he thought to be Spitfires slightly above, but as soon as they
appeared 'up sun' they attacked the rear of the squadron. Flight Lieutenant
Robinson was able to get a five second burst of fire at the leading Me109,
which was attacking him head-on; it immediately rolled over and went
down through cloud at 9,000 feet. He claimed the aircraft as probably
destroyed. Later Pilot Officer Tim Vigors sighted two Me109s and caught
up with them 15 miles north-west of Beachy Head. He fired at both aircraft,
which went into a diving spin and then disappeared from view in the clouds
below.

No.41 Squadron were also again engaged in action at the same time over
Ashford, clashing with Me109s. The squadron lost Sergeant Len Garvey
who was killed; his aircraft P7375 crashed on Church Farm, Stanford. Pilot
Officer G.G.F. Draper was also shot down and slightly wounded, but he
managed to bale out and on landing, was admitted to Willesborough
Hospital. His Spitfire P7282 crashed to earth at New Barn Farm, Postling.
No enemy aircraft were claimed during this action.

The Station Diary records that on this date Major Taylor and Major
Moffatt of the United States Army Air Force arrived to spend a week at the
Station. Instructions were given that they were to be shown everything.

**31st October 1940: Officially considered as the last day of the battle.
Some 300 Luftwaffe aircraft are lost in this month for
no apparent strategic benefit.**

Thursday, 31st October, Hornchurch put up a few patrols, but the weather,
with drizzle in the Channel and rain over most of England and France,
prevented any real enemy raids that day.

The final cost to men and machines over the four months of fighting was recorded as:

German aircraft lost – 1,887   German aircrew killed – 2,662
RAF aircraft lost – 1,023   RAF aircrew killed – 517

The part of RAF Hornchurch in the Battle of Britain should not be underestimated nor forgotten. Although it did not perhaps receive the same media attention as stations such as Biggin Hill, Tangmere, and Duxford, the record of RAF Hornchurch was second to none. Sixty-eight airmen of Winston Churchill's famous 'Few' gave their lives in the cause of freedom, during the Battle of Britain, while operating from RAF Hornchurch, and its satellite airfields of Rochford and Manston. Their names are listed with honour within this book.

CHAPTER 8

AFTER THE STORM
November – December 1940

Although the Battle of Britain was now over, London and other major cities in Britain were now taking the full brunt of the Luftwaffe's night bombing raids, to which the RAF was finding it extremely difficult to put up any real defence. The few squadrons of night-fighters were equipped with aircraft like the Bristol Blenheim, and the Bolton-Paul Defiant, which had been taken off day fighter duties, after suffering badly against enemy fighters. These aircraft battled nightly, with only limited success against the German raiders, using primitive night detection radar and searchlight co-operation.

The Luftwaffe, however, continued with its tactics of fighter-bomber sweeps during daylight hours, mainly using Messerschmitt 109s, with a single bomb slung under the fuselage, and attacking various targets when the opportunity arose.

On 1st November 1940, RAF Hornchurch suffered its first casualty of the new month, when an aircraft of No.41 Squadron, flown by Pilot Officer N.M. Brown, struck a barrage balloon cable over Dagenham and crashed. The Spitfire was a complete write-off, but the pilot escaped from the wreckage uninjured. This accident had been due to bad visibility over the local area, and the close proximity of the balloon barrage to the airfield: it was only two or 3 miles away.

The next day, No.41 Squadron were on patrol over Kent, when one of their pilots, Pilot Officer Edward Wells, a New Zealander, sighted an unidentified aircraft in the distance; he broke away from the squadron and, on catching up with the aircraft, found it to be an Me109. He fired a few bursts of machine gun fire into the enemy aircraft, and saw it fall in flames; he claimed it as destroyed.

Another squadron, new to Hornchurch, arrived on 10th November, when No.64 Squadron flew down from Coltishall, with their CO, Squadron Leader Donald MacDonell. He had led the squadron during the Battle of Britain, while it was stationed at RAF Kenley.

One of the pilots newly arrived at Hornchurch with No.64 Squadron, was an American, Flying Officer Arthur Donahue. In his book, which he wrote in 1942, entitled *Tally Ho! Yankee in a Spitfire*, he recalls his impressions of Hornchurch at that time:

The station personnel at our new aerodrome greeted us

warmly. We were replacing a squadron, which had been there through most of the Blitz, and were being moved up north to rest, just as we had been in August.

With wisdom born of previous moves, I made a beeline for the Officers' Mess as soon as I was free, and 'signed in'. The best rooms are first come – first served; I got a very nice double room for myself and Jonah.

I was particularly delighted because our room had a fireplace, for fireplaces are an English institution that I love most of all. This was a very old station that had been first established in the First World War. In the entry to the Mess, there were on display pieces of Zeppelins that had been shot down by planes operating from here in 1916.

A second Spitfire squadron were stationed at this aerodrome; I found out that their CO had been a roommate of mine in hospital in August. In peacetime he had been a world-famous athlete (Don Finlay).

Our first shift of readiness was to be from dawn to one o'clock the next day, which was Armistice Day – of all days to be going back into action. The day begins with my elderly batman waking me up, by coming into my room at about 6.30 am, to get my uniform, shoes and flying boots. I sink back to sleep again to be wakened by his voice saying 'Its 7.30 am now sir.' I wash, shave and dress. Dressed, I walk down the hallway to the large dining hall, where other pilots of the squadrons are drifting in, clomping with their big boots, and rubbing their eyes sleepily. Copies of all the morning London papers are laid out on a table in one corner of the hall; some of us pick up copies to read, while we're eating breakfast. Breakfast consists as usual of cereal, bacon and eggs, toast, marmalade and tea.

Finally we pile into waiting lorries; we get going and drive through the darkened buildings of the aerodrome, and across the parade ground to the Sergeants' Mess. After a short while, half a dozen of them come trooping out, pulling on their Irvin jackets as they come.

We can hear the roar of a Spitfire's Rolls-Royce engine at full throttle, getting its morning 'run up' as we near the 'B' Flight's headquarters. In the office at our flight building, I leaf through the log sheets for the various aircraft of the flight, until I find the one for the machine I'm using. In this is maintained a record of inspections, refuellings, and flights. I check to see that the mechanics and armourers have signed it in the columns required, indicating that the necessary inspections have been made on the aeroplane, engine, instruments, radio and guns. It also confirms that it has been filled with gas, oil, and cooling liquid; I initial it in the column headed 'Pilot', and now I can relax.

Art Donahue left No.64 Squadron in late February 1941. He was sadly listed as missing in action on 11th September 1942, while flying with No.91 Squadron. When intercepting a Junkers Ju88, his Spitfire was damaged by enemy fire, and he was seen to ditch into the Channel; he was not found.

On 11th November, a raid developed over France in which aircraft of the Italian Air Force, the Corpo Aereo Italiano, were involved. Italy's dictator Benito Mussolini had sent a small contingent of his air force, as a gesture to Hitler in his struggle against the RAF, but they were to be totally outclassed. Pilot Officer Edward Wells was again flying that day on patrol; he recalls the following encounter with the Italians:

I remember very clearly my first encounter with the Italian aircraft over England. On that day, No. 41 Squadron were scrambled, and ordered to gain maximum height, on a vector towards North Foreland. Unfortunately, my Spitfire was slow to start, so the squadron left without me. Within a minute or so my engine fired, and as I was keen to join the squadron, and already knew the vector to follow, I set off at full boost hoping to catch them up. But the sky is a very big place, and by the time I was over Southend there was still no sign of them.

Shortly after this and still climbing, I had to enter cloud. At about 10,000 feet I broke cloud to find myself surrounded, or so it seemed to me, by a very loose and open formation of biplanes, flying just above the cloud. I could not recognise them, but I assumed them to be a friendly training flight, which seemed to have lost its way, and strayed into a highly operational area. Almost at once two or three of them opened fire on me, at what seemed extreme range. I found this behaviour to be unacceptable, irritating and even slightly dangerous. I turned on the nearest biplane and gave him a good burst of 3 to 4 seconds. He immediately disappeared into cloud, and was not seen again. I repeated this performance with three more different aircraft, by which time I had exhausted all my ammunition (Spitfires in those days, had only about 12 seconds fire time).

By then I decided to give up any hope of rejoining No.41 Squadron, and I returned to Hornchurch. Here the Intelligence Officer, who saw my gun ports blasted open, was all agog to know what had happened to the rest of No.41 Squadron. When I told him I had never made contact with them, but that I had been attacked by a formation of biplanes, he was as astonished as I had been. A quick look at the identification chart in the dispersal hut, and I was able to positively identify the aircraft as Italian Fiat CR42 fighters. I claimed only one damaged, as I had seen some parts fly off one of the targets, before he disappeared into cloud. I now believe that all four of the

CR42s must have fallen into the sea, somewhere between Southend and North Foreland.

As far as I know, the Italian Air Force never came to England again!

Earlier that day, he had also claimed a Henschel 126 German spotter aircraft, five miles north-east of Cap Gris Nez, which he claimed as a probable.

It was also on this date that No.222 Natal Squadron were posted to RAF Coltishall in Norfolk, to take a well earned rest. While stationed at Hornchurch during the Battle of Britain, they had fought with distinction, claiming 19 enemy aircraft destroyed, and a further 50, either as probably destroyed or damaged. They had lost nine pilots in achieving this.

On 14th November, in view of the full moon, and rumours of reprisals for the interruption of the Molotov Banquet in Berlin by Bomber Command, and the beating up of the Italian Fleet by the Fleet Air Arm, night-flying pilots of the Hornchurch squadrons were at 30 minutes readiness during the night. But their services were not required in 11 Group; the Germans concentrated on Coventry instead of London.

Twelve Spitfires of No.41 Squadron were involved in combat on 17th November, when they encountered a formation of about 70 Me109s, at 25,000 feet over the Thames estuary. During the fighting No.41 were able to claim five of the enemy destroyed and one damaged. Unfortunately they suffered the loss of Pilot Officer Eric Lock, who was wounded in the right arm and both legs; he had been attacked by an Me109 of JG54. He was forced to crash-land his Spitfire P7554 at Martlesham Heath, Suffolk. After landing, he spent the next two hours trapped inside the cockpit of his aircraft, until he was rescued by two soldiers, who then carried him for two miles on a makeshift stretcher. He was to undergo over 15 operations in hospital, to remove cannon shell splinters from his legs, and did not leave hospital until May 1941.

A Spitfire, flown by Pilot Officer Aldridge, was also damaged during this combat; he too had to crash-land, but escaped uninjured.

During November, every squadron at Hornchurch was stood down, for one day a week, for relaxation and recuperation. Flying Officer Peter Brown remembers how one day their CO, a former Olympic hurdler, had other ideas:

Don Finlay, our CO, decided that for the squadron day off, we should all go on a cross-country run, because he thought we should all be physically fitter. The pilots did not think much of the idea, but the CO was adamant about it. We all got together, and met outside the Officers' Mess for the six mile run, dressed in a motley selection of sporting attire. Our CO led us out, but after only a few minutes into the running, he mistimed a jump, and ended up falling into a stream. I finished somewhere around the middle order; our CO came in sixth. We never repeated the exercise.

On 21st November, enemy air activity was once again confined to a few reconnaissance flights, by single aircraft at around mid-day. A section of No.603 Squadron was vectored on to one of these raids. A Heinkel 111 was sighted near Faversham, and although the enemy aircraft was brought down, it was by an unfortunate accident.

Sergeant Ronald Eric Plant, who attacked, failed to breakaway after his attack, and collided with the enemy aircraft. Both aircraft crashed together and burst into flames. Sergeant Plant baled out, but was killed, his body was found near Teynham. His Spitfire P7387 crashed at Bullards Farm, Widdeham. It was unfortunate that the squadron's 100th enemy claim was achieved in this manner.

Again, on 23rd November, aircraft of the Italian Air Force were intercepted by Spitfires from Hornchurch. As previously the Italians were outclassed, because of the obsolete biplanes and bombers they were flying. Air Vice-Marshal David Scott-Malden was a pilot officer with No.603 Squadron at the time, and he remembers that day:

> I can remember 603 Squadron's engagement with the Italian raid over the south-east of England. We were flying with No.41 Squadron, whose CO was Don Finlay. I think I spotted these biplane CR42s first, and reported to our leader, who said something like, 'Can anybody see what they are?' I clearly remember shouting out excitably over the R/T, 'They're Wops', which was the ungracious name given to Italians at this time. I can remember the CO then keeping dead silent, and heading the whole squadron of 603 towards this formation; then Don Finlay calling up over the R/T and saying, 'Where are you going, what have you seen? I heard somebody say Wops.' But we all kept quiet, because we wanted this lot for ourselves.

Seven Italian aircraft fell to the guns of No.603 Squadron, who suffered no loss to themselves. Pilot Officer Scott-Malden claimed two Fiat CR42s damaged. No.41 also claimed an Me109 that day, shot down by Don Finlay, when five 109s were sighted over Tonbridge, Kent during a morning patrol. No.603 Squadron were up on patrol over the Channel on 29th November, when they sighted a Dornier 17, off Ramsgate. David Scott-Malden takes up the story:

> I never really suffered any injuries during the war, except one bogus time, when 603 were attacking a Dornier over the Channel; it seemed to be doing some sort of reconnaissance sortie. When the pilot saw us he dived to sea level; we attacked and he put up a very stout resistance, and I was hit by the rear gunner. I heard this clatter, and noticed there were holes all over my aircraft, so I headed back to Hornchurch.
>
> I called up over the R/T, and told the people at Hornchurch,

that I was struggling back to base, that my left arm was dead, but I could manage the throttle and the stick with my right arm.

They had the blood wagon and fire engine ready for when I landed. I managed to get the wheels and flaps down without too much trouble. I landed and they said 'Stay where you are, and we will come and get you'. Well at that moment my left hand mysteriously started to work; I hadn't wanted to look at it, because I didn't like the sight of blood, but now it was working. I said, 'It's okay I can get to dispersal.' When I got to dispersal, I could find nothing wrong, so it was a bit of a puzzle. But when I looked into the cockpit, I found the armour-piercing core of a shell in a hole in the armour plating; this was lying on the fuse box, which is under your left arm in a Spitfire.

What had happened was that the cannon shell had just come through the armour plate; the rest of the shell was in splinters, and had hit the funny bone in my elbow and paralysed it. I thought I was totally wounded, and out of action, but in fact it hadn't even broken the skin. So that was my only entirely bogus emergency. Every time I went down to dispersal afterwards, they would say, 'How's the wounded hero today?'

On 14th December, another new squadron arrived. This was No.611 'West Lancashire' Auxiliary Squadron who flew their Spitfire MkIs down from Digby, to relieve No.603 Squadron, who, in return, flew back up to Scotland, for a much needed rest. No.611 Squadron was to operate mainly from Rochford, led by their CO Squadron Leader Eric Bitmead.

As Christmas approached, a carol singing service was organised at the RAF Hornchurch Station church for 21st December. Peter Brown, a Flying Officer with No.41 Squadron at that time, remembers the event:

'A' Flight was persuaded to attend by Flight Lieutenant Norman Ryder, our flight commander, and a great leader in the air. He felt we should go and share the occasion, and meet the other station personnel, who we rarely got to see, such as the administration and Ops Room people.

It was also on the morning of 21st December that 12 aircraft of No.64 Squadron were given orders at 10.35 am, to fly a standing patrol over the Maidstone area; this they proceeded to do at a height of 15,000 feet. Five minutes later, No.611 Squadron at Southend, were also given orders to patrol the same line. After a while both squadrons met up in the skies over Kent, but no enemy activity had yet been sighted. Pilot Officer Trevor Gray flying with No.64 Squadron reported:

We had been on patrol for some time when we noticed a condensation trail above us, heading south. Squadron Leader Don MacDonell, our CO took us up after it. When he saw we

were not gaining on it fast enough, he ordered us to break
formation, so we could go after it at the speed of the fastest
Spitfire, and not the slowest.

The condensation trail in fact belonged to a Messerschmitt Me110, of No.7
Long Range Reconnaissance Staffel of Lehrgeschwader II, who operated
from Grimbergen in Belgium. The crew, Leutnant Helmut Fisher and
Unteroffizier Kurt Schaefer, had been given orders to observe and report on
any shipping in the Thames estuary near Southend, and also to photograph
Detling airfield.

The Germans flying at 33,000 feet had now spotted the Spitfires below
them. They pushed full throttle for home, but within four to five minutes, a
couple of the fastest Spitfires had managed to climb and get within firing
range. Pilot Officer Trevor Gray was the first to get within 500 yards of the
Me110, and fired several bursts of fire from long range; one burst hit Kurt
Schaefer wounding him mortally. The pilot of the Me110 swung the aircraft
around the sky, in an effort to lose his attackers, which now consisted of
over a dozen aircraft. Flight Lieutenant Barrie Heath of No.611 Squadron
states in his report:

> I came within range of the enemy at 32,000 feet, and was
> about to attack when he dived steeply. I dived after him,
> waiting until about 20,000 feet, while a Spitfire did an astern
> attack. I then fired a five to six second burst, closing from
> three hundred yards to one hundred yards. At 5,000 feet I had
> to pull out, as I could no longer hold my plane in the dive.

After both Pilot Officer Gray and Flight Lieutenant Heath had tried to bring
down the Me110, two more pilots, Flight Sergeant Maurice Choron and
Pilot Officer Lawson-Brown, tried their luck.

The combat had started at a very high altitude, but had now descended
several thousands of feet, causing the front windscreens of the Spitfires to
frost over; this caused the pilots great problems in an attack. Pilot Officer
J. Lawson-Brown reported:

> I only had a view of about 3 inches in diameter, when I
> cleaned the safety glass with some Glycol solution; some of
> the Perspex was frozen up. I made a quarter attack at 700 feet,
> firing one short burst at 250 yards range, when I was about
> five miles out to sea off Eastbourne. I then came in below
> astern, and fired two short bursts at 250 yards range; then
> closing in, two more at 50 yards range. During the attack the
> enemy aircraft lost height steadily from 300 feet to 50 feet.
> With the fourth and final burst of my attack, I raked the enemy
> aircraft from stem to stern, by pulling the stick back. Then I
> had to break to port, and make a steep climbing turn, to avoid
> being forced into the sea by the enemy aircraft. I circled once,

but could not see anything, and so I set course for Hornchurch.

The Me110, which had crossed the coast at Eastbourne, continued to be harried by the chasing Spitfires. But, one by one, the Spitfires were forced to break off their attacks because of shortage of fuel, some of them having to land at other airfields, or force-land in the Kent countryside, not being able to make it back to Hornchurch.

The Me110 managed to make it back across the Channel, and landed at an airfield at Mardyk, near Dunkirk. The pilot Helmut Fisher survived. His aircraft had taken much damage, with over 30 hits to the airframe. He was to meet one of his opponents, Trevor Gray, 39 years later when he visited Surrey in 1979, and they became good friends.

On 24th December 1940, Wing Commander Harry Broadhurst took over command of RAF Hornchurch from Group Captain Cecil Bouchier. Harry Broadhurst had joined the RAF in 1926, having previously been in the Royal Artillery. He had gained experience flying on the North-West Frontier. Back in England in 1931, he flew with No.41 Squadron on Bristol Bulldogs. By the early 1930s he was thrilling the crowds at the Hendon Air Pageants, leading his tight aerobatic formation of three aircraft, which were roped together. When war came he commanded No.111 Squadron, and by January 1940 he commanded RAF Coltishall. When the Germans invaded, he was posted out to France to command No.60 Wing. Returning to England in May, he was given command of RAF Wittering. With Harry Broadhurst now in command at Hornchurch, and leading from the front, the coming year of 1941 was going to be far from ordinary.

But what of Christmas 1940 at RAF Hornchurch? The Christmas programme was as follows:

December 25th. Station dance at Sutton's Institute, 8 pm to 12 pm.
December 26th. 'Cinderella' – A musical pantomime by the station band and other station personnel at the station workshops at 6 pm.
December 28th. 'Co-Optimists' with Phyllis Monkham at the Station Workshops at 6 pm.
December 31st. Station dance at Sutton's Institute from 8 pm till 1 am.

There was also the following message received from the Chief of Air Staff addressed to all RAF units at home; this read:

> I send warmest greetings for Christmas and best wishes for the New Year to all ranks of the Royal Air Force. Your splendid work of the past 12 months gives me full confidence that the coming year will be one of great achievements. I am proud of you all and thank you.

In the year that followed, RAF Hornchurch would again be in the front line, bringing the fight to the Germans over occupied France, engaged with sweeps and fighter escorts for Bomber Command, as Britain hit back.

ROLL OF HONOUR

The 68 Pilots & Aircrew killed during the Battle of Britain while flying operational from RAF Hornchurch are listed below.

Rank	Name	Squadron	KiA
F/O	J.L.Allen	No.54	24.7.40
F/Lt	R.C.V. Ash	No.264	28.8.40
Sgt	B. Baker	No.264	2.9.40
Sgt	S. Baxter	No.222	14.9.40
P/O	J.V. Benson	No.603	28.8.40
Sgt	A. Berry	No.264	24.8.40
P/O	N.G. Bowen	No.266	16.8.40
F/O	J.G. Boyle	No.41	28.9.40
P/O	J.W. Broadhurst	No.222	7.10.40
P/O	F.W. Cale	No.266	15.8.40
P/O	P.M. Cardell	No.603	27.9.40
P/O	H.H. Chalder	No.41	10.11.40
P/O	D.G. Cobden	No.74	11.8.40
Sgt	G.R. Collett	No.54	22.8.40
F/Lt	J.L.G. Cunningham	No.603	28.8.40
F/O	J.W. Cutts	No.222	4.9.40
P/O	A.E. Davies	No.222	30.10.40
P/O	R.B. Dewy	No.603	27.10.40
P/O	H.P.M. Edridge	No.222	30.10.40
Sgt	F.W. Ely	No.74	31.7.40
P/O	A. Finnie	No.54	25.7.40
F/O	D.R. Gamblen	No.41	29.7.40
Sgt	L.A Garvey	No.41	30.10.40
F/O	C. W. Goldsmith	No.603	28.10.40
Sub/Lt	H.L.Greenshields	No.266	16.8.40
P/O	F.S. Gregory	No.65	13.8.40
F/O	F. Gruszka	No.65	18.8.40
P/O	H.R. Gunn	No.74	31.7.40
Sgt	F.B. Hawley	No.266	15.8.40
S/Ldr	H.R.L. Hood	No.41	5.9.40
P/O	P. Howes	No.603	18.9.40
S/Ldr	P.A. Hunter	No.264	24.8.40
Sgt	J.I. Johnson	No.222	30.8.40

Rank	Name	Squadron	KiA
P/O	C.E. Johnson	No.264	28.8.40
P/O	J.T. Jones	No.264	24.8.40
Sgt	F.J. Keast	No.600	8.8.40
P/O	P.L. Kenner	No.264	28.8.40
Sgt	M. Keymer	No.65	22.8.40
P/O	F.H. King	No.264	24.8.40
Sgt	D.I. Kirton	No.65	8.8.40
P/O	G.A. Langley	No.41	15.9.40
P/O	J.G. Lecky	No.41	11.10.40
Sgt	P.D. Lloyd	No.41	15.10.40
P/O	D.K. MacDonald	No.603	28.8.40
F/Lt	H.K. MacDonald	No.603	28.9.40
Sgt	W.H. Machin	No.264	24.8.40
P/O	H.K.F. Matthews	No.603	7.10.40
Sgt	W. Maxwell	No.264	26.8.40
F/O	D.H. O'Neill	No.41	11.10.40
P/O	A.P. Pease	No.603	15.9.40
F/Sgt	N.T. Phillips	No.65	8.8.40
P/O	W.A. Ponting	No.264	24.8.40
P/O	L.L. Pyman	No.65	16.8.40
Sgt	J.W. Ramshaw	No.222	4.9.40
F/Lt	F.W. Rushmer	No.603	5.9.40
S/Ldr	H.C. Sawyer	No.65	2.8.40
Sgt	E. Scott	No.222	27.9.40
F/O	W.J.M. Scott	No.41	8.9.40
F/O	I.G. Shaw	No.264	24.8.40
P/O	D.N.E Smith	No.74	11.8.40
Sgt	R.C. Turner	No.264	28.8.40
F/O	R. M. Waterston	No.603	31.8.40
F/Lt	B.H. Way	No.54	25.7.40
F/Lt	J.T. Webster	No.41	5.9.40
P/O	H.L. Whitbread	No.222	20.9.40
P/O	D. Whitley	No.264	28.8.40
S/Ldr	R.L. Wilkinson	No.266	16.8.40
P/O	J.H.R. Young	No.74	28.7.40

APPENDIX A

Royal Flying Corps and RAF Squadrons
stationed at Sutton's Farm 1915-1919

Squadrons	Aircraft Types
No.23 Squadron, detachment to Sutton's Farm October 1915	BE2c
No.39 Squadron, April 1916 – October 1918	BE2c, BE2e,BE12a
	Bristol F2b
No.46 Squadron, July – August 1918	Sopwith Camel F1
No.51 Squadron, May – June 1919	Sopwith Camel F1
No.66 Squadron, July 1917	Sopwith Pup
No.78 Squadron, September 1917 – December 1919	BE 2c, BE12, FE9
	Sopwith 1½ Strutter
	Sopwith Camel F1
No.189 (Night Training) Squadron, April 1918 – March 1919	Sopwith Pup and Snipe

Sutton's Farm Squadron Commanders 1916-1918

No.39 Squadron

Officers	Dates
Major T.C.R. Higgins	19.4.16
Major W.C.H. Mansfield	13.6.16
Major A.H. Morton	26.7.16
Major H.G.H. Murrey	20.3.17
Major J.C. Halahan	7.7.17
Major W.H.D. Acland	9.8.17

No.46 Squadron

Major P. Babington	8.8.18

No.51 Squadron

Major H.L.H. Owen	–.5.19

No.66 Squadron

Major G.L.P Henderson	–.7.17

No. 78 Squadron

Major C.H. Rowden	5.7.17
Major G. Allan	26.4.18
Major C.J.Truran	12.8.18

No. 189 Squadron

Major H.S. Powell	18.2.18

APPENDIX B

RAF Hornchurch Station Commanders
1928-1940

Wing Commander K.R. Park, MC, DFC	1.4. 1928
Squadron Leader F.O. Soden, DFC	8.3. 1929
Squadron Leader L.H. Slatter, OBE, DSO, DFC	25.10.1929
Wing Commander E.R. Manning, DSO, MC	4. 4.1930
Wing Commander C.H. Nicholas, DFC, AFC	22. 7.1933
Wing Commander A.S.G. Lee, MC	22.12.1935
Wing Commander M.B. Frew, DSO, MC, AFC	2. 4.1937
Wing Commander C.T. Walkington	27.7.1938
Group Captain C.H. Nicholas, DFC, AFC	4.10.1939
Group Captain C.A. Bouchier, OBE, DFC	21.12.1939
Group Captain H. Broadhurst, DSO, DFC, AFC	23.12.1940

APPENDIX C

Squadrons operational from RAF Hornchurch
3rd September 1939 – 31st December 1940

Squadron	Dates	Sqdn Code Letters	Aircraft
No.19	25th May – 5th June 1940	QV	Spitfire Mk1
No.41	28th May – 8th June 1940 26th July – 8th August 1940 3rd September – 23rd February 1941	EB	Spitfire Mk1/IIa
No.54	Sept 1939 – 28th May 1940 4th June – 28th July 1940 8th August – 3rd September 1940	KL	SpitfireMk1/IIa
No.64	10th November 1940 –	SH	Spitfire Mk1
No.65	September – 2nd October 1939 28th March – 28th August 1940	YT	Spitfire Mk1
No.74	September 1939 – 14th August 1940	ZP	Spitfire Mk1
No.92	23rd May – 25th May 1940	QJ	Spitfire Mk1
No.222	28th May – 4th June 1940 28th August – 11th Nov 1940	ZD	Spitfire Mk1
No.264	22nd – 28th August 1940	PS	Boulton-Paul Defiant
No.266	14th – 21st August 1940	UO	Spitfire Mk1
No.600	2nd October 1939 – 14th May 1940 4th July 1940 – September 1940	BQ	Bristol Blenheim
No.603	27th August-13th December 1940	XT	Spitfire Mk1/IIa
No.611	14th December –	FY	Spitfire Mk1

APPENDIX D

Hornchurch Squadron operational radio call-signs during the Battle of Britain

Squadrons	Call-Signs
No.41 Squadron	Mitor
No.54 Squadron	Rabbit
No.65 'East India' Squadron	
No.74 'Trinidad' or 'Tiger' Squadron	Dysoe
No.222 'Natal' Squadron	Cotal
No.264 'Madras Presidency' Squadron	
No.266 'Rhodesia' Squadron	
No.600 'City of London' Auxiliary Squadron	
No.603 'City of Edinburgh' Auxiliary Squadron	Viken

APPENDIX E

Hornchurch's Battle of Britain Squadron Commanders

Squadron		Dates
No.41	S/Ldr Hilary Richard Lionel Hood	April 1940 – 5th Sept 1940 (killed)
	S/Ldr Robert Charles Franklin Lister	8th Sept 1940 – 14th Sept 1940
	S/Ldr Donald Osborne Finlay	14th Sept 1940 – August 1941
No.54	S/Ldr James Anthony Leathart	26th May 1940 – 18th October 1940
	S/Ldr Donald Osborne Finlay	26th August 1940 – 28th August 1940 (wounded)
No.65	S/Ldr Henry Cecil Sawyer	8th July 1940 – 2nd August 1940 (killed)
	S/Ldr Arthur Lawrence Holland	14th August 1940 – 28th August 1940
No.74	S/Ldr Francis Lawrence White	1st March 1940 – 8th August 1940
No.222	S/Ldr John Hamar Hill	31st July 1940 – January 1941
No.264	S/Ldr Philip Algernon Hunter	March 1940 – 24th August 1940 (killed)
	S/Ldr George Desmond Garvin	24th August 1940 – 8th December 1940
No.266	S/Ldr Rodney Levitt Wilkinson	28th June 1940 – 16th August 1940 (killed)
	F/Lt Dennis Armitage	16th August 1940 – May 1941
No.600	S/Ldr David de B. Clarke	20th June – 12th September 1940
	S/Ldr Hugh Maxwell	15th Sept 1940 – November 1940
No.603	S/Ldr George Denholm	4th June 1940 – April 1941

APPENDIX F

Pilots and Aircrew who served at RAF Hornchurch during the Battle of Britain

No.41 Squadron

F/O D.A. Adams
P/O E.S. Aldous
P/O F.J. Aldridge
Sgt J.W. Allison
Sgt R.A. Angus
Sgt A.C. Baker
F/O H.C. Baker
Sgt C.S. Bamberger
Sgt R.A. Beardsley
P/O G.H. Bennions
P/O R.J. Boret
F/O J.G. Boyle
F/O M.P. Brown
P/O N. McHardy Brown
Sgt R.A. Carr-Lewty
Sgt L.R. Carter
P/O H.H. Chalder
F/O G.W. Cory
Sgt E.V. Darling
P/O G.G.F. Draper
S/Ldr D.O. Finlay
Sgt R.C. Ford
F/O D.R. Gamblen
Sgt L.A. Garvey
Sgt T.W.R. Healy

S/Ldr H.R.L. Hood
Sgt I.E. Howitt
P/O G.A. Langley
P/O J.G. Lecky
S/Ldr R.C.F Lister
Sgt P.D. Lloyd
P/O E.S. Lock
F/O A.D.J. Lovell
Sgt J. McAdam
F/O J.N. Mackenzie
P/O D.E. Mileham
F/O O.B. Morrough-Ryan
Sgt J.K. Norwell
F/O D.H. O'Neill
F/Lt E.N. Ryder
F/Sgt J.E. Sayers
F/O W.J.M. Scott
F/O E.A. Shipman
Sgt F. Usmar
F/O J.R. Walker
F/O R.W. Wallens
F/Lt J.T. Webster
P/O E.P. Wells
S/Ldr H.West

No. 54 Squadron

Sgt A. Aitken
P/O J.L. Allen
P/O W. Armstrong
P/O S. Baker
P/O A.R. Campbell
P/O E.J. Coleman
Sgt G.R. Collett
P/O G.W. Couzens
Sgt J. Davis
F/O A.C. Deere
P/O E.F. Edsall
S/Ldr D.O. Finlay

P/O A. Finnie
Sgt D.G. Gibbins
F/O C.W. Goldsmith
F/O C.F. Gray
F/O D.G. Gribble
Sgt L.W. Harvey
P/O W.P. Hopkin
P/O P. Howes
F/O J.L. Kemp
Sgt W. Klozinski
P/O W. Krepski
Sgt N.A. Lawrence

No.54 Squadron (continued)

S/Ldr J.A. Leathart
F/O D.A.P. McMullen
P/O L. Martel
F/O H.K.F. Matthews
F/Lt S.T. Meares
Sgt J.K. Norwell
Sgt R.H. Robbins

Sgt B.L. Robertson
P/O M.M. Shand
Sgt D.J. Steadman
Sgt L. Switon
F/Sgt P.H. Tew
F/O D.R. Turley-George
F/O B.H. Way

No.65 Squadron

P/O B. Drobinski
P/O B.E.F. Finucane
P/O W.H. Franklin
P/O E.D. Glaser
F/O S.B. Grant
P/O F.S. Gregory
F/O F. Gruszka
P/O K.G. Hart
Sgt C.R. Hewlett
Sgt G. Hill
Sgt M.H. Hine
S/Ldr A.L. Holland
Sgt M. Keymer
Sgt J.R. Kilner
Sgt D.I. Kirton

F/Sgt R.R. MacPherson
F/Lt W.H. Maitland-Walker
Sgt P. Mitchell
F/O J.B.H. Nicholas
F/Lt C.G.C. Olive
Sgt H.C. Orchard
F/Sgt N.T. Phillips
F/O L.E. Pyman
F/O J.K.Quill
F/Lt G.A.W. Saunders
S/Ldr H.C. Sawyer
F/O T. Smart
Sgt R.L. Stillwell
P/O W. Szulkowski
F/O R.G. Wigg

No.74 Squadron

F/Lt S. Brzezina
P/O D.G. Cobden
F/O D.H.T. Dowding
P/O B.V. Draper
Sgt F.W. Eley
F/O J.C. Freeborn
P/O H.R. Gunn
P/O D. Hastings
Sub/Lt D.A Hutchinson
F/O D.P.D.G. Kelly
F/Lt A.G. Malan
W/O E. Mayne

F/Lt W.E.G. Measures
Sgt E.A. Mould
F/O J.C. Mungo-Park
F/O W.H. Nelson
F/O P.C.B. St. John
Sgt W.A. Skinner
P/O D.N.E. Smith
P/O H.M. Stephen
P/O P.C.F. Stevenson
P/O H. Szczesny
S/Ldr F.L. White
P/O J.H.R. Young

No.222 Squadron

P/O W.R. Assheton
P/O F.B. Bassett
Sgt S. Baxter
Sgt O.R. Bowerman
Sgt R.A. Breese
P/O J.W. Broadhurst
Sgt J.H.B. Burgess
P/O J.M.V. Carpenter

Sgt D.J. Chipping
P/O I.H. Cosby
F/O J.W. Cutts
P/O A.E. Davies
P/O G.G.A. Davies
Sgt P.O. Davis
Sgt J.T. Dunmore
P/O H.P.M. Edridge

No.222 Squadron (continued)

P/O E.F. Edsall
Sgt D.G. Gibbins
Sgt R.H. Gretton
F/O I.L.M. Hallam
S/Ldr J.H. Heyworth
S/Ldr J.H. Hill
Sgt I. Hutchinson
Sgt J.I. Johnson
Sgt R.B. Johnson
F/O D.A.P. McMullen
Sgt R.G. Marland
F/Lt G.C. Matheson
S/Ldr H.W. Mermagen

Sgt L.F. Patrick
Sgt R.B. Price
Sgt N.H.D. Ramsey
Sgt J.W. Ramshaw
F/Lt A.I. Robinson
Sgt E. Scott
Sgt A.W.P. Spears
P/O C. Stewart
F/Lt E.H. Thomas
F/O B. van Mentz
P/O T.A. Vigors
P/O H.L. Whitbread

No.264 Squadron

F/Lt R.C.V. Ash
F/O J.R.A. Bailey
Sgt B. Baker
F/Lt A.J. Banham
Sgt F.J. Barker
P/O E.G. Barwell
Sgt A. Berry
P/O P.D. Bowen
Sgt A. Campbell
F/Lt E.W. Campbell-Colquhoun
P/O S. Carlin
F/O W.F. Carnaby
Sgt V.R. Chapman
Sgt W.E. Cox
Sgt V.W.J. Crook
P/O C.C. Ellery
Sgt C.S. Emeny
S/Ldr G.D. Gavin
Sgt F. Gash
P/O R.S. Gaskell
P/O H.I. Goodhall
P/O G.H. Hackwood
Sgt O.A. Hardy
Sgt L.H. Hayden
F/O F.D. Hughes
S/Ldr P.A. Hunter
P/O C.E. Johnson
P/O J.T. Jones
P/O P.L. Kenner
P/O F.H. King
F/O W.R.A. Knocker
Sgt A.J. Lauder

Sgt W.H. Machin
Sgt A. Martin
Sgt W. Maxwell
P/O A. O'Connell
F/O D.K.C. O'Malley
F/O H.H. Percy
P/O W.A. Ponting
Sgt G. Robinson
Sgt L.P. Russell
F/O I.G. Shaw
F/O F.W. Shepherd
P/O D.M.A. Smythe
F/O I.R. Stephenson
F/O R.W. Stokes
P/O A.J. Storrie
P/O F.C. Sutton
P/O S.R. Thomas
Sgt E.R. Thorn
P/O F.A. Toombs
Sgt R.C. Turner
P/O T.D. Welsh
P/O D. Whitley
P/O M.H. Young
Sgt R.B.M. Young

No.266 Squadron

P/O D.L. Armitage
F/Lt S.H. Bazley
Sgt R.G.V. Barraclough
P/O N.G. Bowen
P/O F.W. Cale
P/O H.H. Chalder
Sgt A.W. Eade
Sub/Lt H. Greenshields
Sgt R.H. Gretton
Sgt F.B. Hawley

P/O W.R. Jones
Sgt D.E. Kingaby
P/O C.L. Logan
P/O R.J.B. Roach
P/O J.F. Soden
S/Ldr D.G.H. Spencer
P/O R.M. Trousdale
S/Ldr R.L. Wilkinson
P/O W.S. Williams

No.600 Squadron

Sgt A.V. Albertini
P/O R. Atkinson
P/O S. Baker
Sgt E.C. Barnard
F/Lt J.G.C. Barnes
P/O C.E. Blair
F/O B.H. Bowring
F/O A.D.M. Boyd
Sgt J.W. Brown
P/O J.C. Bull
Sgt A.G. Burdekin
Sgt P.S. Burley
Sgt A.W. Canham
F/Lt D.L. Clackson
S/Ldr D.B. Clark
Sgt R.J. Coombs
Sgt L.E.M. Coote
P/O G.A. Denby
AC L. Dixon
P/O K.C. Edwards
Sgt E.J. Egan
P/O J.L. Frost
P/O A.J. Glegg
Sgt E.J.F. Grant
Sgt F.W.W. Green
F/O D.N. Grice
P/O R.C. Haine
Sgt W.R.H. Hardwick
F/Lt T.N. Hayes
P/O C.A. Hobson
Sgt R.M. Holland
P/O G.H. Holmes
P/O H.B.L. Hough

Sgt P.E. Huckin
P/O S.F.F. Johnson
P/O J.R. Juleff
Sgt F.J. Keast
P/O M. Kramer
P/O R.L. Lamb
P/O B.D. Larbalestier
Sgt E.S. Lawler
F/Lt S.P. le Rougetel
Sgt C.S. Lewis
S/Ldr H.L. Maxwell
Sgt E.W. Moulton
AC A.E. Owen
LAC P.G. Pearce
Sgt F.S. Perkin
F/Lt C.A. Pritchard
F/O A.J. Rawlence
AC H. Reed
Sgt A.H. Riseley
P/O J.R. Ritchie
F/O G.E.T. Scrase
Sgt B. Senior
AC A. Smith
Sgt E.C. Smith
F/Lt E.S. Smith
Sgt F.J. Tearle
Sgt T.W. Townsend
Sgt J.I.B. Walker
AC J.B.W. Warren
P/O N.J. Wheeler
Sgt P.C. Whitwell
P/O W.D. Wiseman

No.603 Squadron

Sgt I.K. Arber
Sgt G.J. Bailey
P/O N.J.V. Benson
P/O R. Berry
F/Lt J.C. Boulter
Sgt A.D. Burt
P/O J.R. Caister
F/O B.J.G. Carbury
P/O P.M. Cardell
F/Lt J.L.G. Cunningham
Sgt A.S. Darling
S/Ldr G.L. Denholm
P/O R.B. Dewey
F/O P.G. Dexter
F/O G.K. Gilroy
F/O C.W. Goldsmith
F/Lt J.G.E. Haig
F/O P. McD Hartas
F/O R.H. Hillary
P/O P. Howes
P/O K.A. Lawrence
P/O D.K. MacDonald
F/Lt H.K. MacDonald
F/O B.R. MacNamara

P/O J.F.J. MacPhail
P/O L. Martel
F/O H.K.J. Matthews
P/O D.A. Maxwell
P/O J.S. Morton
P/O P. Olver
F/O A.P. Pease
F/O C.D. Peel
F/O D.J.C. Pinckney
P/O H.A.R. Prowse
P/O W.P.H. Rafter
P/O W.A.A. Read
F/Lt I.S. Ritchie
F/Lt F.W. Rushmer
Sgt A.R. Sarre
F/O F.D.S Scott-Malden
P/O J.F. Soden
F/O B.G. Stapleton
P/O D. Stewart-Clark
Sgt J. Stokoe
Sgt P.H.R.R. Terry
F/O R. McG. Waterston
P/O A.L. Winskill

APPENDIX G

Hornchurch Squadrons Battle of Britain enemy claims

The honour of the most enemy aircraft destroyed during the Battle of Britain period is credited to No.603 'City of Edinburgh' Squadron with 58 enemy aircraft confirmed.

Top scoring pilot during the Battle of Britain

Until recently this honour was credited to the Polish pilot Sergeant
Josef Frantisek of No.303 Squadron with 17 enemy aircraft destroyed and 1 probable.
Now recent research shows that Flight Lieutenant Eric Lock of No.41 Squadron claimed 20 enemy aircraft destroyed with 7 probably destroyed.

Number of enemy aircraft destroyed during the Battle of Britain by individual squadrons at Hornchurch and their losses

Squadron	Enemy aircraft destroyed	Own aircraft losses
No.41 Squadron	45	32
No.54 Squadron	34	20
No.65 Squadron	10.5	15
No.74 Squadron	23	11
No.222 Squadron	19	15
No.266 Squadron	8	11
No.264 Squadron	7.5	10
No.603 Squadron	58	30
Total 205		**Total 144**

APPENDIX H

Serial numbers of known aircraft used at Hornchurch during the Battle of Britain. Their final fate or their arrival date at the squadron is listed, and the pilots who flew them, if known.

Spitfire aircraft flown from RAF Hornchurch during the Battle of Britain

No.41 Squadron

Serial No.	Date of arrival or final fate	Pilot
K9890	13.7.40	Sgt Darling
K9993	19.6.40	F/Lt Ryder
N3038	Shot down on 29.7.40	F/O Gamblen
N3054		P/O Mackenzie
N3059	Damaged in combat on 11.9.40	Sgt Hewitt
N3098	Forced landed 5.9.40	Sgt Carr-Lewty
N3100	Damaged in landing on 29.7.40	F/O Scott
N3108	22.3.40	P/O Morrough-Ryan
N3112	Damaged in combat on 29.7.40	F/O Mackenzie
N3113	Crashed on landing on 29.7.40	F/Lt Webster
N3118	Shot down on 24.9.40	Sgt McAdam
N3123	18.2.40	P/O Langley
N3126	21.1.40 – Wrecked in landing 5.8.40	P/O Mackenzie
N3162	Damaged in combat on 5.9.40	P/O Lock injured
N3163	24.12.39	P/O Wallens
N3225	Damaged in combat on 5.10.40	F/O Lovell
N3234	20.7.40	F/O Boyle
N3264	Crashed on landing on 29.7.40	P/O Bennions
N3266	Damaged in combat on 17.9.40	P/O Chalder
N3267	Shot down on 7.10.40	F/O Adams
N3280	20.10.40	Sgt Baker
P7281	24.10.40	P/O Mileham
P7282	Shot down on 30.10.40	P/O Draper
P7283	24.10.40	F/Lt Ryder
P7284	24.10.40	Sgt McAdam
P7299	25.10.40	F/O Mackenzie
P7300	24.10.40	Sgt McAdam
P7314	24.10.40	P/O Lock
P7322	24.10.40	P/O McHardy-Brown
P7326	24.10.40	P/O Wells
P7354	24.10.40	F/O Brown
P7371	Forced landing on 25.10.40	Sgt Beardsley
P7374	24.10.40	Sgt Healy
P7375	Shot down on 30.10.40	Sgt Garvey killed

P7382	25.10.40	F/Lt Lovell
P7384	25.10.40	Sgt McAdam
P7442	Forced landing on 25.10.40	P/O Mackenzie
P7443	24.10.40	F/Lt Ryder
P7448	26.10.40	F/O Cory
P7507	26.10.40 – Hit barrage balloon cable	
	& crashed on 1.11.40	P/O McHardy-Brown
P7508	27.10.40	P/O Lock
P7509	Borrowed from No 603 Sqdn Oct 40	P/O Mackenzie
P9324	Shot down on 15.9.40	P/O Langley killed
P9335	11.10.40	P/O Wells
P9394	Damaged in combat on 30.9.40	Sgt Beardsley
P9427	13.9.40	P/O Aldous
P9428	Air collision with R6635 5.9.40	S/Ldr Hood killed
P9429	Forced landing on 28.7.40	F/O Lovell
P9430	Shot down on 7.9.40	Sgt McAdam
P9447	Shot down on 11.10.40	P/O Lecky killed
P9500	Forced landing on 6.9.40	Sgt Usmar
P9512	Forced landing on 12.10.40	Sgt McAdam
R6597	29.9.40	F/O Brown
R6604	Forced landing on 24.9.40	Sgt Darling
R6605	Shot down on 14.9.40	S/Ldr Lister injured
R6610	Damaged in combat 17.9.40	Pilot not known
R6611	30.7.40	F/O Scott
R6612	Damaged in combat on 15.9.40	Pilot not known
R6619	Damaged at Hornchurch 28.9.40	P/O Bennions
R6635	Air collision with P9428 5.9.40	F/Lt Webster killed
R6687	1.6.40	P/O Walker
R6697	6.9.40	F/Lt Ryder
R6755	Shot down on 27.9.40	F/Lt Ryder
R6756	Shot down on 8.9.40	F/O Scott killed
R6765	17.10.40	Sgt Garvey
R6883		F/O Wallens
R6884	1.7.40	Sgt Howitt
R6885	Shot down on 5.9.40	F/O Lovell
R6887	Damaged in combat on 17.9.40	P/O Mackenzie
X4017	5.10.40	Sgt Cory
X4021	Shot down in combat on 5.9.40	F/O Wallens
X4027	Sent from No.74 Sqdn.	Sgt Bamberger
X4042	Air collision on 11.10.40	F/O O'Neill killed
X4052	19.9.40	Sgt McAdam
X4060	12.10.40	P/O Adams
X4068	13.9.40	F/O Lovell
X4069	13.9.40	F/O Lovell
X4101	Forced landing on 20.9.40	P/O Bennions
X4178	Shot down on 15.10.40	Sgt Lloyd killed
X4235	Shot down in combat on 11.9.40	P/O Langley
X4253	5.10.40	F/O Brown
X4317	Damaged in combat on 18.9.40	P/O Bennions
X4318	Forced landing on 5.9.40	F/O Morrough-Ryan
X4325		F/O Lovell
X4338	7.9.40	Sgt Usmar
X4343	Damaged in combat on 11.9.40	P/O Bennions
X4344	Damaged in combat on 30.9.40	F/O Lovell
X4345	Shot down on 28.9.40	P/O Aldous injured
X4346	6.9.40	Sgt Howitt

X4409	Forced landing on 17.9.40	P/O Baker
,,	Shot down on 28.9.40	P/O Chalder died later
X4426	Shot down on 28.9.40	F/O Boyle killed
X4545	Struck parked A/C on 2.10.40	Sgt Norwell
X4547	2.10.40	
X4554	Air collision with Spitfire 11.10.40	Sgt Carter
X4558	Forced landing at base 9.10.40	S/Ldr Finlay
X4559	Shot down on 1.10.40	P/O Bennions injured
X4560		P/O McHardy-Brown
X4584		P/O Adams
X4589	7.10.40	P/O Lock
X4592	8.10.40	F/O Brown
X4604	14.10.40	F/O Mackenzie
X4609	17.10.40	Sgt McAdam

No.54 Squadron

Serial No.	Date of arrival or final date	Pilot
L1042	26.7.40	P/O Turley-George
L1093	29.5.40	P/O Hopkins
N3097	Shot down on 15.8.40	Sgt Lawrence
N3110	Destroyed in airfield attack 31.8.40	
N3160	Forced landing on 12.8.40	P/O Edsall
N3173	9.3.40	P/O Gray
N3184	Shot down on 21.7. 40	P/O Kemp
N3192	Damaged in F/Landing 24.7.40	Sgt Collett injured
P9326	1.9.40	
P9367	12.6.40	P/O Coleman
P9369	Damaged in F/Landing 8.8.40	Sgt Squire injured
P9387	Forced landing on 25.7.40	P/O Turley-George
P9389	Shot down on 24.8.40	P/O Stewart
P9446	Damaged in combat on 10.7.40	Sgt Mould
P9549	Damaged in combat on 24.7.40	Sgt Tew
R6705	Shot down on 9.7.40	P/O Garton killed
R6707	Shot down on 25.7.40	F/Lt Way killed
R6708	Shot down on 22.8.40	Sgt Collett killed
R6709	12.6.40	P/O Gray
R6710	Damaged in combat 24.7.40	P/O Matthews
R6812	Damaged in combat, crashed 24.7.40	P/O Allen killed
R6814	12.7.40	P/O Edsall
R6815	Forced landing on 12.8.40	P/O Kemp
R6816	Shot down in combat on 25.7.40	P/O Finnie killed
R6832	Shot down on 28.8.40	F/Lt Deere
R6892	25.6.40	P/O Gray
R6893	9.7.40	P/O Gray
R6895	Damaged in airfield attack 31.8.40	F/Lt Deere injured
R6898	13.7.40	P/O Howes
R6899	13.7.40	P/O Gribble
R6901	Failed to return from Ops 7.9.40	P/O Krepski missing
R6913	23.7.40	Sgt Norwell
R6914	Damaged in crash-landing 12.8.40	P/O Turley-George
R6962	28.7.40	
R6969	Damaged in combat 25.8.40	P/O Shand injured
R6973	17.8.40	S/Ldr Leathart
R6974	17.8.40	P/O Campbell

R6981	Shot down on 15.8.40	F/Lt Deere
R6984	2.8.40	
R7015	Shot down on 15.8.40	Sgt Klozinski injured
R7017	28.7.40	P/O McMullen
R7019	Forced landing on 15.8.40	P/O Matthews
R7021	28.7.40 (See also 603 Sqdn)	Sgt Klozinski
X4019	Damaged in combat 24.8.40	P/O Campbell injured
X4021	1.8.40	
X4022	1.8.40	
X4053	Shot down on 28.8.40	S/Ldr Finlay
X4054	Shot down by Hurricane 31.8.40	Sgt Gibbons
X4108	16.8.40	P/O Matthews
X4163	13.8.40	P/O Howes
X4235	Damaged in airfield attack 31.8.40	Sgt Davis
X4236	Destroyed in airfield attack 31.8.40	P/O Edsall
X4238	25.8.40	P/O Gray
X4276	29.8.40	S/Ldr Leathart

No.65 'East India' Squadron

Serial No.	Date of arrival or final fate	Pilot
K9789	27.2.40	
K9903	21.3.40	F/Lt Olive
K9904	22.3.39	Sgt Hine
K9905	Shot down on 8.8.40	F/Sgt Phillips killed
K9909	Failed to return 22.8.40	Sgt Keymer missing
K9911	Shot down on 8.8.40	Sgt Kirton killed
K9913	28.3.40	
K9915	Shot down on 16.8.40	P/O Pyman killed
K9919	4.4.40	
L1094	Damaged in combat on 22.8.40	Sgt Orchard
N3101	2.4.40	F/O Nicholas
N3128	Crashed on take-off at night 2.8.40	S/Ldr Sawyer killed
N3161	3.4.40	Sgt Stillwell
N3163	8.8.40	P/O Glaser
N3164		F/Sgt Franklin
P9436	Forced landing on 5.8.40	Sgt Walker injured
P9516	12.7.40	Sgt Kilner
P9555	16.8.40	
P9562	18.8.40	P/O Chappell
R6602	Damaged in combat on 14.8.40	P/O Pyman
R6610	4.8.40	
R6617	Crashed on take-off on 7.8.40	F/Lt Olive
R6618	Destroyed in enemy raid on 16.8.40	
R6620	Damaged in combat on 23.8.40	P/O Smart
R6712	Damaged in raid on airfield 12.8.40	P/O Hart
R6713	Shot down on 18.8.4	F/O Gruszka killed
R6714	10.7.40	Sgt Keymer
R6764		P/O Hart
R6766	Shot down on 13.8.40	P/O Gregory killed
R6775	12.7.40	F/O Quill
R6777	12.7.40	
R6799	12.7.40	S/Ldr Sawyer
R6803	8.8.40	F/O Wigg
R6818	Forced landing on 20.8.40	P/O Hart

R6883		F/Lt Olive
R6884	Damaged in combat on 14.8.40	Sgt Keymer
R6886	Damaged on 18.8.40	Sgt Hewlett
R6982	6.8.40	
R6987	11.8.40	S/Ldr Holland
X4059	9.8.40	Sgt Kilner
X4232	21.8.40	P/O Drobinski
X4233	21.8.40	Sgt Hart

No.74 'Tiger' Squadron

Serial No.	Date of arrival or final fate	Pilot
K9863	Damaged in operations on 10.7.40	P/O Freeborn
K9870	Damaged in operations on 8.8.40	P/O Hastings
K9871	Shot down in operations on 13.8.40	P/O Szezesny
K9878	1.3.39 (See also 222 Sqdn)	F/O Mungo-Park
K9951	2.5.39	F/Sgt Mayne
K9953	2.5.39	Sub/Lt Wallace
L1001	Damaged in practice flight on 24.7.40	F/O Nelson
L1089	12.12.39 (See also 222 Sqdn)	P/O Freeborn
L1094	Sent to Hornchurch on 15.8.40	W/O Mayne
N3091	Shot down in combat on 13.8.40	F/Lt Brzezina
P9306	9.7.40 – Now preserved at the Museum of Science & Industry, Chicago	P/O Stevenson
P9336	Shot down in combat on 28.7.40	Sgt Mould
P9379	Shot down in operations on 31.7.40	P/O Gunn killed
P9380	Damaged in operations on 8.8.40	P/O Freeborn
P9393	Shot down in operations on 11.8.40	P/O Stevenson
P9396	Shot down in combat on 28.7.40	Sgt Mould wounded
P9397		P/O Dowding
P9398	Shot down in operations on 31.7.40	Sgt Eley killed
P9399	Force-landed on 10.7.40	P/O Cobden
P9492	3.6.40 (See also No.222 Sqdn)	Sub/Lt Hutchinson
P9446	1.6.40	Sgt Mould
P9465	Damaged in combat on 8.7.40	P/O Stevenson
P9466	Damaged in combat on 10.9.40	Sgt Mould
P9492	3.6.40	P/O Stephen
P9547	Shot down in combat on 28.7.40	P/O Young killed
R6603	10.8.40	
R6706	Damaged in operations on 28.7.40	P/O Freeborn
R6716	10.7.40	
R6757	Shot down in operations on 11.8.40	P/O Cobden killed
R6759	Damaged in combat on 13.8.40	F/Lt Kelly
R6771	13.7.40	F/Lt Kelly
R6772	13.7.40	
R6773	13.7.40	P/O Hastings
R6779	Damaged in operations on 28.7.40	P/O Stevenson
R6780	12.7.40	
R6830	Write-off on delivery to 74 Sqdn on 13.8.40	
R6839	29.7.40	F/Lt Brzezina
R6840	29.7.40	F/O Freeborn
R6962	Shot down in operations on 11.8.40	P/O Smith killed
R6982	2.8.40	
R6983	Badly damaged in operations on 31.7.40	F/Lt Kelly
X4068	9.8.40	

No.222 'Natal' Squadron

Serial No.	Date of arrival or final fate	Pilot
K9795	Forced landing on 15.10.40	P/O Edridge
K9799	Damaged in operations on 2.9.40	
K9826	Shot down in combat on 30.8.40	P/O Edridge injured
K9878	4.9.40	
K9939	Shot down in combat on 30.10.40	P/O Edridge died later
K9947	23.9.40	P/O Marland
K9960	17.6.40	
K9962	Shot down in combat on 4.9.40	Sgt Ramshaw died later
K9993	Shot down in combat on 20.9.40	P/O Assheton injured
L1010	Crashed on operations on 3.9.40.	Sgt R.Johnson injured
L1011	18.9.40	
L1031	3.9.40	Sgt Burgess
L1041	2.10.40	
L1089	Forced landing on 15.10.40	Sgt Dunmore
N3119	Shot down on 30.10.40	P/O A.Davies killed
N3169	Forced landing on 7.9.40	Sgt Burgess
N3203	Destroyed in combat on 20.9.40	P/O Whitbread killed
N3233	Damaged in combat on 31.8.40	F/Lt I. Robinson wounded
P9318	Damaged in combat on 29.10.40	Sgt Burgess
P9323	Shot down in combat on 30.8.40	Sgt Spears
P9324	21.3.40 (See also No.41 Sqdn)	P/O Vigors
P9325	Shot down in combat on 30.8.40	Sgt Baxter safe
P9328	Damaged in combat on 9.9.40	
P9337	Shot down in combat on 31.8.40	P/O Davies injured
P9360	Destroyed on airfield by raid on 31.8.40	
P9364	Failed to return on 27.9.40	Sgt Scott killed
P9375	Damaged in operations on 30.8.40	P/O Carpenter
P9378	Shot down in combat on 4.9.40	P/O Carpenter
P9397	Damaged in operations on 15.10.40	
P9434	Damaged in combat on 30.10.40	P/O Carpenter
P9443	Shot down in combat on 30.8.40	F/Lt Matheson injured
P9469	Shot down in combat on 7.10.40	P/O Broadhurst killed
P9492	Forced landing on 30.9.40	Sgt Hutchinson injured
P9505	Destroyed on airfield by raid on 31.8.40	
P9542	Damaged in operations on 14.9.40	F/O Van Mentz
R6628	Shot down in combat on 30.8.40	Sgt J.Johnson killed
R6638	Forced landing on 11.9.40	P/O Assheton
R6685	6.9.40	F/Lt Thomas
R6702	Forced landing due to combat on 27.9.40	Sgt Gretton injured
R6719	Forced landing due to combat on 30.8.40	Sgt Hutchinson
R6720	Shot down in combat on 30.8.40	P/O Assheton
R6772	Shot down in combat on 18.9.40	Sgt Hutchinson injured
R6773	Destroyed in crash landing on 26.10.40	Sgt Davis
R6809	20.9.40	
R6837	Damaged in combat on 4.9.40	F/O Van Mentz
R6840	Crashed near Hornchurch on 20.9.40	P/O Edsall
X4024	Damaged in operations on 14.9.40	
X4057	Shot down in combat on 5.9.40	Sgt Chipping injured
X4058	Crash-landed on 9.9.40	P/O Vigors
X4067	23.9.40	
X4089	Damaged in combat on 7.9.40	F/O Van Mentz
X4249	Shot down in combat on 14.9.40	Sgt R. Johnson
X4265	Damaged in combat on 14.9.40	Sgt Hutchinson

X4275	Crashed while landing on 14.9.40	Sgt Baxter killed
X4278	Shot down on 4.9.40	F/O Cutts missing
X4280	Damaged in operations on 2.9.40	F/Lt I. Robinson wounded
X4341	7.9.40	P/O Marland
X4416	17.10.40	F/Lt Thomas
X4540		F/O Van Mentz
X4546	29.9.40	
X4548	Damaged in operations on 27.10.40	P/O Edsall injured
X4610	17.10.40	

No.266 'Rhodesia' Squadron

Serial No.	Date of arrival or final date	Pilot
K9850	Damaged in enemy raid on airfield 18.8.40	
K9864	Damaged in combat on 16.8.40	P/O Soden injured
L1043	18.6.40	P/O Mitchell
L1088	Damaged in enemy raid on airfield 18.8.40	
N3095	Destroyed in combat on 16.8.40	P/O Bowen killed
N3127	Damaged in enemy raid on airfield 18.8.40	
N3189	Failed to return on 15.8.40	Sgt Hawley missing
N3181	Damaged in combat on 15.8.40	F/Lt Armitage
N3168	Destroyed in combat on 15.8.40	P/O Cale killed
N3240	Failed to return on 16.8.40	S/Lt Greenshields killed
N3245	Damaged by enemy raid on airfield 15.8.40	
P9312	Destroyed in combat on 16.8.40	F/Lt Bazley injured
R6762	Damaged in enemy raid on airfield 18.8.40	
R6768	Shot down in combat on 16.8.40	S/Ldr Wilkinson killed
R6780		Sgt Gretton
R6881	13.8.40	P/O Williams
R6920	Damaged in enemy raid on airfield 18.8.40	Sgt Kingaby
R6991	17.8.40	Sgt Eade
X4030	Damaged in combat on 16.8.40	Sgt Eade
X4061	Destroyed by enemy raid on airfield 18.8.40	
X4063	Damaged by enemy raid on airfield 18.8.40	
X4066	Destroyed by enemy raid on airfield 18.8.40	
X4172	17.8.40	
X4173	17.8.40	Sgt Eade
X4174	17.8.40	F/Lt Armitage
X4175	17.8.40	Sgt Barraclough
X4253	21.8.40	F/Lt Armitage

No.603 'City of Edinburgh' Squadron

Serial No.	Date of arrival or final date	Pilot
K9795	29.9.40	
K9803	Damaged in combat on 18.9.40	Sgt Bailey
K9807	Shot down in combat on 5.10.40	P/O Morton injured
K9916	Shot down on 17.7.40	F/O Peel killed
L1020	15.9.40	P/O Stapleton
L1021	Forced landing on 29.8.40	P/O Hillary
L1024	Damaged in combat on 1.9.40	
L1025	Destroyed on landing on 15.9.40	
L1040		P/O Stapleton
L1046	Failed to return on 28.9.40	P/O D.MacDonald killed

L1049	18.9.39	F/O Morton
L1057	Crash-landed at base on 7.9.40	P/O Pease
L1067	Shot down on 30.8.40	S/Ldr Denholm
L1075	17.10.40	
L1076	Shot down on 28.9.40	F/Lt H.MacDonald killed
N3056	Shot down on 2.9.40	Sgt Stokoe injured
N3099	29.9.40	
N3100	18.9.40	
N3105	Shot down on 28.8.40	P/O Benson killed
N3109	Shot down on 7.10.40	F/O Matthews killed
N3196	Forced landing on 7.9.40	P/O Stapleton
N3244	Shot down on 27.9.40	P/O Cardell killed
N3267	Damaged in combat on 29.8.40	P/O Boulter injured
N3288	31.5.40	P/O Gilroy
P1030	Crash-landing after combat on 1.9.40	P/O Cardell
P7286	Damaged in combat on 27.10.40	P/O Maxwell
P7287	17.10.40	
P7288	29.10.40	P/O Olver
P7289	20.10.40	P/O Winskill
P7294	24.10.40	
P7295	17.10.40	
P7297	17.10.40	
P7307	20.10.40	
P7309	Shot down in combat on 25.10.40	P/O Olver injured
P7311	17.10.40	F/O Pinckney
P7315	17.10.40	S/Ldr Denholm
P7324	17.10.40	P/O Stapleton
P7325	Shot down on 25.10.40	P/O Soden injured
P7327	17.10.40	
P7328	17.10.40	
P7346	27.10.40	
P7350	Damaged in combat on 25.10.40	P/O Martel
P7365	Crash-landed on 27.10.40	P/O Dewy killed
P7387	28.10.40	
P7388	28.10.40	
P7389	28.10.40	
P7439	Shot down on 27.10.40	F/O Goldsmith killed
P7449	Damaged in operations on 24.10.40	
P7496	25.10.40	P/O Gilroy
P7509	29.10.40	
P7528	27.10.40	P/O Stapleton
P7529	27.10.40	F/O Pinckney
P9394	30.8.40	
P9440	Damaged in combat on 15.10.40	
P9459	Forced landing on 29.8.40	F/Lt Rushmer
P9467	Shot down on 7.9.40	Sgt Sarre injured
P9499	6.9.40	P/O Berry
P9553	Shot down on 2.10.40	P/O Dexter injured
R6619	10.9.40	
R6626	20.7.40	P/O Berry
R6751	Failed to return on 28.8.40	F/Lt Cunningham
R6752	Damaged in combat on 2.9.40	P/O Haig
R6753	Shot down on 29.8.40	F/O Pinkney
R6754	Shot down in combat on 30.8.40	Sgt Sarre
R6835	Damaged on 31.8.40	F/O Carbury injured
R6836	Sent from No.266 Sqdn.	F/O Pinckney

R6989	Damaged in combat on 28.8.40	F/O Ritchie injured
R7019	Destroyed in combat on 15.9.40	S/Ldr Denholm
R7020	6.10.40	
R7021	Shot down on 30.8.40	Sgt Sarre
X4019	7.10.40	
X4163	Damaged in combat on 30.8.40	F/O Waterston
X4164	20.8.40	S/Ldr Denholm
X4185	Shot down on 3.9.40	P/O Stewart-Clarke inj.
X4248		P/O Boulter
X4250	Forced landing at base on 7.9.40	S/Ldr Denholm
	Forced landing on 27.9.40	P/O Dexter
X4259		F/Lt H.MacDonald
X4260	Forced landing in France on 6.9.40	P/O Caister P.o.W
X4261	Shot down on 5.9.40	F/Lt Rushmer killed
X4263	Forced landing on 4.9.40	Sgt Sarre
X4264	Shot down on 5.9.40	P/O Rafter injured
X4266		P/O Berry
X4271	Shot down on 31.8.40	P/O Gilroy
X4273	Shot down on 31.8.40	F/O Waterston killed
X4274	30.8.40	P/O Lawrence
X4277	Shot down on 3.9.40	P/O Hillary badly burned
X4323	Shot down in combat on 18.9.40	P/O Howes killed
X4324	Shot down on 15.9. 40	P/O Pease killed
X4327	Shot down on 14.9.40	P/O Robbins injured
X4347	8.9.40	F/O Scott-Malden
X4348	8.9.40	P/O Stapleton
X4349	8.9.40	
X4415	14.9.40	S/Ldr Denholm
X4489	24.9.40	P/O Boulter
X4490	24.9.40	
X4593	8.9.40	
X4594	8.10.40	F/O Pinckney
X4613	17.10.40	

Other Aircraft Types

No.264 'Madras Presidency' Squadron flying Boulton-Paul Defiant aircraft at Hornchurch during the Battle of Britain

Serial No.		Pilot/Gunner
L6957	Damaged on 28.8.40	Sgt Lauder / Sgt Chapman
L6963		S/Ldr Garvin / Sgt Hardy
L6965	Shot down on 24.8.40	P/O Gaskill injured / Sgt Machin died
L6966	Failed to return on 24.8.40	P/O Jones / P/O Ponting both missing
L6967		F/O Stephenson / Sgt Maxwell
L6985	Shot down on 26.8.40	F/Lt Banham safe / Sgt Baker missing
L6996		P/O Whitley / Sgt Turner
L7003		P/O Stokes / P/O Corner
L7005	Crash-landed on 26.8.40	Sgt Thorn / Sgt Barker slightly injured
L7006		P/O Percy / P/O Smythe
L7013	Forced landing on 24.8.40	F/Lt Colquhoun / P/O Robinson
L7018		P/O Thomas / Sgt Shepherd
L7021	Shot down on 28.8.40	S/Ldr Garvin injured / F/Lt Ash killed

L7024	Damaged on 26.8.40	P/O Goodhall / Sgt Young
L7025	Shot down on 26.8.40	F/O Stephenson injured / Sgt Maxwell missing
L7026	Shot down on 28.8.40	P/O Kenner / P/O Johnson both killed
L7027	Failed to return on 24.8.40	F/O Shaw / Sgt Berry both missing
L7028		P/O Jones / P/O Ponting
N1535	Failed to return on 24.8.40	S/Ldr Hunter / P/O King both missing
N1536		P/O Barwell / Sgt Martin
N1556		P/O Hackwood / P/O Storrie
N1569	Badly damaged on 28.8.40	P/O Bailey / Sgt Hardy
N1574	Shot down on 28.8.40	P/O Whitley / Sgt Turner both killed
N1576	Badly damaged on 28.8.40	P/O Carnaby/ P/O Ellery
N1581		P/O Barwell / Sgt Young
N1628		F/Lt Banham / Sgt Shepherd
N1630		P/O Goodhall / Sgt Young
N1672		P/O Welsh / Sgt Hayden
N1673		F/Lt Colquhoun / P/O Robinson

No.600 'City of London' Squadron
flying Bristol Blenheim Mk1. & Beaufighter

Serial No.		Pilot & Crew
L1295		P/O Denby / Sgt Lewis
L1403		F/O Boyd / P/O Davis
L1521	Destroyed during enemy raid on Manston airfield on 14.8.40	No aircrew casualties
L4095		Sgt Ingram / Sgt Davidson
L6545		F/O Smith / P/O Hough & Wiseman
L6599		
L6684	Crashed on approach to landing at Hornchurch on 7.9.40	Sgt Sanders / Sgt Davies both killed
L6777		
L6786		Sgt Holmes / Sgt Moulton
L6791		F/Lt Hayes/ Sgt Holmes/ Sgt Pearce
L8372		F/Lt Hayes / Sgt Ingram
L8665	Shot down on 8.8.40	F/O Grice / Sgt Keast / AC1 Warren all killed
L8670		Sgt Coombs / Sgt Hardwick
L8679	Crashed due to engine failure on 9.8.40.	F/O Le Rougetel / Sgt Smith unhurt
L8730		
R2065	2 Beaufighter aircraft arrive	
R2071	on Squadron 13th/14th.9.40	F/O Smith

APPENDIX I

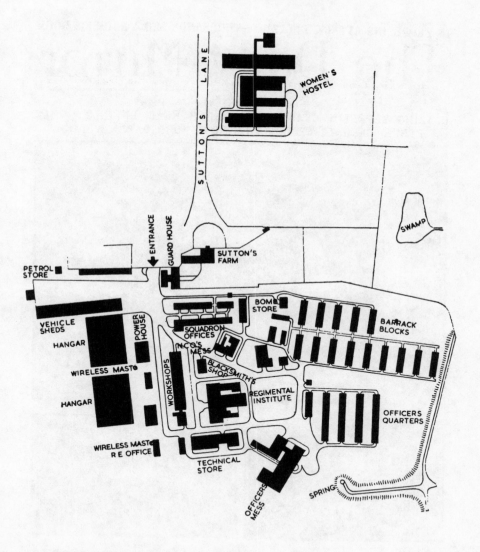

The Sutton's Farm airfield site plan of buildings as they stood in 1918. The RAF Hornchurch site (1939/40) consisted of a grass Flightpath of 1,200 yards from north to south or vice versa, 850 yards from south-east to north-west or 830 yards from east to west. There were three C-type hangars, petrol storage tanks to hold 72,000 gallons and also 4,000 gallons of oil, while the ammunition magazines held over 1,000,000 rounds.

APPENDIX J

The Daily Mirror front page for 4th September 1916, after Lieutenant William Leefe-Robinson had shot down the Airship SL.11, which crashed to earth at Cuffley in Hertfordshire.

THE FRINGE OF GLORY
1940

I have touched the fringe of glory
and flown the high blue sky,
I was there, when men of courage
had said they – and I –
could meet the storm that threatened,
oppose it and deny.

Oh, how they flew, outnumbered,
and fiercely stemmed the tide.
I knew those men of courage
and watched them as they died.

They're gone, but not forgotten
and bravely played their part.
The foe who would destroy us
had met the Lion-heart.

And now, in dimming memory,
yet overwhelming pride
I know that I was honoured
to be there at their side.

I still look up, and listen,
and hear the Merlins roar,
see vapour trails, criss-crossing,
of many years before.

And then I stand, and silence
succeeds the angry noise
of men in mortal combat,
some hardly men – just boys.

For England, Mother England,
Another Crispin's Day
Look up, as I, and see them
and with me, truly say
They Hold the Fringe of Glory
and God will them repay.

R.W. 'Wally' Wallens DFC
Squadron Leader RAF (Ret'd)
41 Squadron Hornchurch 1940

THE CRYING CRIMSON SKY

(An ode to Hornchurch's Few)

They flew high in the azure blue
And kept their fears aside,
As hordes of invading eagles
Trespassed in their skies.

They looked down on their Mother Earth,
The fields, the lakes and dales,
The Country Pub, the Cricket Green,
The workers in the fields.

Now in their early youth they had to go and fight,
Up amongst the swirling clouds and dizzy twirling heights,
The growl of Merlin engines, the chatter of the guns,
The falling burning parachute, the screaming falling bombs.

Though tired and outnumbered they continued with their fight,
Looked on from below by loved ones conscious of their plight.
And when the day was over, the crimson sky would cry,
For all those who did not return,
'Her Lost Spitfire Boys'.

Now the years are passing and memories will fade, it's true,
But England will not forget her famous 'few'.
The airfields now stand empty,
Where now children laugh and play,
Where once England's youth fought from day to day.

So when you walk through the Country Park,
And see a crimson sky,
Spare a thought and remember
Our lost 'Spitfire boys'
Our lost 'Spitfire boys'.

Richard C. Smith

BIBLIOGRAPHY

The following books listed below are recommended by the author as essential background reading for those interested in Sutton's Farm, RAF Hornchurch, and the Battle of Britain

Aces High, Chistopher Shores & Clive Williams, Grub Street 1994

Battle of Britain Then and Now MkV, Winston Ramsey, After the Battle 1980

Fighter Squadrons in the Battle of Britain, Anthony Robinson, Arms & Armour 1987

Fighter Squadrons of the RAF and their aircraft, John Rawlings, Macdonald & Co 1969

First Things First, Eric Smith, Ian Henry Publications Ltd 1992

Fly for your Life, Larry Forester, Frederick Muller Ltd 1956.

Men of the Battle of Britain, Kenneth G. Wynn, Gliddon Books 1989

Paddy Finucane Fighter Ace, Doug Stokes, Kimber 1983

Nine Lives, A/Cdr Alan Deere, Wingham Press Ltd 1992

Raiders Approach, S/Ldr H.T. Sutton, Gale & Polden 1956

Sir Keith Park, Vincent Orange, Methuen 1984

Sky Tiger, The Story of Sailor Malan, Norman Franks, Kimber 1980

Smoke Trails in the Sky, Tony Bartley, Kimber 1984

Spitfire The History, Morgan and Shacklady, Key Publishing Ltd 1987

Suttons Farm and RAF Hornchurch 1915-41, S/Ldr H.T. Sutton,Crown Copyright 1953

Tally Ho-Yankee in a Spitfire, A.G. Donahue, Macmillan & Co Ltd 1943

Tigers, The Story of No.74 Squadron, Bob Cossey, Arms & Armour 1992

The Air Battle of Dunkirk, Norman Franks, Grub Street 2000

The Last Enemy, Richard Hillary, Macmillan & Co Ltd, 1942

The Narrow Margin, Derek Wood and Derek Dempster, Tri-Service Press Ltd 1990

The Zeppelin Fighters, Arch Whitehouse, Robert Hale Ltd 1968

Documents and Squadron Operations Books etc, consulted at the Public Record Office, Kew, London.

No.19 Squadron	Operations Book	AIR/27/252
	Combat Reports	AIR/50/10
No.39 Squadron	Operations Book	AIR/27/406
No.41 Squadron	Operations Book	AIR/27/424

	Combat Reports	AIR/50/18
No.54 Squadron	Operations Book	AIR/27/511
	Combat Reports	AIR/50/21
No.65 Squadron	Operations Book	AIR/27/593
No.74 Squadron	Operations Book	AIR/27/640
	Combat Reports	AIR/50/32
No. 92 Squadron	Operations Book	AIR/27/743
No. 222 Squadron	Operations Book	AIR/27/1371/1372
	Combat Reports	AIR/50/85
No.266 Squadron	Operations Book	AIR/27/1558
No.264 Squadron	Operations Book	AIR/27/1553
No.600 Squadron	Operations Book	AIR/27/2059
No.603 Squadron	Operations Book	AIR/27/2079
	Combat Reports	AIR/50/167
RAF Hornchurch	Operations Book	AIR/28/384
1915-1941		

INDEX

1928 – 1940

Personnel